PELICAN BOOKS

TOWARD A DEMOCRATIC LEFT

D0778368

Michael Harrington was born in 1928 at St Louis,
Missouri, and educated at Holy Cross, Yale and the
University of Chicago. He was associate editor of the
Catholic Worker from 1951 to 1953. His social work
at the Catholic Worker House in New York led to
studies of American industry, social alienation and
institutionalized poverty. A member of the Socialist
Party since 1953, he has participated in the civil rights
and disarmament movements of the past decade. He
is chairman of the board of the League for Industrial
Democracy and an adviser to the government on problems of poverty and unemployment.

Mr Harrington made his reputation as a leading social
critic with his book, *The Other America* (Penguin
Special s223), which provided the intellectual stimulus
underlying the national antipoverty programs of the
Kennedy and Johnson administrations. His next book,
The Accidental Century (Pelican A880), considered
the cultural and intellectual crisis brought about by the
'accidental revolution', in which an unplanned social
and creative technology has haphazardly reshaped our
lives and put in doubt all our ideologies and beliefs.

MICHAEL HARRINGTON

TOWARD A DEMOCRATIC LEFT

A Radical Program for a New Majority

PENGUIN BOOKS INC
BALTIMORE, MARYLAND

Penguin Books Inc., 7110 Ambassador Road,
Baltimore, Maryland 21207, U.S.A.
Penguin Books Australia Ltd, Ringwood,
Victoria, Australia

First published by Macmillan 1968
Published in Pelican Books 1969
Reprinted 1969
Copyright © 1968, 1969 by Michael Harrington
Afterword: The Road to 1972
Copyright © Michael Harrington, 1969

Printed in the United States of America

In memory of Al Gervis
and Edward Michael Harrington

And for the Next Generation

CONTENTS

ACKNOWLEDGMENTS

Traditionally, authors' acknowledgments end with a note of thanks to the wife for the comfort and support she provided during the difficult days of composition. I begin these acknowledgments with this tribute to my wife, Stephanie Gervis Harrington, because she has been so much more than that. The very idea of this book arose out of conversations with her, and at every moment of its writing she was an indispensable source of suggestions and criticisms as well as a lovely help-mate. This book is hers even more than *The Accidental Century*, which was inscribed with her name.

None of the chapters has been previously published in the form in which they appear here. Yet portions of earlier drafts of material in this book appeared in *Commentary, Dissent, Harper's,* the *Village Voice* and *World View*, and I am grateful to those publications for facilitating my work.

My participation in the fiftieth anniversary conference of the School of Applied Social Science at Case Western Reserve University helped me to formulate some basic themes.

A grant from the Stern Family Fund to the League for Industrial Democracy helped to support part of the research and writing of *Toward a Democratic Left* at a critical point in its gestation, an act of generosity that is deeply appreciated.

I wish also to state a special debt to the *Wall Street Journal*, whose news columns are as informative as its

editorial opinions are quaintly reactionary. The reformist, and even anti-capitalist, data of this staunch
defender of the *status quo* are worthy of particular
note.

My association with the League for Industrial Democracy has allowed me to work with some of the finest
civil-rights, trade-union, intellectual and youth activists
in the land, and I believe that the League must continue as a major educational institution of the democratic Left.

And finally, this book is, as the dedication says, quite
literally for the next generation.

CHAPTER ONE

UTOPIAN PRAGMATISM

The American system doesn't seem to work any more.

The nation's statesmen proclaim that they seek only to abolish war, hunger and ignorance in the world and then follow policies which make the rich richer, the poor poorer and incite the globe to violence. The Government says that it will conduct an unconditional war on poverty and three years later announces that life in the slums has become worse. And supposedly practical people propose that the country make a social revolution but without the inconvenience of changing any basic institutions.

Before the escalation of the tragic war in Vietnam signaled the retreat from all his domestic social promises, Lyndon Johnson's rhetoric soared. Ending poverty and abolishing racism were, he said, 'just the beginning.' He looked forward to nothing less than a Great Society, 'a place where men are more concerned with the quality of their goals than the quantity of their goods,' where leisure would mean 'a welcome chance to build and reflect, not a feared cause of boredom and restlessness,' where the city would serve 'the desire for beauty and the hunger for community.'

An excellent case can be made for dismissing this talk as windy futurism.

America has not yet even bothered to fulfill the hopes of the last generation of reform. In 1944, for instance, Franklin Roosevelt advocated a genuine, legally guaranteed right to work (if the private sector failed to provide a man with a job, the public sector would be obliged to

create a useful employment for him). By the time a conservative Congress got through with this fine affirmation
in the Employment Act of 1946, the President's binding
pledge had been degraded to a pious wish. There followed two decades in which intolerable rates of unemployment were chronic. In November 1966, the Department of Labor showed that, if one defined joblessness
realistically, the black and white poor of the urban slums
were living under Depression conditions during the
greatest boom in the economy's history and twenty years
after the society had committed itself to full employment.

This Department of Labor report is typical of the Sixties. For the Government of the United States has carefully counted, classified and computer-taped all of the
outrages which it does so little about.

The statistics would frighten a Jeremiah, but the laws
must be written to satisfy stolid businessmen. Housing is
a case in point. In 1949 Senator Robert Taft concluded
that the private sector would not provide decent dwellings for the poor and urged the construction of better
than 200,000 low-cost units a year. That was not done.
Then, in 1966, the White House Conference on Civil
Rights totted up the deficit that had accrued from ignoring Taft's advice, surveyed the new needs and concluded
that America must construct 2,000,000 housing units annually, 500,000 of them for the impoverished. The next
year Mr Johnson advocated 165,000 low-cost units, or
about a third of what his own conference had told him
was desperately needed. However, there was not the
slightest possibility that Congress would honor this
utterly inadequate request, since it is in the habit of
appropriating funds for about 35,000 units a year. Mr
Johnson then persuaded the insurance industry to put up
$1 billion, but even if that Federally guaranteed invest-
ment were to be spent exclusively on housing for the poor
(it will not be), it would yield only 80,000 new units.

So the Administration's own figures convict it of perpetuating – and even worsening – conditions the Ad-

ministration says lead to social explosions. After the next riot the Federal statistics thus predict, another commission will presumably be empaneled to explain why it took place.

This contradiction between bold words and sordid deeds does not, however, stop at the water's edge. The United Nations officially designated the Sixties as the 'Development Decade.' After five years of this effort, the Secretary General bluntly admitted the failure of this hope and pointed out that the gap between the fat and the starving lands was increasing. Fully informed of this trend, the affluent economies proceeded to reduce the percentage of their national products devoted to foreign aid, shifted disbursements from grants to loans and, in the Kennedy Round, rejected all the urgent pleas for the reform of world trade addressed to them by the developing countries.

Given these intolerable contrasts of American pretense and practice both at home and abroad, we have good reason to suspect the new utopias urged by men who will not even carry out the old reforms. This is particularly true when President Johnson suggests that fundamental transitions in the nation's life and values are to be achieved almost effortlessly. The corporations and the unions, the racial majority and the minorities, the religious believers and the atheists, the political machines and the reformers are all supposed to unite in making a gentle upheaval. And in a society where making money has traditionally been the most respected activity, spiritual considerations are suddenly going to come first.

Yet it would be wrong to dismiss all these unfulfilled promises as mere dishonesty. These pathetic utopias of the practical men are an admission – and a reflection – of the fact that the United States must take some first steps toward utopia in the best sense of that word. It is of some moment that tough-minded manipulators have been driven to visions even if they do little about them. Then there are now the rudiments of a public awareness of the national plight, and the case for radical change can therefore be made with the help of official figures. Finally, our documented inadequacies make a precise statement of what needs to be done, and the program for reform can thus be more specific than ever before.

But this analysis should not be taken to argue that all that is required is to draw the humane conclusions implicit in the public premises. Nor should it be thought, as some of those struggling to end the war in Vietnam have said, that the nation's problems are simply a function of the pride and perversity of Lyndon B. Johnson. Our social irrationality is not a product of the Presidential psyche nor of faulty logic but a coherent, consistent feature of our social structure. There are powerful, organized and, I am sure, sincere forces committed to the maintenance of the injustices chronicled by the Government. They are not the bloated Wall Street plutocracy of Leftist myth, and that is why it is all the more difficult, and all the more imperative, to recognize them. They most certainly do not enjoy seeing people suffer at home or in the Third World of Africa, Asia and Latin America, and they just as certainly refuse, out of a sophisticated self-interest, to do what is necessary to end their agony.

To take America's urgent goals seriously and to make the system work again will demand vigorous democratic conflict and a vivid social imagination. Such an undertaking, which is the work of the democratic Left, challenges an orthodoxy which prevails both in the groves of Academe and in the smoke-filled rooms.

I

America believes in utopian pragmatism.

The pragmatism of this formula is familiar enough. All of the politicians and most of the professors hold that this country is blessedly unideological land where elections are naturally won at the Center rather than on the Right or Left. The utopianism of this no-nonsense creed is not so obvious, since it is either shamefaced or unconscious.

It is found in the assumption that the world has been so benevolently created that the solutions to problems of revolutionary technological, economic and social change are invariably to be discovered in the middle of the road. Not since Adam Smith's invisible hand was thought to vector a myriad of private greeds into a common good has there been such a touching faith in secular providence.

Utopian pragmatism became fashionable after World War II, in part as a reaction to the rigid intellectual categories popular during the Depression. In that era Marxism was regularly vulgarized so as to project a United States which was the mere reflex of oversimplified class antagonisms. This attitude produced more than its share of crudities and, as befits a dialectical method, therefore provoked its own negation. In the postwar years semi-affluence intensified the revulsion from this theory, and many thinkers proceeded to ignore the crises of the Fifties, Sixties and Seventies on the grounds that the bread-lines of the Thirties had not returned. So it was said on all sides that America is a pluralist nation in which power is shared, statesmen are quite properly the brokers of interest groups and endless progress is possible as long as no one gets too principled.

The notion that America is a unique place exempt from the polarizations of the class struggle is hardly new. At the beginning of the century Werner Sombart was already claiming that the abundance of roast beef and apple pie explained the absence of a mass socialist movement in this country. But the current belief in utopian pragmatism goes far beyond this simple sociology. Everything in American life – its geography, its constitutional institutions and even its latest technology – are seen as conspiring to deliver this society from the European curse of ideology. And these happy accidents are, often enough, supposed to have converged in the best of all possible worlds.

Here, for instance, is how Samuel Lubell pictures

American politics: 'To win the Presidency each party must appeal to a cross section of voters, to Midwesterners as well as Easterners, to employers as well as to factory workers. Extreme differences must be conciliated, thus putting a premium upon the arts of compromise which have helped hold this country together.' In this vast land, Lubell says, the basic drama is not the battle of Left and Right but 'the constant struggle for national unification.' So the sectional deal becomes one of our most typical arrangements.

Others, like James MacGregor Burns, trace the diffuseness of American politics back to a conscious decision. The Madisonians are said to have been so intent on thwarting the triumph of factionalism that they fragmented power through an intricate system of checks and balances. Since practically every group had a veto over every other group, even a clear and democratic majority was forced to the arts of wheedling. At its worst, Burns says, this structure could produce a 'deadlock of democracy.' Yet, in a bow to the prevailing optimism, he still believes that the 'overlapping, jostling, crisscrossing, mutually interdependent networks of leaders and followers' are a prime, and praiseworthy, source of stability in the society. In the end, however, Burns is an academic who does understand the need for changing ancient habits.

More recently the futuristic potential of economic and social accounting has been seen as reinforcing the hallowed anti-ideological ideology. Government intervention, according to Daniel Patrick Moynihan, is more and more a matter for experts drawing on the latest academic research. Therefore the days of the 'mile-long petitions and mass rallies' are over; there is a decline 'in the moral exhilaration of public affairs at the domestic level.' Where the social classes once fought, the specialists now discuss. Max Ways of *Fortune* magazine has taken up this theme on behalf of private enterprise. Now that there is going to be neutral problem-solving rather than passionate political contention, he proposes that the corporations contract to redesign the society (a view which will be examined in Chapter 4).

There is clearly a great deal of truth in these various explanations of the American reality. Yet even as history they tend to be overly neat. America has the most violent and bloody trade-union history of any advanced nation, and the workers, as Seymour Martin Lipsett has documented in *Political Man*, support the Democratic Party more cohesively than their counterparts in class-conscious Britain back the Labor Party. But most important of all, the utopian pragmatists underestimate the significance of the realigning elections in the nation's past. There were great issues at stake in the Republican victory of 1860, the triumph of the East and the Midwest over the Populist South and West in 1896, the New Deal victories of 1934 and 1936. At such moments an entirely new political context was created. Then the deals, the compromises and the coalition took place within a transformed framework.

In the turmoil of the Thirties there were thinkers who saw only the dialectical leaps of society; in the semi-affluence of the Fifties and Sixties the fashion was and is to notice only the evolutionary increments. Both perspectives distort. But what is at issue is not a scholarly quarrel over the past but a political debate over the future. For even if it were true that this country has stumbled through its history without any particular idea of where it is going, it can no longer afford to do so.

In *To Move a Nation*, Roger Hilsman gives a summary description of the utopian pragmatist way of doing things: 'Rather than through grand decisions or grand alternatives, policy changes seem to come through a series of modifications of existing policy, with the new policy emerging slowly and haltingly by small and usually tentative steps, a process of trial and error in which policy zigs and zags, reverses itself and then moves forward in a series of incremental steps.' My thesis, simply put, is that this method cannot possibly cope with the profound social crises which have been officially defined – and then catalogued – by the United States Government.

It has been recognized (ironically, on the initiative of defense planners) that the evils of the society are not random but systematic. In the megalopolitan complexes, for instance, inadequate transportation, central-city decay, racial segregation and high rates of unemployment all reinforce one another. Reality itself is, in short, demanding 'grand decisions or grand alternatives' whether American history likes it or not. The decision to rebuild Europe under the Marshall Plan was not an 'incremental step,' and neither is a commitment to rebuild America.

In a sense, the emerging situation is so radical that it changes at least some of the evidence on which Lubell and Burns base their analyses. The interdependence of the United States is becoming so marked that one could even say that the country is finally nationalizing itself and thus is moving toward a Left-Right, rather than a regional, opposition. For a few years after the murder of John F. Kennedy the Dixiecrat-Republican Congressional coalition which symbolized the deadlock of democracy was defeated, and there were those who thought that America had escaped from the paralysis of its Madisonian institutions. But in 1967 that famed alliance for reaction returned more vigorous than ever. So even in Burns's and Lubell's own terms, the need for truly decisive change is becoming more and more insistent.

A personal anecdote might make this point clearer. In 1964, immediately after President Johnson appointed Sargent Shriver to head the War on Poverty, I spent two weeks as a consultant to the task force which eventually drew up the Economic Opportunity Act of 1964. At my first meeting with Shriver I told him that the billion dollars the White House then planned to invest in the project was 'nickels and dimes' ('Oh really, Mr Harrington,' Shriver said. 'I don't know about you, but this is the first time I've spent a billion dollars'). But as the days went on I became conscious that the intellectual deficit was even greater than the financial. The task-force members were dedicated, often brilliant. Yet all of us suffered from the fact that, during the Eisenhower years, few people had thought of what to do about poverty. When the moment for action finally came, practical men were hamstrung because not enough visionaries had preceded them.

But the limitations of utopian pragmatism did not just bedevil the War on Poverty. They led Lyndon Johnson to miss one of the greatest opportunities in recent American history. For his incredible personal triumph in the landslide of 1964 was also a failure of leadership.

In the aftermath of that election there were many who believed that the victory had been so total that the country had turned a political corner. Now, said Samuel Lubell, there was a decisive majority which 'opened a new political epoch.' And in 1965 Congress seemed to confirm this optimistic analysis. There were Federal aid to education, Medicare, a civil-rights law, anti-poverty action, a Cabinet seat for the cities, and so on. It seemed that, were it not for the escalation of the war in Vietnam, Mr Johnson would have achieved his youthful ambition of becoming a second Franklin Roosevelt. Yet, for all the very real achievements of the Johnson Administration in those days, 1964 and 1965 marked the end of an old era, not the beginning of a new one.

John F. Kennedy had been stymied by the Dixiecrat-Republican coalition that had ruled Congress since 1938. He was forced to adopt a strategy of prudence in order to win a few Southern Democratic congressmen to his side. So he regularly proposed bills that were judged inadequate by his own planners. If these managed to pass, they were further compromised in the process. By the year of Kennedy's death there was hardly a political analyst in the land who did not agree with Burns that democracy had become deadlocked.

The emotional shock of the President's assassination

made it possible for Mr Johnson to move even before November 1964. But it was Barry Goldwater who truly prepared the way for the liberal legislative triumphs of 1965. Goldwater's campaign strategy was precisely an attempt to force a realigning election. He proposed to win the South away from the Democratic Party and, by uniting it with Republican strength in the Midwest, create a completely new political context. In fact, Goldwater drove the moderates and independents into the Johnson camp, and a fantastic coalition was assembled, stretching from Martin Luther King Jr, to Russell Long and from Walter Reuther to Henry Ford.

In *The Making of the President 1964*, Theodore H. White describes a debate that took place within the Johnson staff during the election: 'Among the speech-writers the dialogue was different from the dialogue among the strategists. What was the object of the Johnson campaign, asked some of the speech writers – to "broaden the base" or "to shape the mandate." It was a luxurious internal argument open only to men certain of victory. Should they state a campaign whose purpose was to harvest the greatest majority in American history? ... Or should they press the campaign in another way? To spend in advance some of the certain margin of victory by putting before the people such hard, cleaving issues as must lose a few million votes but would shape an explicit mandate to give the President clear authority for the new programs of his next administration.'

White believes that Johnson both expanded the safe middle ground and shaped his mandate. In fact, he sought new votes but not new ideas. This was one reason why his Congressional troubles started even before the Democratic defeats of 1966. The program Johnson put forth in 1964 and legislated in 1965 was essentially the culmination of the New Deal. Most of the measures in it – such as Medicare – had been debated for a generation and had been postponed because of the strength of the Dixiecrat-Republican coalition. There was a clear popu-

lar majority in favor of these bills and, once Barry Goldwater performed the invaluable service of getting the
reactionary coalition out of the cloakroom and onto the
ballot, it was inevitable that this social legislation would
be passed. So the 1964 election finally vindicated the
New Deal of Franklin Roosevelt. It did not, however,
inaugurate the Great Society of Lyndon Johnson, for,
among other things, no one really knew what that Great
Society was supposed to be.

Even before the 1966 election the very same Congress
which had been so enthusiastic about completing the
New Deal became recalcitrant about rent subsidies, the
Teacher Corps and Model Cities. These were, for all
their inadequacy, new ideas and principles, and the President had neglected the opportunity to win the American
people to them under the euphoric conditions of the
1964 election. More broadly, his obsession with consensus
had kept Mr Johnson from informing the electorate
about the conflict-ridden practicalities of the future. He
helped Henry Ford and other captains of industry to
make their belated peace with Franklin Roosevelt, and
he even persuaded them to join in a united front with
Walter Reuther. But he secured this agreement on the
conquests of the Thirties by avoiding the divisive challenges of the Sixties and Seventies.

So it is necessary to speak of major social changes as
the Sixties come to an end, even though the forces of
reform and renewal are everywhere on the defensive. For
the history I have just sketched makes it clear that the
democratic Left cannot wait for political victory and only
then begin to work out a program. When Franklin Roosevelt began to improvise the New Deal after his electoral
triumph in 1932, his audacious pragmatism accomplished
many things – but it did not end the Depression. Now the
problems before the nation are infinitely more complex
than the gross catastrophe which confronted the Thirties,
and the Johnson Administration proves that they are not
susceptible to jerry-built solutions. Therefore it is precisely

in the dark days when the horrible war in Vietnam has put an end to innovation that we must prepare for an advance that cannot even be foreseen. For the next time the nation decides to start moving again, there must be a democratic Left with some idea of where it is going.

Last generation's reforms will not solve this generation's crises. For all the official figures prove that it is now necessary to go far beyond Franklin Roosevelt. And this, as Washington has so magnificently documented, cannot be done by trusting in the incremental zigs and zags of utopian pragmatism somehow to come out right. The country has no choice but to have some larger ideas and to take them seriously.

2

Liberalism, as it has been known for three decades, cannot respond to this challenge unless it moves sharply to the democratic Left.

One consequence of that extraordinary consensus which Barry Goldwater organized among his enemies was to make the traditional liberal domestic program the official, national ideology of the United States. Everyone except the Neanderthals agreed on Federal management of the economy, the goal of full employment, Medicare, formal legal equality for Negroes and, above all, economic growth. There was even a vague unanimity about a misty future called the Great Society. So liberalism was no longer a subversive, prophetic force. It had arrived at the very center of the society.

To be sure, the liberal demands were adopted more on principle than in practice. Harry Truman's call for universal national medical insurance was turned into a Medicare program which covered some of the needs of people over sixty-five and some of the poor. In this area, and in many others, a struggle is still demanded to get the nation to honor its own commitments. But that is a matter, however important, of quantitative change. And liberalism, which is as far Left as this country has ever gone, must propose qualitatively new innovations if it is to be true to its own traditions.

The most intelligent and radical of the American youth sensed this impasse before any scholar defined it. They began to scandalize their liberal elders, charging them with having become agents of the corporations and the Establishment. The theories in which the young expressed their anger were intemperate, unhistorical, much too sweeping and contained a substantial truth. In *The New Industrial State*, John Kenneth Galbraith, the chairman of Americans for Democratic Action, provided a brilliant, reasoned analysis which substantiated many of the most bitter attacks on the liberal movement which he led.

'Except as he may stress more equitable distribution of income,' Galbraith wrote, 'the reformer's goals are identical with those of the industrial system. Except as he concerns himself with the poor he has become the political voice of the industrial system. It is an effortless role; no loud controversy is involved, there are no unseemly quarrels, no one need be persuaded. It is merely necessary to stand modestly at attention and take a bow as the Gross National Product goes up again, perhaps by a record amount. Reformers who so spend their time are, in effect, unemployed.'

In other words, what used to be the Left is now the Center. Yet the problems that remain are even greater than the ones that have been solved. So liberalism must recover from its own intemperate victory, and it can do this only by a move toward the democratic Left. In saying this I do not propose a socialist reorganization of society even though I most emphatically favor it. The horizon of this book is set roughly twenty years in the distance and it is not, alas, realistic to expect that the American people will decide to transform capitalism during that period. So I use the term 'Left' here to describe a program and movement which socialists and radicals can

– and must – support but which appeals to the more traditional American aspirations for reform as well.

I make no secret of the fact that I believe that extending democracy into significant areas of economic and social life, as I urge here, is a first step toward a completely new society. For myself, I make these proposals in precisely this transitional sense. Yet it is not at all necessary to agree with the socialist philosophy which I outlined in *The Accidental Century* in order to favor these ideas. They are grounded in liberal, religious and humanist, as well as socialist, values, and their urgency is attested to by the statistical authority of the United States Government itself.

Moreover, recent, and very hopeful, events make it particularly important thus to locate a radical program midway between immediate feasibility and ultimate utopia. For if the radical youth of the Sixties have rightly understood that liberalism must transcend its now established truths, they have been quite vague about what that means. They are precise about the bureaucratic, technocratic and hypocritical society they reject, but, despite some anarchist yearnings, they have not really addressed themselves to the problem of how one can actually infuse a complex technological order with a democratic and humane spirit.

A hazy apocalypse is no substitute for an inadequate liberalism. This can be seen most dramatically in the confusions of the Left with regard to the revolutionary movements of the world. In analyzing the failures of a purely negative radicalism in this area, it becomes clear why the Left must state what it is for as well as what it is against.

The tendencies toward totalitarianism in the Third World of Asia, Africa and Latin America are not the invention of agents from Moscow, Peking, Havana or anywhere else. The bureaucratic and terrorist accumulation of capital in a developing nation is a rational, intolerable response to a real problem and it appeals to elites in the ex-colonies whether they are 'pro-Communist' or not. As Senator J. William Fulbright put it: 'The reconstitution of a traditional society requires great discipline and enormous human sacrifice: not only must the rich be persuaded to give up privileges which they regard as their birthright, *but the poor who have practically nothing must be persuaded to do with even less in order to provide investment capital.*' (Italics added.)

In this setting, the terms 'socialism' and 'Left' are often used to express meanings diametrically opposed to the definitions made by the people of Europe and America in the course of their struggles. These words were originally intended to express the possibilities of a rich society producing for popular need under popular control, but they are now regularly employed to rationalize a coercive system in which the masses work harder for less and any independent organization, be it a union or a political party, is treated as a dangerous claimant for a scarce surplus. So on the basis of economics as much as, if not more than, ideology, the states of the Third World tend toward dictatorship when they seek to develop themselves.

The terrible necessities of this process are not necessary at all. They are, as Chapters 7, 8 and 9 will demonstrate, the invention of Western power; they are imposed from without, and they can be substantially changed. But what is particularly relevant here is the simple-minded reaction of some Leftists to the complexities involved. France and the United States are cases in point.

French youth played a heroic, vanguard role in leading the opposition to the Algerian war. The socialists were divided on the issue, the Communists were afraid of acting because they were not at all sure the workers would follow them, and the students, professors and intellectuals courageously fought their own Government and the terrorists of the Right. But in the course of denouncing the colonialist horrors which France was perpetrating, many in the youthful resistance assumed that, if only the imperial power were withdrawn, then it would be a simple matter to create a regime of socialism and liberty in North America. When De Gaulle finally made his historic settlement with the National Liberation Front, the first half of the process described by Senator Fulbright was successfully concluded: the privileges of the rich had been successfully challenged. But then came the second part of the current development equation, the struggles against poverty – and, more often than not, against the poor.

At this point the loss of French expertise imposed a terrible social cost on the new republic. Unemployment became chronic, production declined, and there was an internal crisis which led to Boumedienne's coup against Ben Bella. For a considerable period the country was dependent on the largess of the United States in order to feed its own people. And at the beginning of 1968 those Algerians who proclaimed themselves 'revolutionary' were mainly in an underground opposition. Thus did reality take its revenge on the libertarian fantasies of the French Left. The ideas of the youth were as shallow as their deeds were courageous.

There were analogous tendencies in the American movement to end the war in Vietnam. Here again students played a major role. Very few of them belonged to the various Communist organizations, and most were sincere democrats who were horrified at what their own Government was doing. Yet more than a few saw only the fight against American policy. They were romantic about what would come after the peace, supporting the Vietcong, or indifferent, not thinking about the problem at all. In their justified rage against Washington they did not concern themselves with the agonizing choices before the Vietnamese when the killing stopped. They saw Ho Chi Minh only as the hero of nationalist resistance and not as the man who had forcibly collectivized the peasants of the North. He was both.

These Vietnamese and Algerian examples are instances of a larger truth: it is not enough simply to be against the *status quo.* In the Third World the economic necessities as they have been artificially defined by the West provide a strong argument for anti-democratic rule. In such circumstances to think that the work of human liberation is accomplished simply by dismantling the old order is often to make way for a new tyranny. In the advanced nations the application of science to production collectivizes intelligence and creates huge, impersonal organizations. Thus there are tendencies toward an inhuman, manipulative society in the poverty of the ex-colonies and the affluence of the big powers. So in addition to excoriating the past and present, one must propose the future.

The old liberalism does not offer an adequate response to these massive historic trends and can even be used as a screen for corporate collectivism. And so long as the new Leftism is only an opposition it may help people to change their masters but not to free themselves. To deal with the crises it has officially certified at home and abroad, the United States will have to be quite concrete. It must, among other things, redefine economics, recover its passion for equality and, in the doing, reduce the profit motive to fourth-rate importance and raise the non-profit motive to the first rank.

3

According to the prevailing, but not universal, notion of economics in the Western world, it is uneconomical:

for advanced countries to trade with impoverished nations so as to improve the relative position of the latter and help close the global gap between the rich and the poor;

for private capital to be invested in balanced economic development in the Third World;

for the corporations to abolish the slums of America;

for urban space to be 'wasted' on beauty, history or civility;

to subsidize the humanities and not just the physical and social sciences.

These are only a few examples. They express the fact that there is much more money to be made by investing in the misshapen development of the world economy and in the distortion of affluence than in human decency. Decisions to act in this way are not necessarily made by malevolent men and are, often enough, the work of sincere people. It is just that these choices are economical and justice is not.

Here is how Charles J. Hitch and Roland McKean, the authors of one of the most influential books of political economy in recent times, *The Economics of Defense in the Nuclear Age*, put the prevailing orthodoxy: 'But always economics or economizing means trying to make *the most efficient use* of the resources available in all activities and in any circumstances.' (Italics added). The crucial phrase is, of course, 'the most efficient use.' With some important exceptions, economists have understood this term in a quantitative, commercial sense. That which produces the most units in the shortest time at the cheapest cost and therefore yields the highest profit is 'economic.'

There are economists who have made a much broader and humane reading of the textbook doctrine. Theodore Shultz had demonstrated that education made a relatively greater contribution to increased production in the United States than the combined inputs of capital and labor. Fritz Machlup of Princeton pleaded with his colleagues, 'We must not put economic values to one side and other values – say ethical, social, political or human – to the other side.' And in a speech to the Urban American Conference, John Kenneth Galbraith argued that market determination of land value, though once justified, made it impossible for society to take social or aesthetic considerations into account. He therefore proposed to take a great deal of property out of the speculative realm altogether by making it public.

But on the whole, professionals have understood the 'most efficient use' of resources in the crass, obvious sense of the phrase. Moreover, it has been this definition that has guided Government policy. And yet the most urgent needs of the times – economic progress in the less developed countries, an end to poverty and racism in America, the design of a humane environment for human beings – are not economical within this definition. Suburban sprawl is a more 'efficient' use of resources than the abolition of slums; rigging the world market to tax the poor for the benefit of the rich is more 'efficient' than the other way around (the first point is documented in Chapter 4, the second in Chapter 7).

These facts of life have been recognized in one relatively small area of American life: television. The Ford and Carnegie foundations, the White House, and even Congress, have come to realize that commercial television slights some rather important values. As Robert Sarnoff of RCA stated an excellently uneconomical philosophy in a 1967 speech, 'Although non-commercial television may attract only a small fraction of the audience, *its value cannot be measured in these terms alone.* It should be measured by the vitality of its service to minority interest. The results of such efforts often find their way to the majority of the people, helping to enrich and elevate the quality of life.' (Italics added.)

Sarnoff's rejection of the commercial measure of television time which his company – and all the others – have so religiously used is a gain. Yet the conclusions he drew from this insight illustrate another important theme of this book: that executives usually propose to serve the public interest in a way that maximizes their own corporate interest as well. Sarnoff rejected two suggested methods of financing public television: the Carnegie notion of a tax on sets and Ford's idea of a non-profit domestic satellite company which would use its surplus to underwrite a quality network. Both of those reforms might cost the industry something, so Sarnoff held that the funds be paid from the general – taxpayers' – revenues. (This was not an isolated instance but a typical case of the moneymaker's perspective on social service. Chapter 4 fills out the details.)

In any case, foundations, businessmen and politicians all recognize that television cannot be made to serve truly social ends as long as it is operated on commercial principles. Such a shocking admission can be made in this area of the economy because public television will not cost very much and will not require any structural innovation in the society. And the chief beneficiaries of such an undertaking (and I still support it even though this is the case) would be the educated middle class. As will be seen, such a discriminatory expenditure of Federal funds in favor of the well-off is the one form of un-economics the Congress usually approves.

Decent housing for the poor is as uneconomical as good television for the cultured, but General Sarnoff's philosophy is not normally applied in this case. It would be too dangerous. To end the slums will take the expenditure of billions of dollars, the creation of new institutions of democratic planning and a system of fiscal priorities which would actually subsidize the poor to the same degree as the middle class and the rich. That comes to a little more than a contribution for good video theatre. Yet the democratic Left cannot permit the redefinition of economics to be confined to the genteel, middle-class side of American life – public television, highway beautification and the like. Therefore one of the most basic strategies of the Left will be to commit the state to make massive public investments which are not 'economical' in the traditional sense of the word.

In short, there must be a social determination of what is economic. Building homes for the impoverished is not profitable from the point of view of a corporate investor because it does not provide a high enough rate of return on capital. But the social investor – which is to say the democratic society – has a different point of view. Poverty is, of course, enormously costly in terms of increasing the risks of crime, fire, disease and every other ill, and America already pays a high price for being unjust. But much more basically, human beings are being squandered, and this is a tragic waste from the point of view of both the individual and the society.

As the Harvard psychiatrist Robert Coles told a Senate sub-committee in 1966, 'I have found in the most apathetic or lawless people enough unused energy and side-tracked morality to make of them different people, given different circumstances in their actual, everyday life.' But in order to reach these people – and the millions of the Third World – the democratic Left must carry out a concerted attack on the old notion of the 'efficient' uses of resources.

John Maynard Keynes anticipated this point even though he was a radical conservative rather than a revolutionist. In his *General Theory of Employment, Interest and Money*, he wrote that 'strict business principles' led people to prefer wholly wasteful expenditures to the partly wasteful. It was, he said, more acceptable to finance unemployment relief by a loan than to put people to work recreating the society and financing the improvements with a subsidized interest rate. So it is today. America would rather administer a humiliating, utterly inadequate, annual dole than to make a massive multi-billion-dollar investment in people for an abolition of poverty which will yield enormous human and social profit.

In saying these things I am not advocating charity. For, as later chapters will show, the power of the American state has been used to reinforce the maldistribution of wealth in the society, and the rich and the middle class have received more handouts than the poor. In these circumstances it would be justice, not *noblesse oblige*, to channel public funds to those who most desperately need them. In the process, the nation might even resurrect one of its most hallowed, and forgotten, ideals: equality.

The current rediscovery of the problems of the American underclass is not, by far and large, a response to an egalitarian movement. It came as a result of mass pressure only in the sense that the country would never have noticed its own poverty were it not for the Negro movement. In their struggle for equality before the law, black Americans also laid bare the inequalities of the economy and probably did more for their white fellow citizens than for themselves. Beyond that, the War on Poverty derived from reformist conscience at the top of the society rather than from revolutionary consciousness at the bottom. The Cold War slackened and social criticism became less suspect, the intelligentsia less complacent; John Kennedy awakened the idealism of the youth and middle class; and in the wake of the ghetto riots of the mid-Sixties there was a fearful advocacy of amelioration. When, for instance, Henry Ford came out in support of the anti-poverty effort in 1966, he did so out of the explicit worry that, if these miseries were not attended to, they might menace the *status quo*. The Detroit riots of 1967 proved him prescient.

So there is now considerable talk of raising minimum standards up to a semi-humane level, but no one speaks of increasing the justice of the society. For despite many journalistic, and even scholarly, proclamations of recent social 'revolutions,' the American system of inequality has shown a depressing vitality in the last two decades. In 1947 the poorest 20 percent of the population received 5 percent of the income, and it held this same 5 percent share in 1964 (all figures are taken from the Current Population Report of the Department of Commerce, the Federal agency assigned to record this Federal scandal). The second lowest fifth got 12 percent in 1947 and 12 percent in 1964. In short, 40 percent of the American people were held to a 17 percent share of the income throughout the entire postwar period. The 5 percent at the top got about the same portion as that 40 percent. These figures, it must be realized, underestimate the evil, since they are taken from tax returns; and the highest income recipients hire expensive lawyers and accountants in order to conceal as much of their wealth as possible, while the rest of the nation pays as it goes.

Such a stagnant, unfair distribution of wealth mocks the American egalitarian spirit. But more than that, the regressive division of wealth within America and throughout the globe has been encouraged by Washington. For one of the most important economic mechanisms to be described in this book shows that in a world, or in a society, dominated by the economic power of large corporations (or, for that matter, by fat Communist bureaucracies), policies to foster the economic common good will, in the absence of determined political countermeasures, strengthen the existing order of injustice. When foreign aid is given, trade pacts are negotiated or the domestic pump is primed, it is 'natural' that the rich individuals and institutions will be the brokers of the public investment and the greatest gainers from the publicly induced prosperity.

So the democratic Left must not only commit itself to 'uneconomic' investments in human beings but must do so in such a way as to increase the equality of the society. It is important that people have 'enough' – and morally imperative that they should have what is rightfully theirs. Henry Ford seeks ameliorations to keep the natives happy at home and abroad; and every summer the mayors of the Big American cities throw a few crumbs into the ghetto in the hope that a riot can be bought off. That is social engineering. And, by way of sharp contrast, the democratic Left is concerned with justice.

Finally, these broad changes in social philosophy will challenge the primacy of the profit motive as the principle of social and individual life.

Businessmen, as I pointed out in *The Accidental Century*, have been the main subverters of the classic capitalist ethic. The gigantic corporation is a private collective that engages in planning, administers prices and dispenses with the test of the market by generating its own future capital rather than by borrowing it. There is still a diminishing function for the money market and the law of supply and demand, but it really does not have much to do with the dominant industrial sector of the society. As a result, the Horatio Alger myth, whatever validity it had in the past, is now a nostalgic lie.

A growing number of young people have been recognizing the new facts of life. In 1964 the *Wall Street Journal* reported that 14 percent of Harvard's senior class entered business, as opposed to 39 percent in 1960. In 1966 a Harris poll found that the trend was deepening. Only 12 percent of a sample of college seniors were looking forward to business careers – and twice as many wanted to be teachers. In that year the *Wall Street Journal* 'Labor Letter' also noted that corporate personnel officers were stressing the social contribution of the private sector, with a company like General Electric recruiting trained youth to the struggle against air pollution rather than to the making of money. And in 1967 *Newsweek* reported that business executives were worried because the Peace Corps was attracting a disproportionate number of the brightest students from the finest colleges.

Late in 1967 Albert R. Hunt of the *Wall Street Journal* summarized the trend: 'It looks as if selling refrigerators to Eskimos may be only a little harder than selling the virtues of a corporate career to today's collegians.' Hunt reported that in a poll at wealthy Stanford University only 8 percent of the freshman class were intending to have business careers.

But then perhaps the most authoritative testimonial to the possibility of dispensing with the profit motive comes from a millionaire businessman and stock speculator. I speak once again of John Maynard Keynes.

In 1925 Keynes wrote, '. . . the moral problem of our age is concerned with the love of money, with the habitual appeal to the money motive in nine tenths of the activities of life, with the universal striving after individual security as the prime object of endeavor, with the social approbation of money as the measure of constructive success, and with the social appeal to the hoarding instinct as the foundation of the necessary provision for the family and for the future.' Yet, as I noted earlier, Keynes was not a revolutionary, and his *General Theory* explicitly defended 'the environment of private wealth ownership.' How is the contradiction resolved?

Two years after his attack on the love of money Keynes published a sophisticated and paradoxical distinction. There were two separate issues, he said, and one concerned the efficiency of capitalism, the other the desirability of the system. 'For my part,' Keynes wrote, 'I think that capitalism, wisely managed, can probably be made more efficient for obtaining economic ends than any alternative system yet in sight; but that in itself is in many ways objectionable.' Eventually, Keynes believed, the economy would become so productive (he even imagined a zero interest rate for capital) that society would no longer need to be immoral in order to be efficient. At that point, 'The love of money – as distinguished from the love of money as a means to the enjoyments and realities of life – will be recognized for what it is, a somewhat disgusting morbidity; one of those semi-criminal, semi-pathological propensities which one hands over with a shudder to the specialists in mental disease.'

This distinction between money as means and money as an end is crucial if the issues are not to be muddled. For the immediate future, and even into the visionary middle distance, almost everyone is going to be raising his standard of life and even pursuing luxuries. One accepts, then, a modicum of self-interest and anti-neighborliness at this point in history. Moreover, it is absolutely imperative that an economy produce a surplus (a 'profit,' if you will) in excess of what is consumed in order to provide for future investment and, above all from the point of view of the democratic Left, future social investment.

Yet these relatively functional concepts of money-making are a far cry from the profit mythology which is still taught to innocent school children in this society. For Americans are told that buying cheap and selling dear, gaining an advantage over one's neighbor, making a killing out of a rise in the value of stock or land which the individual did nothing to promote are the basic principles which should guide the citizen and the society. It is indeed a 'somewhat disgusting morbidity' that the country thus reverences.

Many college students have, as noted earlier, turned their backs on this dog-eat-dog ethic. More generally, educators have a major contribution to make on this count. They can begin to teach the young about economic reality and assign personal greed a relatively modest role in the society. And they can discuss the humane, co-operative motives which can induce people to action. Indeed, there are many signs that the youth have understood the necessity for such a pedagogy before it occurred to their teachers.

But homilies will not change the motivational structure of an entire society. What is needed in addition is action to create an environment in which it is more 'natural' to help one's fellow man than to profit from him. And this is precisely what follows from the main argument of this book. An analysis of international and domestic social issues shows over and over that there is an objective need for more public, as opposed to private, investment; for social, as opposed to individual, consumption; and for giving aesthetic and other non-commercial values a claim on material resources. These reforms, it should be emphasized, are required in order to redeem the existing, official pledges of the United States of America. If they are carried out, however, they will have a profound by-product. For as the social, non-profit and aesthetic sectors of the society expand, more and more people will be able to live their lives and express themselves in the actual practice of a cooperative, rather than a competitive, ethic. And that fact will be the most powerful sermon of all.

4

Finally, the ideas in this book are not presented as blueprints for legislative draftsmen but as practical intimations of a new civilization.

I am not proposing another exercise in futurism, an attempt to guess the inventions that will take place in the next twenty or so years. There are already distinguished study commissions engaged in that undertaking. Throughout this book I simply assume that unprecedented change will be a commonplace, as in the recent past. If the pace of the next twenty years is only as headlong as that of the last twenty, that will provide imperative enough for the kinds of political, social and economic reform urged here. If, as is quite possible, there is some unforeseen scientific breakthrough, then a transformation of our minds and institutions becomes even more urgent. In either case, America desperately needs a democratic Left.

I do not here pretend to have made an exhaustive description of that Left. I have identified some of the most important evils in the society and tried to see them not as isolated outrages but as part of a social system in motion. They are typical instances of what is grievously wrong with America rather than a comprehensive inventory. And the solutions are put forth to illustrate new ways of thinking, to initiate, rather than to close, the discussion.

And yet in saying that there must be first steps toward a new civilization I do not mean to effect a vague rhetoric. Along with the social tragedies, the Government has also catalogued the awesome possibilities that are already present among us. It is quite clear that this nation, and the world, are in for profound, qualitative change; that we are heading, willy-nilly, for a new epoch in man's history.

The National Commission on Technology, Automation and Economic Progress reported that, if America were to take all of its productivity gains from 1965 to 1985 in the form of increased leisure, it would then be able to choose between a twenty-two-hour week, a twenty-seven-week year and retirement at thirty-eight.

There are now around sixty million housing units in the United States. By the year 2000 it will be necessary to build an *additional* seventy million, or more than now exist. This means, in the Johnson Administration's phrase, the construction of a 'second America.' On what principles and according to what design?

By 1975, according to the special Counsel to the Senate Sub-committee on Anti-Trust, three hundred corporations will own 75 percent of the industrial assets of the world.

George Ball, formerly of the State Department and now chairman of the foreign-operations branch of Lehman Brothers, predicted in 1967, 'Before many years we may see supernational corporations incorporated under treaty arrangements without a domicile in any particular nation state.' Such entities, one might add, could well turn out to be more powerful than the United Nations.

There are thus fundamental choices to be made, choices which will affect the relation of man to himself, his fellow citizen and the entire world. And yet all that America has really done is to take note of this tremendous fact and then file it in the Library of Congress. As a result, the system no longer seems to work, for it cannot keep its own promises.

That is why there must be a democratic Left.

was staffed by businessmen. And for all the talk against economic royalism there had, after all, been a conservative premise underlying most of Roosevelt's policies: that the point of Federal reform and intervention was to get the old order working by providing it with a new, and more favorable, context. As Keynes himself wrote to Roosevelt, 'You have made yourself the trustee for those in every country who seek to mend the evils of our condition by reasoned experiment within the framework of the existing social system.' It was a paradox that this approach was carried out over the political dead bodies of those whom it was designed to benefit most, and it was enthusiastically supported by working people, Negroes, the poor and their middle-class allies.

The positive emotions still evoked by the New Deal are radical and liberal and are clearly related to these class antagonisms which presided over its birth. But, beginning with the Second World War, the corporations gradually came to recognize that the welfare state could be made to serve the interests of those who had most vigorously opposed it. In 1964 this understanding was solemnized when big business supported Franklin Roosevelt's protégé for President and opposed a free-enterprise adventurer.

As a result of these transformations, a welfare state which was supposed to solve the problems of the vast majority increasingly began to exacerbate them. For, as this chapter will document, it is a rule of our economic and social life that, in the absence of conscious political counter-pressures, the state intervenes more on behalf of the rich than of the poor and lavishly subsidizes the very crises it deplores. This pattern is not the result of a Wall Street conspiracy (though the corporations do have a much more effective lobby than the popular organizations). It is just the 'natural' tendency of a society in which the Government insists that economic priorities be determined according to the values of the private sector.

Herbert Hoover defended the classic theory that Washington should simply act as a night watchman for free enterprise; Franklin Roosevelt proposed that the Federal power should act as a sort of Keynesian underwriter for the system. At the time, the contrast between these two views – and the programs they implied – was radical. Now, however, FDR's innovations are not only inadequate to the challenges of the Seventies and Eighties but are themselves a source of some of our most serious difficulties.

In 1952 Adlai E. Stevenson delivered a campaign speech in the hallowed American mode of appealing to every possible voter from a podium placed in the middle of the road. Though his words were probably more a rhetorical ploy to the Right than anything else, they nevertheless defined a serious truth: 'The strange alchemy of time has somehow converted the Democrats into the truly conservative party of this country – the party dedicated to conserving all that is best, and building solidly and safely on those foundations.' In 1964 the captains of industry, such as Henry Ford, got around to agreeing with Stevenson.

The New Deal, for all its achievements and the popular idealism which inspired it, has become the *status quo*. Its genuine gains, such as Social Security, must be defended and extended, of course. But the real task, for the democratic Left and for the nation, is now to go beyond the New Deal. Far beyond it.

I

In the spring of 1967 Gardner Ackley, chairman of the President's Council of Economic Advisers, gave a speech that was enthusiastically hailed, and reprinted, in the *Wall Street Journal*. Ackley's remarks are a perfect summary of the economic ideology which the nation received from the New Deal. It might be called Smith-Keynesianism.

First there is the avowal of the Adam Smithian faith: 'If one were to examine all the thousands of decisions made daily by the managers of the modern corporation, I think he would be struck by the relatively small number in which significant questions of conflict between public and private interest arise. In the vast majority of these decisions, businessmen need not explicitly consider the public interest; nor does government have reason for concern. What sources of material are cheapest, what product sells best, what production method is most efficient – these are questions to which answers that maximize profit in most cases also maximize public welfare.' Clearly the United States Government trusts in the invisible hand.

Then there is a surprisingly candid avowal of the Keynesian partnership between the corporations and government. If, Ackley says, you take 120 important members of the Business Council, 'the influence of these 120 men – and other members representing smaller firms – extends to a substantial fraction of American industrial activity.' And one is told quite openly how this power meshes with that of the state: 'The majority of the members of the Business Council can gather in a fair-sized room, and often do – usually in the company of a few high government officials.'

How did the United States thus come simultaneously to believe in the magic of the market and in the necessity for government intervention to correct it? The answer is found in one of the ironies of the American past: that Franklin Roosevelt's decision to take more vigorous Federal action against the Depression in 1935 was also a move away from planning and toward free-enterprise economics. The 'first' New Deal, as Arthur Schlesinger, Jr, shows in his brilliant account of the period, thought in terms of some kind of coordinated planning. There was considerable business support for this strategy because it provided a rationale for price fixing and ignoring the 'laws' of the market; and social reformers like Rexford Tugwell and A. A. Berle were for it because it offered the possibility to plan for the needs of the people.

The 'second' New Deal, which emerged toward the end of Roosevelt's first term, like the progressive movement at the turn of the century, expressed its hostility to the corporations by championing competition. Under the leadership of Louis Brandeis, the Second New Dealers argued that the Government should prime the pump and then let the plan of economic forces take over. So a move to the Left took the trust-busting form of looking back to the heroic days of capitalism and led to a strange intellectual amalgam, Adam Smith's John Maynard Keynes.

At first many executives petulantly refused the favored position which Government had offered to them. But eventually they got over their principles and entered Mr Ackley's fair-sized room.

There are other groups which are much more democratically based than the Business Council and which try to influence Federal policy – the unions, for example. But these organizations do not control the production and investment decisions of a 'substantial fraction of American industrial activity.' Indeed, there is only one power center in the entire nation that is potentially stronger than Mr Ackley's 120 men, and that is the Government of the United States. However, rather than counterpoising itself to the Business Council, Washington shares that room with it. In saying this, there is no suggestion that the executives and officials are conspiring against the American people. One can assume that all the participants in these meetings are genuinely convinced, along with the chairman of the Council of Economic Advisers, that in most cases the self-interest of private companies is the social interest of America ('answers which maximize private profit . . . also maximize public welfare'). The sincerity of these gentlemen is not at issue. The disastrous consequence of their assumption is.

On January 30, 1967, Lyndon Baines Johnson unwittingly showed how un-idyllically Smith-Keynesianism works out in practice. On that day the President transmitted a message to Congress on 'Protecting Our National Heritage.' He was concerned with the problem of pollution and he had his own version of the fair-sized room: 'It is in private laboratories and in private board rooms that the crucial decisions on new fuels, new control technology and new means of developing power and locomotion will be made. We should support private efforts now to expand the range of their alternatives and make wiser choices possible.'

Then Mr Johnson restated the optimistic thesis that private profit and public good usually go hand in hand: '*Out of personal interest, as out of public duty*, industry has a stake in making the air fit to breathe. An enlightened government will not only encourage private work toward that goal but will join and assist where it can.' (Italics added.)

Now the pollution problem which Mr Johnson was attacking had been caused, to a considerable extent, by a myriad of private decisions that minimized the nation's health rather than maximized its welfare (they involved, to recall Mr Ackley's phrase, 'what sources of material are cheapest,' and this criterion pointed straight to an anti-social allocation of resources). Moreover, on the very day on which the President was affirming the congruence of corporate interest and public duty, there were two interesting newspaper dispatches. The New York *Times* reported from San Francisco that Mr Arjay Miller, the president of Ford, said that air pollution confronted the motor industry with the 'threat of over-regulation by government.' And the *Wall Street Journal* Washington office wrote about the reaction to Johnson's Federal proposals: 'Business concerns, which have favored state control of anti-pollution programs, will probably fight hard against the proposal.'

This prediction came true. When Lyndon Johnson signed the Air Quality Act of 1967, he publicly pretended that the law gave the Secretary of Health, Education and Welfare 'new power to stop pollution before it chokes our children and strangles our elderly – before it drives us indoors or into the hospital.' In fact, Congress had denied Mr Johnson and Washington such powers and relegated the crucial decisions to the state level. As the *Wall Street Journal* realistically interpreted the event, 'This was a major victory for such industrial groups as the coal producers, who vigorously opposed toughening Federal standards.'

The men in those private board rooms who created the problem will, in short, struggle to see that it is not solved (or, as will be seen in Chapter 4, they will themselves propose to solve it for a handsome price and in the wrong way). This attitude is not the product of malevolence but of a rational desire, hostile to the public welfare, to protect investments, use the cheapest fuels, and so on.

2

So the pursuit of profit and of common good do not, as is assumed in the Smith-Keynesian scheme of things, necessarily coincide. But the problem is not just that private interests are quite capable of creating public crises such as air pollution. More basically, the Smith-Keynesian approach encourages Washington to subsidize the companies in their social wrong-doing.

The 1966 *Report* of the Council of Economic Advisers contains a somber description: 'Almost without exception, the central core cities, which are the heart of the metropolitan area, have experienced a gradual process of physical and economic deterioration. Partly as a result of people's desire for more space and home ownership, and made possible by the development of the automobile, central cities have been losing middle- and upper-income families to the suburbs. This movement accelerated when cities became caught in a vicious spiral of spreading slums, rising crime and worsening congestion. . . . This process created an almost impossible financial situation for many cities.'

The Council then added some of the dreary details. Many families have moved to the suburbs but their jobs have stayed behind in the metropolis. So there are vast migrations of commuters who come into the central city each day. At the same time, urban land values for commercial uses have been on the increase and consequently tall, densely packed buildings have become the rule. As a result, hordes of people must travel to a particular area and the transportation system is strained to the limits. By the end of the day, hundreds of thousands have experienced the social cost of congestion, traffic jam and frayed nerves.

So far, this is a standard, mid-Sixties statement of a familiar chaos. But when the Council raises the issue of responsibility for this crisis, it suddenly becomes diplomatic and evasive. The *Report* tells how the real-estate developers do not have to bear the cost of the daily problems which they create, and local governments are thus forced to make large investments in transportation. Then comes a most delicate remark: 'From the point of view of efficiency, these investments often should have been made in facilities for mass transit. Instead, *for many reasons*, they have been primarily in automobile expressways, which only increase the congestion at the center.' (Italics added.)

Among the 'many reasons' the Council failed to specify, two are of particular importance here: the automobile and real-estate industries. They are among the most important instrumentalities for 'planning' our urban crisis. And it was not just that their urge for private profit was in conflict with the public interest, like the run-of-the-mill air polluters. More than that, they were able to carry out socially injurious policies with Federal aid. In documenting this statement, let me again make it clear that I do not for a moment want to suggest a conspiracy (although in the case of real estate there was some old-fashioned collusion and thievery). In an economy in which the majority of the ten largest industrial corporations sell either cars or gas, it is not so surprising that they were able to bend Government policy to their own purposes. They might have even done so in Mr Ackley's fair-sized room. The archaic real-estate industry is, of course, much less powerful on the national scene than the automobile manufacturers and oil companies (it tends to dominate local governments rather than Washington). It just drove to its subsidy in a car.

In short, the public investments in transportation and housing in postwar America were not made to suit the needs of the society as a whole and indeed had the effect of reinforcing the misery of specific groups, such as the black and white poor. These expenditures did, however, serve the short-range interests of middle- and upper-income people and certain powerful industries – although in the long run they helped to create tragedies which threaten every citizen.

One of the most pernicious things about this process was its invisibility. When the poor are granted a subsidy, it is plain for everybody to see, for it takes the form of a segregated, high-rise housing project or a welfare payment. But when the middle class and the rich get their handouts, the dole is managed discreetly. For instance, Alvin Schorr has estimated that in 1962 the subsidies for the housing of the upper-income fifth were twice as great as those for the lowest fifth ($1.5 billion as compared to $820 million). But the well-off got their charity in the form of tax deductions on mortgage payments and in other esoteric ways. The recipients of the princely benefits from under the table were thus allowed to remain contemptuous of those who received the smaller, but highly visible, support.

However, this discriminatory system is not simply unjust to individuals. It is part of the larger pattern whereby the Federal Government invests in the crisis of the cities.

The car is, of course, the beneficiary of enormous public subsidies. Roads are, after all, among the few things which conservative Republican Congressmen are hell-bent to socialize. The total cost of the interstate system was estimated in the mid-Sixties at $46.8 billion and, if past experience is any guide, will almost certainly be higher than that. In June of 1965 there were some $14 billion of Federally supported highway projects approved or under construction. Had such a sum been then invested in the abolition of poverty, there probably would have been talk of Red revolution.

It is said in defense of this massive public investment that the funds are supplied by a 'user' charge. But, as Senator Claiborne Pell has pointed out, the car pays a curious kind of tax, for it is immediately returned to the driver in the form of new and better roads. If, Pell noted, Washington would collect a similar charge from all railroad passengers and then return it to the railroads for capital improvements, there might not even be a passenger rail crisis. But then, even if this tax were not so discriminatory, the 'user' charges do not even begin to pay the automobile's way. For the car imposes huge indirect costs on the society. Some of the most obvious are the salaries of highway patrolmen, the cost of traffic systems, the price of parking lots. And Charles Abrams has computed the annual cost of the traffic jam – in terms of time and wages lost, extra fuel consumption, vehicle depreciation, etc – at $5 billion.

But there is a much more profound, though less evident, cost of the present transportation policy: it has increased the agony of the poor and intensified racial discrimination. In the Watts area of Los Angeles, the White House Conference on Civil Rights reported in 1966, workers had to travel two hours, transfer to several bus lines and pay half a dollar each way to commute to jobs or visit employment offices. 'These transportation difficulties,' a Conference report said, 'discourage job seekers and impose unfair costs on workers least able to meet them.' It did not add that this tragic situation, which contributed to inciting a riot, was created with massive assistance from the taxpayers' moneys. (In the next section of this chapter there is more Government documentation on how the Government helps promote that despair in the ghettos which it deplores.)

Then, at the end of the subsidized road which facilitated the flight of the middle class from, and the decay of, the cities, there stands the subsidized suburban home.

The White House Conference stated the outrageous truth when it noted: 'Federal housing policy until recently was geared almost exclusively to a market of middle-class families who desired to live in the suburbs. This was, and remains, a market from which Negroes and the poor are virtually excluded.' The state generously provided the credit for suburbia (through the Federal Housing Administration, the Veterans Administration, the Federal National Mortgage Association) with one hand while, with the other hand, it was spending money to entice the middle class back into the central city through urban renewal. If you were well off, you couldn't lose either way.

There were some cases, such as the Title I scandals, where speculators simply robbed the public. But more often the real-estate industry stamped the public programs with a private purpose in the full, legal light of day. It was, after all, just good political and economic business for Washington to stake the middle class in suburbia. Investing money to transform the plight of the most miserable in the land was, as Chapter 4 will detail, 'uneconomic.' And even when the Federal funds did get into the central city they were used, as James Q. Wilson of Harvard has summarized the evidence, 'in some places to get Negroes out of white neighborhoods, in others to bring middle-class people closer to downtown department stores, in still other places to build dramatic civil monuments and in a few places to rehabilitate declining neighborhoods and add to the supply of moderately priced housing.' For the poor there were the visible pittances; for the white middle class and rich, these invisible but lavish charities.

There is a public document which ironically gives an unwitting summary of this whole process. It is the 87th Congress' Highway Cost Allocation Study, published in the beginning of 1961. The study laboriously tots up every conceivable increment in values which resulted from the roads, including the increase in land prices and the creation of better opportunities for skilled workers. Then, in what seems to be a casual aside, it was noted that these Federal expenditures may well have had three other effects. They were the decline of the central cities, the deterioration of mass transit systems and the crisis of the railroads.

3

At this point it is necessary to become even more precise about the crises which Federal policy has helped to create. For there are two caricatures of the current American plight which confuse the issue. One is a seemingly radical attack on suburbia by muckrakers; the other is a sophisticated argument for complacency made by reputable scholars (who, strangely enough, themselves favor some excellent reforms). In dealing with these antagonistic distortions the nature of the problem should become clearer.

There is no question here of a scathing, total denunciation of suburbia. In some books of the Fifties and folk-rock protests of the Sixties the suburbanites were pictured as desperate, promiscuous and status-ridden people who have turned their backs on the real world. Yet, as Herbert Gans's brilliant study, *The Levittowners*, demonstrated in detail, this is simply not the case. Gans found a tendency for the upward-bound subjects of his book to broaden their horizons and become more politically and socially concerned, not less so (they came to Levittown in New Jersey from, for the most part, the working class and lower middle class of Philadelphia). And, as the social psychologists have conclusively shown in recent

years, there is less neurosis, psychosis and family pathology in the split-levels Washington bankrolled than in
the tenements it ignored.

Moreover, space and privacy – or, for that matter,
martinis and charcoal cooking – are hardly the evils that
some radical-sounding Puritans make them out to be.
A problem arises only when society treats such goods and
pleasures as if they were its most important values and
purchases them for the white middle class at the expense
of the poor and to the disadvantage of the culture which
flourishes in cities. The crisis I am talking about, then,
is not the one that has been pictured by the aesthetically
outraged opponents of suburban life. It goes much
deeper than that.

But rejecting the bitter simplifications of the muckrakers should not be an excuse for accepting the happy
simplifications of the professors.

Perhaps the most effective defense of the present trends
has been made by some faculty members of Harvard
and the Massachusetts Institute of Technology. I call
them the Cambridge Optimists. In a series of books and
articles – particularly, as far as this discussion goes, in
The Myths and Reality of Our Urban Problems by
Raymond Vernon (Harvard University Press, 1966) and
in the essays by John F. Kain and John R. Meyer in
*The Metropolitan Enigma: Inquiries into the Nature and
Dimensions of America's 'Urban Crisis'* edited by James
Q. Wilson and published by the U.S. Chamber of Commerce in 1967 – they have argued that our difficulties
have been greatly exaggerated. I do not take up their
ideas at some length out of polemical gusto (I share
many of their values and support some of their specific
proposals) but because, through dealing with their complacency, I can more precisely define how the Government's Smith-Keynesian policies have financed our public chaos.

There is no urban crisis, the Cambridge Optimists say,
and that is why the very phrase is in quotation marks in

the title of the Chamber of Commerce volume. As Raymond Vernon puts it, '... the clear majority of Americans who live in urban areas look on their lifetime experience as one of progress and improvement, not as one of retrogression. ... ' And even the poor, though certainly victimized, have better housing than before. As a matter of fact, Vernon continues, most of the talk about the decay of the cities comes from two relatively small groups: the old elite with personal and business ties to the central city; and the discontented intellectuals who prefer the cultural and social institutions of metropolis to the mass entertainments which are the staple of surburban leisure.

In falsifying this realism, John F. Kain and John R. Meyer argue, the prophets of urban doom make the automobile a scapegoat for all the imagined ills which are said to result from suburbanization. In point of fact, they go on, the real reason for the flight from the city is to be discerned in massive economic trends. As transportation improved, industry was freed from its reliance on the downtown railroad yard or the river port; the new technology required single-story, spread-out plants; the work force bought cars, thus decreasing the importance of locating a corporation near public transportation; and the division of labor in the office permitted many mechanized functions to be removed to outlying areas.

To reverse this tendency toward suburbanization, the Cambridge Optimists say, would be incredibly costly. There are, to be sure, those who suffered from this process, mainly the poor and the Negroes, and their needs should certainly be given special attention. But what is basically required is a pragmatic policy adapted to different situations – improved service for the New York commuter corridor is economically feasible but the middle-sized city needs more expressways – and an understanding that the car is going to be a basic means of transportation during the foreseeable future.

So goes the rose-colored thesis. It is knowledgeably argued in terms of detailed statistics; and it ignores the larger agonies and public injustices of the times.

It is certainly right to say that the majority of Americans have raised their standard of living in the postwar period and are, in part, happy about the fact. It may even be that, contrary to the rush-hour impression of the Long Island Expressway or the Los Angeles freeways, that average time per commuter mile has declined in the last generation. But it is utterly mechanistic to think that a quantitative increase in the material well-being of the majority of Americans proves that there is no urban crisis. If social reality were really so banal, then Aldous Huxley's *Brave New World*, where no one is hungry, would be utopia. So it is necessary to look at society as a living entity with ethical responsibilities and emotional responses as well as economic statistics. From this perspective it can be demonstrated that Washington's great concern for middle-class cars and houses injured the entire nation – including the middle class.

First of all, consider again the most obvious victims of the urban crisis: the poor in the central city.

At the end of the 1950s more impoverished Negroes lived in the city slums than at the beginning, in part because of a migration from the rural South to the metropolitan North (that uprooting was also financed by the Government, a point that will be developed shortly). Ironically, a Bureau of the Census underestimate of the amount of dilapidated housing – 'endangering the health, safety or well being of their occupants' – made many experts, some of them living in Cambridge, complacent. In 1967 it turned out that the decline in dilapidated housing during the Fifties had not been, as the Census had previously reported, 1,600,000 but actually less than 100,000 and possibly around zero.

One year before the riots of 1964 Professor Vernon wrote, probably on the basis of this inaccurate Government data, that 'there is no clear evidence of the taut stretching of a rubber band close to its breaking point' in the slums, 'no indication of the building up of a pressure which the political vessel can no longer contain.' By the summer of 1967 the rubber band had snapped in almost every impoverished black neighborhood in the nation.

As usual, the Federal Government has documented the evils it helped to finance. In the Department of Labor's 1967 Manpower Report there was this frank admission: 'Furthermore social and economic conditions are getting worse, not better, in slum areas. . . . [They] have not been reached significantly by the national gains in employment and income. There has been some movement of the least disadvantaged people to better neighborhoods, but their place has been taken by a continuing influx of the poor – many of them disadvantaged farmworkers, lacking the education and skills needed for urban jobs. The poorest, most disadvantaged people, including a rising proportion of Negroes, are caught in the slums, without hope of enough earning capacity to escape from poverty.'

And then the report gave a major reason for this desperate situation: 'The movement of business and industry away from the central city and toward the suburbs during the past decade has created major obstacles to employment of slum residents – barriers much greater than these people themselves perceive.' But this is, of course, precisely the pattern that has been so lavishly underwritten with public dollars.

It would, however, be wrong to take an abstract view of this misery and think that riots are automatically induced by horrible conditions. In their one-dimensional psychology, the Cambridge Optimists assume that a man becomes happier as his material comforts increase. It is on the basis of this notion that they assume that a statistical rise in the standard of living is proof of growing contentment in the society. But that is not the case – and not even among the worst off in the land.

In a two-year study at UCLA of the Watts riot of 1965 Professor Nathan E. Cohen discovered that 15 percent of the Negro population were active at some point during the violence and looting; another 35 to 40 percent were 'active spectators.' More to the point, Cohen concluded that 'support for the riot was as great among relatively well educated and economically advantaged as among poorly educated and economically disadvantaged in the curfew area.' Most interesting of all, Cohen and his co-workers found that the core of the 'militant' groups in Watts was made up of people who are 'educated, tend to come from educated families, are less religious and do not identify themselves as lower class.' (Some of the political implications of this finding will be analyzed in Chapter 10.)

The Detroit rising of 1967 was the most violent of these outbreaks. Yet in Detroit, Negroes had made considerable political gains and had successfully supported a concerned, maverick mayor. Moreover, there was less economic discrimination against black workers in this area than in almost any part of the country, to a large measure because of the policies of the United Automobile Workers Union. In Michigan as a whole, Negroes received around 90 percent of the white wage as compared to around 55 percent nationally. The rioting was indeed begun by some of the most marginal and alienated people – it was triggered by a raid on a speakeasy in the middle of the night – and many looters were probably recruited from the same stratum. But tens of thousands of Detroit Negroes joined in, or sympathized with, the upheaval. And a few months after the event a university survey showed that the people of the riot area most admired not Stokely Carmichael but Martin Luther King, Jr.

But this concentration on the black ghettos should not be taken to suggest that the urban crisis is exclusively, or even primarily, a Negro problem. Within the entire United States, Negroes constitute one third of the poor, which is a viciously disproportionate number but still a minority. And in the central cities themselves, in 1964, 5.6 million of the impoverished were white, 4.4 million were black. This outrage is, in short, integrated – and in Detroit there were apparently Appalachian whites who joined with Negroes in the looting.

So clearly those who have been left behind in the cities are living in the middle of a governmentally induced urban crisis. This is true in a double sense. On the one hand, the employment and housing situations have actually worsened, a trend promoted by various Federal programs; and on the other hand, those who are making gains are desperately aware that they are not receiving what Washington has promised.

The middle class out in suburbia has escaped the most horrible degradations of the slums. But it, too, is nonetheless a victim of the urban crisis, for one cannot simply assume that those who are leading a better material life are therefore happier. In the calculus of pleasure and pain, what weight is assigned to fear? For there is no question that, as the Sixties draw to a close, white and well-off America is afraid. The President's Commission on Law Enforcement and the Administration of Justice reported in 1967 that a survey of two large cities showed that 43 percent of the people stayed off the streets at night, 35 percent did not speak to strangers, 21 percent used cars and cabs after dark rather than mass transit, and 20 percent wanted to move. In the summer of 1967 the Easthampton, Long Island, *Star* reported that the police of the fashionable eastern end of Long Island were receiving phone calls saying that Negro looters were being bussed in from Manhattan, more than a hundred miles away. These reports were, of course, sheer fantasy, yet they are an index of how the urban crisis affects even the most insulated and distant of the well-off citizenry.

But if Negro rioters in 1967 tended to stay in their own ghettos, the professional criminals were more and more commuting to suburbia. In the 'secluded and affluent suburbs,' the New York *Times* reported in December 1967, the burglary rate was increasing faster than in New York City. One reason was that the metropolitan thieves were following the middle class. The other, and more ominous, reason was that the prosperous youth were committing more crimes.

More generally, there was a widespread spirit of middle-class dissatisfaction. The clearest manifestation of it was the revolt of the best of the privileged young against the hypocrisies of the society, a phenomenon which produced the largest activist youth movement since the Depression of the Thirties. But the parents were disturbed, too, and sometimes in a reactionary way. And this has serious political implications for the entire society, not just the poor. For if the fears reported by the Crime Commission come to dominate the country's life, then there is going to be an end to *all* innovation and not just the programs for the poor. Put another way, if the poor, and particularly the Negroes, are locked up for safekeeping in the ghettos, the middle class, though incomparably better off, will be locked up in the suburbs. And a nation that represses social problems with police power will become something of an armed camp – which is not a very happy place for either the wardens or the prisoners.

In other words, the nation's social fabric could be rent in two while the Gross National Product is increasing.

And then there is the question of culture. Professor Vernon downgrades the urban crisis on the grounds that – in part, at least – it has been defined by overreacting intellectuals who treasure the cultural institutions located in the central cities. This is, it seems to me, a strange attitude for a scholar to take. The intellectuals are certainly fit subjects for satire and sometimes apocalyptic in the way they put their feelings about metropolis and megalopolis. But whatever else may be wrong with them, their insistence on the quality of life and the nation's cultural heritage is a positive social good. Moreover, with the vast increase in education now taking place, the size of the group with such concerns is increasing.

It is, then, an issue of some moment that the fate of many of the country's best universities, museums and orchestras is partly dependent on what is done for the most culturally deprived residents of the old urban centers. The policy of ringing a college with a publicly financed and middle-class *cordon sanitaire* – as at the University of Chicago – may work for a while, but eventually if the cities go down they will take these Shangri-las with them. The problem, however, is deeper than the fact that so many cultural buildings are located in, or menaced by, areas of civic decay. The city is the context for a web of personal and creative relationships; it provides a ranging variety of experiences and even just of opportunities for conversation. And such things cannot be crated and sent out to suburbia.

At this point, the complex dimensions of the urban crisis should be more apparent. It is not simply a matter of complaining about the similarity of the houses in a real-estate development, as the superficial muckrakers do. Nor can it be dismissed by pointing out that various statistics are on the march. The poor, the minorities, the frightened middle class and the nation's very spiritual and intellectual future are at stake. Some suffer more than others, most notably in the central city itself, but the entire society is challenged. The publicly subsidized automobile and middle-class house were not the sole cause of all these breakdowns, and an investment of some billions in railroads or mass transit alone will not solve them. But the scandalous fact remains that if one goes to the Council of Economic Advisers, the White House Conference on Civil Rights, the Crime Commission and Manpower reports, or to almost any other public document concerned with social problems, it turns out that the Government has helped to finance practically every crisis it denounces.

The Cambridge Optimists say that most of these transformations were the product of long-range economic trends, like the one toward suburbanization. Yet every factor they cite in this argument – the development of transportation facilities, new technology, the availability of suburban housing for skilled workers – was underwritten by Washington. So the most profound changes in the country's social structure were made through public action but without real public debate. And the reason for this scandal is that America has been operating on the Smith-Keynesian assumption that Washington's programs must be the servant of economic priorities established by the private sector. Within this context business made the only choice of which it was capable: it channeled the Federal dollars toward the most profitable corporate uses and thereby provoked social disasters.

Put another way, it was not beyond the political and economic ingenuity of American society to have chosen another set of priorities in the postwar period. It was not really necessary to have a transportation policy that made riots more likely in Watts; the collective investments could have favored precisely the people with the greatest need. If the poor and the minorities had been treated *as well as* the middle class and the rich – in simple justice they deserve to be treated better since their plight is so much worse – then probably racial discrimination would not have driven people to despairing riot and poverty would not continue to corrupt the ethical pretenses of an affluent society. And if these miseries in the lower depths of America were eliminated, the entire nation would gain.

I would cite a radical truth which I found among the complacencies of the Cambridge Optimists in support of my hopes. It is indeed a momentous fact, as they say, that economic activity is less and less dependent on a particular place, that a company no longer needs to locate near the river or the railroad yard and the worker can live far away from his job. That means that the shape of urban society is increasingly a matter of choice and not of economic or geographical necessity. So far, as this chapter has documented, this new freedom has been used in the worst way. But if the public power can thus plan and finance a crisis, it must also be able to resolve it. That is the extraordinary possibility in the midst of all these errors.

4

So it is necessary to go beyond the New Deal.

That Smith-Keynesianism which was a radical doctrine in the middle of the Depression has become a conservative force. The naïve faith that corporate interest and common good usually coincide is simply not supported by the evidence. The polluters fight for pollution, the automobile makers resist safety standards, the drug companies conceal their profiteering, and so on. Worse, once business got over its idealistically reactionary opposition to the welfare state (the rich in the Thirties fought their self-interest out of ignorant principle), it learned very well how to impose its own purposes on supposedly public expenditures.

The next giant stride in American life will make Keynesianism social rather than Adam Smithian. This is not, let it be noted again, a proposal for democratic socialism. For it is possible for the people to insist that public moneys be spent on public purposes without changing the fundamental relationships of ownership in America. It is just that when tax funds are used to support major transformations of the society, the decisions should be democratically debated and decided on.

But if this perspective is not revolutionary it is profoundly radical. It means that the state will establish its priorities through the democratic process and only then finance them, rather than simply underwriting an economic and social context in which private interests are dominant. To do this would clearly require the creation of agencies for democratic planning and a conscious decision to allocate more of the country's resources according to criteria of social need (some of the specifics are described in Chapter 5). And there is a simple and common-sense argument in favor of such ranging changes. In theory the public already 'owns' and controls the welfare state. Now that must be made practice.

But before turning to the positive proposals, it is necessary to become even more precise about the agonized possibilities of the present policy. Adam Smith's John Maynard Keynes has already intensified the suffering of the poor and the Negroes, as this chapter has shown. But it may well be, as the next chapter will demonstrate, that the current Federal investments in social crisis are preparing for an even grimmer future.

CHAPTER THREE

THE DYNAMICS OF MISERY

A new poverty and a new racism are being created in America.

It is not just that the Federally subsidized economic trends are wreaking social havoc and doing profound injustice. The whole system is subverting one of the proudest pretenses of the nation: that however miserable the present may be, there is always hope for the future. It may well be that we are now witnessing the emergence of a hereditary underclass in which a black caste will be assigned a special portion of despair.

The statistics are, as usual, optimistic, but the possibility of an end to the egalitarian dream remains quite real. In August 1967 the Department of Commerce announced the latest achievements. Poverty had afflicted 22.1 percent of the people in 1959, dropped to 16.7 percent in 1965 and was down to 15.4 percent in 1966. In those years the total number of the other Americans, as the Government computes them, had declined from almost 39 million to less than 28 million. And yet, as the ghetto risings of the summer of 1967 showed, the black poor obviously did not think that things were going so well. In part, this was a consequence of the paradoxical anger of Negro men who were advancing but not fast enough. But there was a less dialectical reason at work, too. In the lower depths of the ghetto, those whose basic strategy is neither revolution nor reform but the sheer struggle to survive understood out of their own bitter experience that somehow all the academic forecasts might be wrong.

There are a number of factors which explain this contrast between official definitions of progress and mass
sensations of hopelessness, and they will be detailed in a
moment. In general, it can be said that the intuitions of
the poor are more realistic than the calculations of the
Federal experts. This does not mean that the data point
inevitably to the institutionalization of a permanent
poverty in the very structure of the society. It does mean
that there must be a powerfully organized political will
if the grim trends are to be reversed. For the misery of
the poor and the Negro, if left to itself, is dynamic. In
the course of documenting the bleak specifics working
toward the social immobility of the poor, some points of
departure for counteraction will be revealed. First, a
profile of the people living in the economic underworld
of the affluent society reveals a potential for political
action. Second, the facts should strengthen a thesis in the
previous chapter: that the other Americans suffer most
horribly from these wrongs but that the entire society
pays an intolerable price for permitting their anguish.
There are, in short, self-interested reasons why the middle
class and the organized workers should join the poor in
actively refuting my pessimistic hypothesis.

Finally, I do not raise the issue of racism in the context of poverty because the majority of the poor are
black. They are not. But the Negro cannot secure equality unless the other America is abolished; and the white
poor cannot be freed from want as long as the black poor
are degraded. Justice for both the white poor and the
Negroes will either be integrated or not at all.

I

Between 1960 and 1965 the United States was in the
midst of an unprecedented boom. One result was that
the national unemployment rate dropped just below 4
percent for the first time in years. During these good
times, the 1967 Manpower Report shows, the average

rate of officially recognized slum unemployment remained virtually unchanged. The unofficial, and actual,
level of joblessness was much worse. How was it that the
impoverished people of the central city were thus unable
to benefit from an economic advance which had been
largely purchased by $20 billion of annual tax relief?

At the 1967 Annual Conference of the League for
Industrial Democracy, John Kenneth Galbraith supplied
an important part of the answer. There are, Galbraith
said, two distinct economies in the United States. One is
based on the scientific technology and sophisticated
organization found in the huge oligopolies which dominate the nation's productive activity. These giant corporations are not, in Galbraith's opinion, socially benign
(his point is discussed in Chapter 5) but they do provide
relatively decent wages to their workers. The second
economy employs the poor. It exploits sweat rather than
machines, is usually based on small, non-union units
and is still very much subject to the cyclical ups and
downs which the big enterprises average out over a
comfortable long run. Here one finds transients, such as
migrant farm laborers and casual restaurant employees,
and the steady workers in the shops of cockroach capitalism.

The paradox is, Galbraith said, that it is possible to
have an inflation in the first economy and a depression
in the second. Let me spell out his point.

In 1965 and 1966, just as unemployment finally
declined to the point where better work would actually
be available for the left-outs, big business faced shortages
of skilled workers and critical materials, and the Government initiated moves to damp down the boom. This
pattern was, of course, profoundly affected by the huge
outlays and pressures on existing capacity caused by the
war in Vietnam; yet this special circumstance should not
be allowed to obscure the basic pattern. In the present
circumstances, as soon as economic growth becomes
dynamic enough to reach down to the laboring poor, it

tends to appear as an inflationary threat to affluent executives. There are then conservative demands to cut back on 'unnecessary' Federal spending, which means, by reactionary definition, social investment.

Two flagrantly contradictory Government documents provide a perfect example of this paradoxical process. The 1967 Report of the Council of Economic Advisers was quite optimistic. The country, the Council said, had finally reached that full-employment equilibrium where 'demand fully matches supply in most labor markets.' This happy event was defined in terms of an official unemployment rate of 4 percent. A few months after the Council announced the good news, the Department of Labor published its Manpower Report. It contained a devastating critique of the official statistics (including those of the Department of Labor) and graphically demonstrated how, despite the theoretical achievement of full employment, people in the central cities were still living in the middle of the Depression.

This shocking conclusion was the result of a special survey undertaken by the Department in November 1966. It embraced ten poverty areas in eight cities (Boston, New York, New Orleans, Philadelphia, Phoenix, St Louis, San Antonio and San Francisco). But instead of just taking the standard definition of unemployment, the researchers developed a much more subtle and realistic index for 'sub-employment.' This counted those who were out of work, but it also made statistical allowance for those working in part-time jobs (who are part-time unemployed), those receiving poverty wages and those who had been forced out of the labor market altogether and thus did not even qualify as statistics.

But perhaps the most chilling factor given consideration in the sub-employment index is the existence of non-persons among the poor. In the slums, the Department of Labor discovered, a 'fifth or more of the adult men expected to be a part of the population . . . were not located by the November surveys.' The Bureau of the

Census has recognized a similar problem of 'under-counting' and is trying to devise a method to deal with it. No one knows the full story. But it does seem clear that there are people in the other America who are so marginal that they do not have even minimal contacts with society, such as a regular address, and therefore are not socially visible enough to become a statistic. This suggests that there are more Negroes, more unemployed and more poor people in the United States than we think.

So the Department of Labor sub-employment index is a much more meaningful measure of slum pathology than the official jobless rate. Some of the incredible figures uncovered by the November 1966 survey are recorded on page 57. They are contrasted with the regular unemployment figures.

This, then, is the first, tragic aspect of the new poverty: its immunity to a boom. The Council of Economic Advisers celebrates full employment, while the Department of Labor shows that hundreds of thousands in the slums have yet to escape the 1930s. This problem could have been avoided if, among other things, there had been a public investment in the social sector, raising the skill level of the poor and consciously creating new and useful jobs for them. Such a strategy would have been anti-inflationary because it would have increased the resources of society. But there was a tax cut and a war in Southeast Asia instead, a point which will be more fully developed in Chapter 5.

A second reason why the plight of the black and the white poor is worse than the Department of Commerce figures imply is particularly poignant: the children of America are 'poorer' than the rest of the society, and there is, therefore, a growth potential for the next generation of the impoverished.

In 1964, when the 'War on Poverty' had just been declared, the Council of Economic Advisers used a rough measure of what it meant to be poor. Poverty, they said, was defined by all those family units, regardless of size and location, with an annual income of less than $3,000. During 1964 the Social Security Administration refined this criterion and the new data became the basis of the 1965 Report of the Council. Under the new guidelines, as updated, an urban family of four with less than $3,200 a year in 1966 was considered poor, and allowances were made for larger and smaller families and for country people who need less money income. The number of the poor was not changed by the 1965 revisions. But, said the Council, 'most important, the estimated number of children in poverty rises by more than one third, from eleven million to fifteen million. This means that one fourth of the nation's children live in families that are poor.'

	Sub-employment in slums November 1966	Official unemployment rate in Metropolitan area for year ending August 1966
Boston-Roxbury	24%	3.7%
New Orleans	45%	not available
New York		4.6%
Harlem	29%	
East Harlem	33%	
Bedford-Stuyvesant	28%	
Phoenix	42%	not available

The most recent figures confirm this tragic fact. In the 1967 definitions, children under eighteen years of age composed 50 percent of the poor people living in families and about 42 percent of all the Americans living in poverty. There is abundant evidence that this means that this group will be disproportionately poor when it reaches adulthood. The Government's study of Selective Service rejectees in 1963 showed that the family is one of the main transmission belts of poverty, that the poor are the children of the poor. If these millions of impoverished young Americans go on to form families of their own – and large families are still the norm in the other America – then it is probable that the recent trend toward a decline in poverty will reverse itself.

This gloomy reading of the statistics can be generalized, for much of the official optimism about poverty rests on one-dimensional, static definitions. It is useful to draw an income 'line' in order to determine the approximate number of people who are poor. But this analytic device should not obscure the living reality: poverty is a dynamic, turbulent social condition which cannot be contained in columns of numbers. There is a huge 'at risk' population (the phrase is Daniel Patrick Moynihan's) which lives only an illness, an accident or a recession away from the other America. Each year there are those who clamber just above the poverty line – and those who sink beneath it.

The most brilliant statistical student of poverty, Mollie Orshanksy of the Department of Health, Education and Welfare, recognized the precariousness of the facts when she spoke of fifty million Americans who 'live within the bleak circle of poverty or at least hover around its edge.' For example, in the Commerce figures, which occasioned more than a little rejoicing, there are more than 3.3 million families with incomes between $3,000 and $3,999. Most of them are not officially counted as poor; and none of them is safe from the threat of poverty. These people may well be above the poverty 'line,' but they are unmistakably within the magnetic field of social disaster.

So the census of the poor has to be taken with a sense of the quality of the numbers. The enormous concentration of poor children at the bottom of the society is a depressing, dynamic fact. It is made all the worse by the incredible inferiority of public education in the slums, where so many children are unfitted for anything but marginal working lives. In the metropolitan-area schools of the United States, the Department of Labor reported in 1967, the average twelfth-grade Negro has a mathematical proficiency which is somewhere between the seventh- and eighth-grade level and a reading proficiency not much higher. This statistic, it should be noted, describes the fortunate black children who did not drop out of school. Since everyone from the Senate Manpower Subcommittee to the President's Automation Commission now proclaims that it takes two years of post-high-school training to be a successful member of the working class, the millions of poor young Americans are at an unprecedented disadvantage.

These various individual scandals of childhood impoverishment, depression joblessness in the middle of a boom and utterly inadequate schools can now be subsumed in a summary point: the newness of poverty.

The old poor, who were typical up until the Thirties, lived at a time when economic opportunity was a secular trend of the economy itself. They suffered terribly, to be sure, and by objective indices of living standard and life expectancy, most were worse off than the impoverished of 1968. But they also participated in that incredible growth of American capitalism, a development which, in Colin Clark's computation, saw a 4500 percent increase in the net income from manufacturing between 1860 and 1953. The farmers often came to the city in good times to better their luck. They were not driven into the metropolis as bewildered, despairing exiles, which is regularly the case today (how this affects black America will be described in the next section).

With all the cyclical ups and downs of those years, the economy had an insatiable need for unskilled and semi-skilled workers. There were jobs for grade-school dropouts and for Eastern European immigrants who could hardly speak English. There was, then, objective reason for hope – and the old poor of the cities were hopeful. The immigrants often brought a language, a religion, even a culture, along with them. The resultant solidarity provided the basis for self-help institutions within the culture of poverty – for political machines, churches, social clubs and the like. In a good many instances aspiration and hunger for learning became a way of life.

These internal resources of the old poor were devoted to the creation of big-city political machines, one of the first welfare systems in the United States. But they also established a base for something more than self-help and group benevolence. In the Thirties militant poverty played a role in a climactic moment in American social history. Millions of the poor participated in the organization of unions, particularly those of the CIO, and in the political struggle for the New Deal. They – and their ethnic drives and community hopes – became an important constituent of a new political coalition which translated the dreams of the liberal reformers and socialists into law – the Wagner Act, Social Security, minimum wage and the like.

The most basic difference between these old poor and the new poor of today is that the economy has changed so fundamentally. The new poor are the automation poor.

There have been, to be sure, overly apocalyptic prophecies about the way in which computers were going to create mass unemployment in the Sixties. Although I did not subscribe to some of the extreme fantasies about the imminent disappearance of work (I located that transformation in the middle to far distance), I am sure that I overestimated the speed of the trend. The tax-cut boom, the direct Federal creation of 700,000 new 'jobs' for soldiers and a million for civilians, through the war in Vietnam, delayed entry into the work force because of expanded education and other factors acted to moderate the revolutionary impact of automated technology. But, as Ben Seligman documented brilliantly in his *Most Notorious Victory*, the radical process of producing more and more goods with fewer and fewer workers is proceeding apace.

The society as a whole has not yet suffered from this trend. The poor have. All of them have been subjected to systematic under-education, and those who have been driven from the land are not even culturally prepared for life in a city. Yet the bottom rungs of the working-class ladder where the unskilled managed to climb into the labor market are being cut off. In 1975, when the skill requirements will be much higher than they are now, the Department of Labor estimates that one fourth (26.6 percent) of the workers twenty-five to thirty-four years of age will be without a high-school diploma. The nation apparently plans that they will be janitors – if they are lucky.

In short, the poverty that will exist in the Seventies is not just a matter of youth, unemployment, totally inadequate education and slums but of all these indignities given a qualitatively new intensity because they occur in the midst of a technological revolution. Thus there is a sinister dynamic at work even as the Department of Commerce announces its statistical triumphs.

2

When the society regained its consciousness of poverty in the Sixties, two errors were often made at opposite ends of the political spectrum. In order to fight reform, conservatives revived that most cherished of middle-class myths: that the poor are essentially lazy free-loaders. And, on the other side, idealistic young people talked of the culture of poverty as if it had created a new 'proletariat,' a class of left-outs driven to struggle heroically for basic change in order to satisfy their immediate needs. Reality has practically nothing to do with the cruel contempt of the Right, but it is, alas, much less romantic than some of the Leftists imagine. It is extremely important to be precise in this regard if one is going to make an accurate assessment of the political potential of the poor.

Consider first the conservative fantasy about high-living welfare chiselers.

The overwhelming majority of the poor who are able to work – about half of the total number of family heads living in poverty – do so. Often, however, as the Department of Labor survey in 1966 demonstrates, their jobs are so low paid or so casual that they are really disguised forms of unemployment. There are still millions of other Americans who spend long hours at back-breaking tasks, such as stoop labor in the fields or dirty work in the kitchen, for a pittance. In the case of those fortunate enough to be covered by minimum-wage regulations, this is done with the full approbation of the law; and those excluded from this protection are even worse off.

Approximately half of the poor are in families where the head is not in the labor market at all. These people are, by an overwhelming majority, too young, too old or too incapacitated to work. Another significant group is composed of women who head large families and are kept home caring for the children. None of those who are thus dependent on some form of public support is exactly living it up. They happen to reside in the stingiest welfare state in the Western world.

In 1967 the Council of Economic Advisers reported that only 22 percent of the poor get public assistance; in 1966 it noted that the majority of the impoverished children in America were not covered under the law, an omission which touches more than ten million of the young. In keeping with the current national adage that the better-off must be taken care of first and the worse-off last, half the money the Government hands out ('public transfer payments') goes to people who are not poor at all; a quarter to those who would be poor if it were not for the aid; and, last of all, a quarter to the poor themselves.

At times the miserly character of American welfare programs is obscene. In his 1967 Economic Report, President Johnson said that state standards in this area are 'miserably low' and cited eighteen states in which a family of four is supposed to live on $45 a month – or less. The President then put forth a seemingly modest, common-sensical idea which, under the prevailing parsimony, is quite radical: that the states be required to pay people what they need to live on and that the definition of need be revised periodically.

In many places government policy encourages divorce. For in a good many states a family is denied funds for impoverished children as long as there is an able-bodied man in the house. This rule establishes a public incentive for a man and his wife to break up: if a husband wants help for his children, he has to leave. Even when this is done, the officially contrived humiliations are not at an end. Local investigators will often make spot checks to be sure that their brutal bargain is being enforced and that the man is not secretly seeing his wife.

So roughly half the poor are dependent on dead-end jobs in the labor market; and the other half must subsist on handouts which, when they are lucky enough to get them, are usually insufficient. But if the poor are most emphatically not pampered in this country, they still do not constitute a social class, much less a revolutionary proletariat. And the basic reason for this is that the culture of poverty contains too many different kinds of people and therefore does not give rise to a common consciousness. There are, however, sub-groups of the poor which do achieve a solidarity and purposiveness and this is of great political importance.

There are heterogeneous elements in all social classes: the young and the old, Northerners and Southerners, big- and small-business men, skilled and unskilled workers. These differences are often the source of tension, and even violent disagreements, within a class. But the fact that people share an economic function tends to impose a long-run community of interest on them. And this is true in the United States despite the widespread conviction that the country is classless. As I noted earlier, American elections follow class lines more religiously than do European.

But poor people have radically different economic roles. One of the most obvious distinctions has already been made: that half of the poor are not tied to the labor market at all. The working poor and the welfare poor are thus subjected to very different kinds of daily experience and may even develop antagonistic needs and attitudes. The matter is further complicated by geography, for the poor are to be found everywhere in the society and are not concentrated like workers and businessmen in the cities or farmers on the land. In 1964 (and the basic reality has not changed much since then) about 47 percent of the poor lived in metropolitan areas and 29.4 percent in central cities. There were 12.7 percent on farms and 39.5 percent in non-farm rural areas.

But there are various sub-groups of the poor within which the members are in sufficiently close contact with one another to share daily experiences and a common consciousness. There are Negroes who have group attitudes derived from a ghetto existence, Mexican-American migrants in California with an ethnic and class solidarity, Appalachians who struggle together against strip mining, and so on. Each one of these insurgencies is tremendously important but there is not enough common interest between these groups to create nation-wide institutions like the AFL-CIO or the Chamber of Commerce.

The other America is also divided on racial lines. According to the 1967 Commerce figures, two thirds of the poor are white, one third non-white (mainly Negro). Among the white poor there are disproportionate numbers from certain ethnic groups, such as the Puerto Ricans, the Southwest Spanish-speaking and the old American stock of Appalachia. As so often happens at the bottom of the society, there is considerable hostility among the different races and cultures partaking of the same misery. This ugly fact should not be taken for granted, and it is possible, as will become clearer in a moment, to revive that brief Populist alliance of the poor whites and blacks which existed after the Civil War. But it is still true that racial difference is one more factor restraining the poor from developing a class consciousness.

Moreover, the fact of poverty is dialectical, for it drives people to both revolt and despair. To the middle-class observer the poor often seem to inhabit a simple hell of violence, broken families, drunkenness and other social pathologies. Yet, as Oscar Lewis has brilliantly documented, some of these attitudes involve a creative, courageous response to an impossible environment. To the law-abiding citizen of the suburbs, a slum gang is a threat to public order and only that; to youth on the streets, it may be an expression of solidarity and a means of self-defense. 'Living in the present,' Lewis writes, 'may develop a capacity for spontaneity, for the enjoyment of the sensual, which is often blunted in the middle-class, future-oriented man.'

And yet there is the other side of poverty, the fact that, to quote Lewis again, 'poverty of culture is one of the crucial traits of the culture of poverty.' The poor live under conditions which debilitate the spirit and rob people of the sense of their own proper worth. The most maimed of the other Americans may participate in a riot or looting, but they do not have that same impulse toward creating permanent organizations of their own as the trade-union workers do.

There is, then, no nation-wide class of the poor. The culture of poverty contains city workers, farmers, the jobless, the indigent and the retired and is located in every section of the nation. And yet there is an objective self-interest which embraces almost all of these people even though their heterogeneous situations do not bring them to a collective awareness of the fact. The poor are particularly victimized by the fact that tax funds are spent on the middle class and the rich and not on those in greatest need. If there were a dynamic political movement, including organized workers and middle-class liberals and radicals, it would provide a context in which the various sub-groups of the poor could find a unity they will probably not achieve on their own (more on this point in Chapter 10).

So the poor are not lazy, as the conservatives think, nor are they revolutionary proletarians, as some radicals hope. They suffer similar miseries, but not in common, and therefore their resistance to injustice is subdivided according to occupation, race and location. But the crucial point is that the resistance does exist. Were there a vital democratic Left it could help transform the entire society.

3

Throughout the postwar period the most dynamic movement involving the poor has taken place among Negroes. One reason is that the new poverty is the mechanism for enforcing the new racism and that black men thus have two motives to fight back – or it must be added, two motives for despair.

The broad outlines of the new racism are familiar enough and, like most social catastrophes these days, have been officially recognized by the Government (in President Johnson's Howard University speech of 1965). The Jim Crow statutes have been eradicated, thanks to the incredible courage of Negroes themselves; laws have been passed to guarantee all men access to the ballot and public accommodations; and the economy keeps the Negro at the bottom of the society anyway, thus providing a perfectly constitutional means of keeping the black man in his 'place.' There are two aspects of this vicious system that are particularly relevant to this chapter: the way in which Washington has paid good tax money to make the urban ghettos worse; the role of technology in imposing a second-class citizenship on black America. This pessimistic analysis will, however, yield one optimistic possibility: that economic action can erode the psychological basis of racism and that intimate hatreds can thus be affected by government action.

First of all, there is the special Smith-Keynesian victimization which did particular harm to the Negro. Agricultural programs which served the interests of rich farmers and, eventually, of giant industrial corporations were a means of exporting social problems from the rural South to the urban North and making them much worse in the process.

The costs of research and development for the farms were long ago socialized by the Department of Agriculture. This governmentally financed application of science to the land was one of the driving forces behind the incredible growth of farm productivity in the United States. Indeed, during the post-World War II period there was a greater technological revolution in rural America than in the factories. Farm output per man hour went up twice as fast as non-farm, and in some years there were fantastic increments: 11.3 percent in 1964–65, 10.4 percent in 1957–58 and 14 percent in 1949–50 (the highest non-farm increase during these years was 6.3 percent). The result was that much more could be produced with far fewer people.

But then it was not just the over-all trend which struck at the farm laborer. There were specific Federal programs to hurt him too. Thus, in the Thirties, the Agricultural Adjustment Act took cotton out of production and reduced the need for hired hands, which was fine for the owner and a disaster for the man who lost his job. More generally, Washington's policies were oriented toward the successful market farmer and had the profound effect of driving small producers, who got no substantial subsidy, out of business while making corporate farming, which was handsomely remunerated, inviting even to city slickers. In 1940 there were over six million farms in the United States, half of them less than a hundred acres in size. In 1967 there were about three million units, most of them larger than one hundred acres.

In effect, the Government was running a curious dis-placed-person program by uprooting poor Southerners, and above all Negroes, and forcing them to migrate from the countryside to the city. This pattern became particu-larly evil in the 1950s when the Civil Rights Movement challenged Southern segregation. For the racists con-sciously used the Federally induced technological trends in order to exile the black opposition to the urban areas. So the U.S. Economic Development Administration re-ported in 1967, 'the push of poor rural conditions rather than the pull of urban economic opportunities' drove ten million people off the land and into the metropolitan areas during the Fifties.

The Government could not have done much worse if it had carefully set out to build more terrible ghettos. Between 1960 and 1965 the white population of the cities declined by 1 percent (immigrants to the suburbs ex-ceeded the population gain by 400,000), while the Negro percentage in the same period went up by a fifth. As a result of this mass migration and a high birth rate, the Negro teen-age population in the slums – this is the group now conventionally referred to as 'social dynamite' by everyone from the FBI to the National Council of Churches – increased by over 50 percent, or at twice the white rate. And there was, as the Economic Develop-ment Administration saw it, a 'startling ... mismatch of jobs and people' when country folk, totally unprepared for city life, arrived in the ghettos.

In short, one of the main reasons why the relief rolls continued to rise in the midst of a boom during the Sixties was Federal agricultural policy.

This narrative of the socialization of public evils would not be complete without a Smith-Keynesian denoue-ment. In August 1967 the *Wall Street Journal* reported that business – and particularly the 'conglomerate enter-prises' which do anything and everything for a profit – were more and more moving into agriculture. So it was, the *Journal* reported, that the Textron company had gone into broiler chickens as well as rocket engines and helicopters. Meanwhile in New York City the public-assistance rolls in June 1964 equalled the Depression peak.

The black DPs from the South joined the earlier migrant generations in the central cities. Then both groups were subjected to the new racism embedded in the new poverty: at the precise moment at which Negroes reached the take-off point in the mass-production society, it began to disappear.

The trek of black Southern farmers to Southern and Northern cities started before World War I. By the beginning of the Twenties there was already sufficient disillusionment with the not-so-promised lands of Detroit, New York and Chicago that Marcus Garvey could recruit masses to the slogan of Back to Africa. In the Twenties the urban good times were so relative for the Negroes that, Horace Cayton and St Clair Drake report, Chicago Negroes actually bettered their living conditions when they went on relief. And yet, in the very midst of the Depression, there was a hopeful development. The CIO, with its philosophy of industrial unionism, was committed to organizing all the workers in a given plant. The historic hostility of the white workers against Negroes whom the companies manipulated as strike breakers was coming to an end. And this opening was widened during World War II when A. Philip Randolph's March on Washington movement forced Franklin Roosevelt to order fair-employment practices in the defense industry.

At this point, if the traditional ethnic scenario of the European immigrants were taken as a model, the Negroes were supposed to deepen their beachhead. Instead, they were driven back.

The Fifties were a period of chronic recession and unemployment during which the poor, both black and white, and many workers were sacrificed to the Republican manias for price stability and balanced budgets. The last to arrive in the mass-production sector were, of course, the first to be fired. Meanwhile, the Federal Government was bankrolling highways and suburbs, exporting rural Negroes to the ghetto, moving jobs to the white outskirts of town, and so on. Ironically, it was in these very years that the American conscience, the exigencies of Cold War politics and a remarkable Supreme Court created a climate in which a brilliant Negro mass movement erupted in the South and challenged the old racism.

So there was economic retrogression in the ghetto at the same time that the black man was making his great political and social strides forward. After the legislative victories of 1964 and 1965 the Department of Labor declared in 1967 that the black slums were worse than ever. In the Hough ghetto of Cleveland, one Labor study in October 1967 reported the percentage of families living in poverty increased from 31 percent to 39 percent during the 'boom' years of 1960–65. Clearly, in order to combat this new racism, the Civil Rights Movement must have a program which proposes full employment, the abolition of the slums, decent education for all, and so on. And hopefully, if such things are to be accomplished (and much of the rest of the book describes how they might be achieved), then economics, which is now used to keep the Negro down, could become a weapon for rooting the racist psychology out of the society.

Prejudice against Negroes in America has many, many springs. It draws strength from the diabolical deeds of slavery, the incompleteness of Emancipation, the profitability of exploiting cheap black labor, white fear, and from many other sources. One of the best current measures of the utter irrationality of racism is the fact that many employed Negroes are overqualified for their jobs! Even when a black man manages to get a good education, he does not get equal pay. Some 35 percent of the nonwhites over eighteen years of age had completed four years of high school in 1965 and 7 percent had finished college, but only 17 percent were in professional, technical, managerial, clerical and sales positions – a much smaller proportion than that of whites with similar education.

It is probably this utterly 'non-functional' discrimination, where there is not even the excuse that a man has been denied the education to qualify for a post, which angers so many young middle-class Negroes and drives them toward the extremes. Huey P. Newton, the leader of the Black Panthers, a California organization which advocates that Negroes carry guns openly (and practices what it preaches), graduated from the Berkeley High School, an integrated institution with an excellent reputation, and attended law school. (At this writing he is accused of shooting a policeman in an altercation in which each side charges the other with firing first.) The leader of the Malcolm X Society in Detroit in 1967 is a lawyer who is the son of a doctor. For it often happens that when the black man fights his way up the occupational ladder he discovers a raw racism, a psychopathology rather than a sociology.

Harry Golden said of the immigrants of his youth that they had to work twice as hard to achieve half as much as the native-born. If that is a fair impression of the barriers faced by the Irish, Jews, Italians and other European groups, then one would say that this country taunts a Negro with the fact that he must work four times as hard to achieve one quarter of what the white gets. The impoverished Puerto Ricans and Mexican Americans will have an easier time in escaping from the culture of poverty than the Negroes, for, once they get the education, most of them can disappear into the larger society.

It is the sickening realization of this barbaric reality that has driven some of the best of the black Americans to despair, nihilism – or to fantasies about the Third World and/or Negro self-determination in the United States. Yet, as the chapters on foreign policy will make quite clear, there is no such thing as a unified Third

World, and, in any case, the impoverished, non-white nations do not have the resources to save themselves, much less the American Negroes. This situation is, to be sure, a consequence of the exercise of white imperialist power and not of the inferiority of the people of Asia, Africa and Latin America. Transforming this evil reality requires, however, the action of a democratic Left in America that includes both black and white.

Proposals for Negro self-determination within America are based on another illusion: that the nationalization of poverty will create wealth. The deficiencies in education and skill which have been imposed on black America within the United States would exist within a black state. Therefore, the only practical strategy for destroying both the new poverty and the new racism requires that the Negro seek access to the mainstream of that very white society which has so outrageously abused him. To some radicals, both black and white, this notion will seem to be a call to Negroes to deny their blackness, admit the superiority of whiteness and homogenize themselves according to the dictates and customs of the middle class. There is both untruth and distorted half-truth in this reaction.

The economic and social programs required to combat the new racism are of such a magnitude that the society is not going to hand them over just for the asking. Politically speaking, Negro leaders will have to organize Negro masses to play a major role in an interracial coalition which will radicalize the entire nation. In the process, black men and women will be asserting their control over their own organizations and their own economic and social destiny. Race pride is clearly a necessary element in this process; it is only the race fantasies which must be excluded from it.

But, secondly, let me admit to a half-truth in the inevitable critique of the program I have suggested: that there will be a certain homogenization if this strategy prevails, that the Negro will have to sacrifice 'soul' in order to get economic justice. That is, I think, partially true and partially, but only partially, deplorable. To the degree that this is not a happy prospect, however, the fault lies with reality and not with the tactic urged here.

In *Civilization and Its Discontents*, Sigmund Freud identified a tragic paradox in human history: that material progress requires the repression of the instinctual life. As society becomes more complex and productive, pleasures are deferred, people become more disciplined, there is long-range calculation, saving and investment. The simpler joys of 'acting out,' of immediate gratification and violent expression are lost – and so are the simpler evils of infant mortality, hunger, disease, shortened life span, and the like. This transition, it should be noted, is characteristic of any technological society, whether it is run by businessmen, commissars or Third World nationalists.

It is one of the strengths of the poor that they have not been dragooned into this work ethic – and it is also a reason for their poverty and misery. It is a distortion to see only one side of this dialectical reality, to dismiss the poor as simply irresponsible as the conservatives do, or to romanticize 'soul' as some radicals do. My Irish ancestors of a hundred years ago in New York were certainly less inhibited and more rollicking than their lace-curtain posterity, and they were often pictured as being as depraved and violent as some racists now think Negroes are. There was a loss and a gain in the process of assimilation.

So if one realistically proposes to end the super-exploitation of the black poor (and the white poor, too, since a place like Appalachia has its own version of 'soul'), there will probably be some loss of spontaneity when there is a gain in economic rationality and the fact will be both poignant and positive. Ultimately, I do not think that mankind need forever submit to Freud's law, a point I discussed in *The Accidental Century*. In the automated world of the twenty-first century, soul may be a necessity as work once was. For now, one must honestly admit that economic progress will require that the Negro, like anyone else, surrender some of the pleasures, as well as all of the horrors, of being poor. And this is true even though a dynamic political movement capable of challenging the new racism must include a black component which is infused with race pride.

And if the economic underpinning of the new racism is indeed destroyed, there will be a psychological dividend. The transformation of the economy can penetrate to some of the secret reaches of race hatred.

Under the new racist dispensation, prejudice is a self-reinforcing mechanism. White America imposes an impossible economic position on the Negro and then in effect equates blackness with menial work, high rates of unemployment, welfare dependency and slum pathology. The whites do not bother to notice that all of these 'qualities' are social artifacts and not free choices or genetic inheritances. There are poor white communities which suffer the very same humiliations, but – and this is a crucial point – they can be dismissed as exceptions to the rule since most whites do not live in the other America. Negroes, however, are more than three times as poor as whites, and if one takes into account the magnetic field of poverty, then the majority of Negroes are well within its reach. So the disabilities of being poor are seen as essential to the Negro and accidental for the white. This allows the ignorant racist to flatter himself with fairy tales of his 'natural' superiority, and it even corrupts the vision of the not so racist white.

But conversely, if there were genuine full employment, decent housing, modern education and all the rest for Negroes, the consequences of this fact would do more to undermine intimate white hatreds than all of the sermons of the priests, ministers and rabbis put together. The race problem is, I am suggesting, to a considerable degree a question of class difference, or, more precisely, of that economic chasm which separates the typical white American from the Negro who has been forced down into the underclass. When black men and women move normally at every level of social and economic life – when their presence is natural and not that of a token model on a TV commercial or an executive for an Equal Opportunity employer – then the eyes of America will literally see differently.

For now, the new racism has the same frightening potential for persistence as the new poverty. Six years ago I wrote in *The Other America* that if all the racist statutes were repealed, the racist economic structure of the United States would take their place. And that, despite the escalation of social rhetoric in the intervening years, is what happened.

4

In January of 1964 President Johnson declared his 'unconditional' War on Poverty. What followed was a totally inadequate, highly conditional program. Those on the democratic Left who welcomed the initiative, as this writer did, saw it as a point of departure, not as the real effort. Yet it was indeed a gain for this society that Johnson, and John F. Kennedy before him, at least placed the issue on the national agenda.

Then, in 1965, the escalation of the Vietnamese war began in earnest. As the special assessments for that tragedy rose to $30 billion or more, social programs were cut back. What was supposed to be a social war turned out to be a skirmish and, in any case, poverty won. Now, given the analysis of this and the preceding chapter, it is possible to outline what an *unconditional* war on poverty would actually be. A good many of the specifics will be detailed in Chapter 5. For now, here are some of the major elements of an attack on the new poverty and the new racism.

Every slum in the United States should be destroyed within ten years, the black ghettos above all.

There must be actual full employment. This would

require a real unemployment percentage equal to the number of people out of work because of illness, moving to a new job, etc. It would not tolerate any involuntary unemployment. It would also mean an end to all poverty jobs and a vast reduction of the number of people who have been forced out of the labor force altogether.

Those Americans not in the labor force should be guaranteed an annual income which will allow them to lead a decent, dignified life.

All schools should be legally required to provide an education adequate to life in the society. Public subsidies for schooling should be provided to the extent that they are needed.

These are the kinds of countermeasures which must be taken if the 'natural,' inherent injustices of the society are not to overwhelm millions. The subsidies for the well-off promoted social chaos, as Chapter 2 documented, but, at this particular time in history, this pattern now takes on an even more sinister cast than ever before. For it amounts to an unwitting conspiracy against at least one fifth of the nation.

The new poverty and the new racism are impervious to ringing declarations and even more dynamic than optimistic statistics suggest. From a democratic point of view, the miseries visited upon the individual poor add up to a collective tragedy: that the classic land of opportunity will condemn some millions of human beings to a hereditary degradation based on class, color or, worst of all, on both.

CHAPTER FOUR

THE SOCIAL-INDUSTRIAL COMPLEX

American corporations, as the last two chapters made abundantly clear, have long scrambled over the common good in pursuit of private profit. In doing this, they were greatly aided by the Adam Smith version of John Maynard Keynes. Now, however, the companies threaten a new, distinctive and paradoxical danger. Instead of creating social problems, they are going to solve them.

In a strangely optimistic speech, Lyle M. Spencer, president of Science Research Associates (an IBM subsidiary), gave an apt and ominous name to this development. He hailed the emergence of a new 'social-industrial complex.' Spencer's enthusiasm is puzzling in that his phrase is borrowed from one of the most somber statements Dwight Eisenhower ever made: the warning against the sinister potential of a 'military-industrial complex' in the United States. And indeed, the phenomenon Spencer describes is quite similar to that coalition of executives and generals which so alarmed Eisenhower in his last address as President. The military-industrial complex bases itself on a permanent war economy and a huge military establishment. This enormous vested interest in annihilation, Eisenhower feared, could subvert the democratic process in matters of war and peace. The social-industrial complex also builds on public expenditure and the 'partnership' of government and business. But its rationale is the Great Society and not the Cold War (much of the spending waits on the end of the tragic conflict in Vietnam).

As Spencer puts it: 'Social causes which in the Thirties were the domain of college professors, labor unions and student demonstrations are today becoming the new business of business.'

What is menacing about this sudden outburst of corporate conscience should be clear from the last two chapters: satisfying social needs and making money are two distinct, and often hostile, undertakings. If they are systematically confused, if social causes become big business, there are disturbing possibilities quite like the ones Eisenhower saw in the military-industrial complex. The first step toward understanding this danger is to see why it is that the private sector became so ethical at a given point in our history.

I

First of all, thought is becoming power to a degree beyond the wildest imaginings of a Platonist philosopher-king. Five years ago Clark Kerr estimated that the production, distribution and consumption of knowledge already accounted for 29 percent of the Gross National Product and was growing at twice the rate of the rest of the economy. In 1966 the president of IBM declared that the nation was fast approaching a time in which more than half the work force would be involved in processing and applying data. In 1967 Harold B. Gores, the head of a Ford Foundation subsidiary, proclaimed that 'learning is the new growth industry.' So higher education is no longer the aristocratic province of a tiny upper-class minority. And both practical politicians and hard-headed businessmen have noticed this momentous trend.

Secondly, the executives of the social-industrial complex, and the nation as a whole, have been tutored by militant Negroes, some of whom can't read. In the Eisenhower Fifties civic virtue was equated with a balanced budget. But, beginning with Martin Luther King's Montgomery bus boycott of 1955, a Negro mass movement rescued America's better self. Eventually, the practical idealism of black men rekindled the spirit of protest on the campus, challenged the churches and the unions and, in effect, prepared the country to respond to John F. Kennedy's summons to action. In the process, social conscience became a political force. Americans suddenly noticed the racial ghettos, the black and white poor, the polluted air and the squalid facilities of the public sector.

But for all the talk about reform, little was done. Three years after the proclamation of the Great Society the Manpower Report noted that the slums had become worse, the people more desperate. In the series of summer riots which began in 1964, America was provided with another motive for change: fear. Some, to be sure, simply wanted to suppress the social problems which gave rise to the violence by brute force and, as Chapter 2 pointed out, if this view triumphs, then the entire society might stagnate for a generation or more. But others were driven by the urban upheavals to seek immediate and ranging solutions to the evils festering in the central cities.

These trends created, as J. Herbert Hollomon put it on behalf of the Department of Commerce, a 'public market.' Hollomon urged private industry to go out and build colleges and create new cities for 400,000 people. Max Ways of *Fortune* called this approach 'creative federalism.' It rested, he said, on 'the rapprochement, during the Johnson Administration, between government and business. The two still have and will always have different responsibilities and aims. But they are beginning to use the same working language, depend on the same kind of people, and get at tasks and decisions in the same way.'

Finally, credit must be given to Barry Goldwater for convincing private enterprise to ratify the massive Federal Presence which the social-industrial complex requires. The ideological unreality of his 1964 campaign forced businessmen to choose between the risks of the market and the stability of a managed economy. The

captains of the greatest industries unhesitatingly chose
the latter course and in the process endorsed not simply
Franklin Roosevelt's welfare state but Lyndon Johnson's
Great Society as well.

The new corporate idealism, then, has a very businesslike basis. The companies have acquired a conscience at
that precise moment when, for a variety of technological,
social and political reasons, there is money to be made in
doing good. And in pursuit of their own private purposes
the executives are going to have much to say about what
Americans think and how they live. The knowledge industry already includes General Dynamics, AT&T,
General Electric, Time Incorporated, Minnesota Mining
and Manufacturing, Bell and Howell, Philco, Westinghouse, Raytheon, Xerox, CBS, Burroughs Business
Machines and Packard Bell. The city building industry
has attracted Goodyear, General Electric, Humble Oil,
Westinghouse, U.S. Gypsum and even Walt Disney Pro-
ductions. And this, clearly, is only the beginning of the
beginning.

2

Charles Silberman of *Fortune* was not being extravagant
when he wrote recently that the knowledge industrialists
are, in their partnership with the Government, 'likely to
transform both the organization and content of education, and through it, of American society itself.' Clearly
such a massive concentration of private power in a traditional public domain is a disturbing fact.

Francis Keppel, the former United States Commissioner of Education, is now the head of General Learning, a knowledge corporation which has been put together by General Electric and Time Incorporated. His
social conscience long predates the business discovery that
thinking is a blue-chip occupation. There is, Keppel concedes, a danger that the companies will dominate, rather
than serve, American education. Yet, he argues, perhaps

the danger has been exaggerated. Of the tens of billions of dollars America spends each year on schooling, the largest single expenditure is for teachers' salaries. After that, the money goes to construction and maintenance and only about 4 percent of the total, or less than $1.5 billion a year, is devoted to instructional materials of all kinds. Therefore, Keppel says, the giant corporations have not really discovered such a huge market and there really isn't a fiscal motive for 'taking over' the system.

Secondly, Keppel points out that decision-making in American education is decentralized, with authority vested in a multiplicity of boards, superintendents and principals. The only way that the knowledge industry can serve a truly public purpose, he believes, is if it is clearly a junior partner and subordinate to the educators. The latter must dictate the content of what is to be taught. The corporations can then supply them with the services and materials they need, but they must not impose a curriculum which is designed to satisfy the needs of private profit rather than those of students.

Keppel's second point involves a crucial distinction. For there are two antagonistic modes of business participation in the solving of social problems which often employ an identical rhetoric. On the one hand, the society can democratically decide on what it wants to teach and the kinds of cities in which it wants to live. It can then contract out the construction work, the preparation of materials and even certain advisory functions to the private sector. But the planning and the programming are clearly kept under democratic, political, rather than corporate control, and the pivot of the whole system is composed of non-profit institutions. This is what Keppel advocates. Or – and this is the sinister potential of the social-industrial complex – America might unwittingly hire business to build a new urban civilization on the basis of the very money-making priorities which brought the old civilization to crisis. The contractor would not simply execute the contract. He would draw it up as well.

Keppel admits that this second, and ominous, possibility exists. He also concedes that the relative smallness of the educational market is not simply a cause for optimism. It could mean that companies will design machines and programs according to corporate specification for private use and then, as a careless, money-making afterthought, unload them on school systems as well. Keppel himself is clearly determined to fight against this tendency. And there have been published reports of an internal struggle within General Learning between the technicians and engineers, concerned with knowledge 'hardware,' and the educators. Yet there is disturbing evidence that there are powerful elements in the industry much less idealistic than Keppel. If they prevail, the intellectual formation of the American young could be subordinated to the pursuit of profit.

And they might well prevail, according to the *Wall Street Journal*. In a number of articles during the past year the *Journal* has paid careful attention to the potential of the knowledge industry. Enthusiastically, even euphorically, this authoritative voice has reported that Keppel's worst fears are already becoming fact.

'It is clear,' the *Journal* said in one analysis, 'both government and industry will play increasingly active parts in deciding what schools will teach and how they will present it.' A little later the paper was more precise on the junior role that would be assigned to educators under the coming dispensation: '. . . new schools to a considerable extent have to be built around the electronic gear that will cram them.'

There are already signs that this is happening. 'A lot of schools have been taken advantage of by industry,' B. Frank Brown, superintendent of schools in Melbourne, Florida, was quoted as saying. 'There are millions of dollars' worth of equipment stored in schools that just isn't practical.' And the United States Commissioner of

Education, Harold Howe II, generalized the point: 'Like the drug for which there is as yet no disease, we now have some machines that can talk but have nothing to say. I would caution the businessman not to venture into hardware unless he is prepared to go all the way into printed materials and programming.'

If, as Howe rightly fears, the technical comes to predominate over the intellectual in American schools, then fundamental decisions about learning will become a function of the corporate struggle for shares of the knowledge market. If this happens, then each producer will push its own particular educational technology. Thus Xerox would be interested in its kind of teaching machines, IBM in computer-run classrooms, CBS in television teaching, and so on. Now obviously machines, computers and television may have an enormous contribution to make to American education. But how is one going to decide among them? If the *Wall Street Journal* estimate is correct, there will be a considerable amount of company jockeying before the basically educational decision is made. At this point, those familiar with the military-industrial complex will be aware of a striking similarity between it and the emerging social-industrial complex.

In the defense sector there are, of course, alliances between particular industries, branches of the service, 'independent' associations for the Army, Air Force, Navy and Marines, and even trade-unions. Each of the elements in this coalition has its own special interest (profit for the companies, prestige and power for the officers, jobs for labor). And they lobby for strategies which are determined not by any objective analysis of the needs of the nation but by their own stake in the decision. The debate over the B-70 bomber during the Kennedy Administration was a classic case in point. A powerful section of the military-industrial complex, led by the Air Force, mounted a determined campaign against the Administration in favor of proposals which had been rejected by three Secretaries of Defense under Eisenhower and by Secretary McNamara under Kennedy.

Something like this pattern is beginning to emerge within the social-industrial complex. 'Business,' to quote the *Wall Street Journal* once more, 'is turning into an important force for pushing embattled domestic proposals through Congress.' An executive of the Department of Housing and Urban Development is quoted as saying, 'Each agency has gradually developed a list of firms interested in its field ... we don't keep them turned on all the time, but we know how to turn them on. ...' At first glance this might seem to portend a happy situation in which the corporations are lending their political power to a public purpose. There are schoolteachers who, after so many years of being treated as irrelevant by practical businessmen, make this optimistic interpretation. But, as the experience of the military-industrial complex demonstrates, such procedures lead straight to private alliances between self-interested executives and ambitious bureaucrats. This trend is already well developed in the cities industry – where, for instance, real-estate men support rent subsidies as a means of attacking public housing – and, as the *Wall Street Journal* rightly realizes, it is going to appear in education too.

A report in the *New Republic* in June 1967 gave a vivid illustration of what this might mean. The Office of Education, it said, was considering a grant of $2 million to build a computer classroom for Menominee Indians in Wisconsin. Westinghouse was to develop the hardware which would eventually serve sixty students. This considerable investment would do nothing to help the nine hundred other children on the reservation who were receiving inferior education from unqualified teachers. And the proposal was made at the precise moment when mechanized teaching is being criticized by some educators because of its impersonality. However, if the *New Republic* is right, the motives behind the decision did not focus on the needs of these particular children but on considerations of governmental-corporate *Realpolitik*. 'The one substantive reason for financing this project,' the article said, 'is the government's interest in building up the education industry; in this instance, picking up Westinghouse's developmental costs so it can compete with other companies, like IBM, which the United States also finances.' So these young Indians might be among the very first students in the land to have their education designed according to the political engineering principles of the B-70 bomber.

During the New York State Constitutional Convention in 1967 there was another illustration of how business might put its aims first and education second. The elected representatives of the people were discussing adopting the principle of universal free college education for all the citizens of the state. Strangely enough at that precise moment, all of the major institutional investors in New York suddenly decided not to bid on $46.6 million in state school construction notes. It was widely rumored that they were fearful that the proposed constitutional provision would make such an investment too risky, and this was taken as a rather blunt hint that the members of the Convention should back off any radical educational commitments to the people. In a not so veiled reference to the influence of Governor Nelson Rockefeller in the Chase Manhattan Bank, the president of the Convention, Anthony Travia, a supporter of the new proposal, remarked, 'Someone has a friend in some bank and it certainly isn't Travia.'

But at this point, the ultimate outcome of many of these trends is in doubt. There have been, to be sure, minor scandals, such as the hawking of programmed instruction door to door during the teaching-machine vogue of a few years back. And Parsons College has shown what an aggressive administrator can do when he runs an educational institution like a business. But the giants in the field have been working cautiously with the long run in mind. The largest single body of experience is found in the Job Corps.

When the Corps was first set up under the Economic Opportunity Act, it was widely hailed as a trail-blazing example of uniting Federal idealism and free-enterprise expertise. Contracts were awarded to corporations like Federal Electric (a subsidiary of IT&T), the ubiquitous Litton Industries, U.S. Industries and Westinghouse Air Brake. In general, the early high hopes have been disappointed. For, as Sar Levitan summed up the experience in 1967, the costs have been high (and the contracts are, in effect, on a cost-plus basis) and the companies themselves have lost some of their enthusiasm. One reason for this latter development is that, with the escalation of the tragic war in Vietnam, executives no longer feel a need to look toward Shriver instead of McNamara.

But, much more particularly, one of the most interesting perspectives on the Job Corps experience is provided by the members and organizers of the American Federation of Teachers. Among the fastest growing unions in the country, the AFT has consistently fought to improve the quality of education as well as the wages and working conditions of its people. Its somewhat disillusioned view of the privately operated Job Corps camps does not really have to do with money. Rather it centers on the feeling that the companies treated the educators in their employ like so many hired hands, that they treated schools as if they were factories.

John O'Leary is a personable young AFL-CIO organizer who worked with AFT in their attempt to sign up the Camp Kilmer Job Corps during 1966 and 1967. Kilmer was operated by the Federal Electric Corporation and its contract established a relationship with Rutgers University, which was supposed to evaluate the project. The first Rutgers report was a controversial criticism of the camp, charging 'flagrant deficiencies.' After much debate, the university decided that its professors were delivering their own opinions and nothing more.

Originally, as O'Leary tells the story of the organizing campaign, eighty academic teachers at Kilmer wanted to form a bargaining unit, and they came to the AFT. The management reacted, O'Leary says, 'as if we were trying to organize a production plant where the workers had less than an eighth-grade education.' Labor-relations experts were imported, group meetings were sponsored, everyone on the payroll received letters. The company, in a classic anti-union maneuver, insisted that the bargaining unit should be expanded to include vocational teachers and fought the issue up through the labor-relations structure. By the time Federal Electric had carried its point at the regional level of the NLRB, the original union membership had either become demoralized or left the camp.

At Excelsior Springs, Missouri, Westinghouse Air Brake fought a similar delaying action after AFT members went out on strike. Ten months after the original action, the union majority had eroded, the election was lost – and management proceeded to fire five of the union leaders (the AFT submitted unfair labor practices charges on this count). At the Parks Job Corps Center in California, managed by Litton Industries, a twenty-day strike led to an election in June of 1967. In the course of that campaign, one of the complaints of the Teachers' and Counselors' union at Parks was that 'Litton bought hundreds of thousands of dollars of Litton teaching materials of questionable value in the classroom from its own educational subsidiary with your tax dollars and forced instructors to use them.'

As a result of these experiences, John Schmid, the State Federations Coordinator of the AFT, concluded that 'it is plain that private industry feels that teachers deserve even less of a voice in the formulation of curriculum than do most boards of education.' This judgment has many implications, but one of them is especially relevant here. As the idealistic, education-oriented activists of the AFT see the Job Corps experience, the private companies have tended to impose factory-style labor relations on a school system. In terms of Keppel's hopes and fears, business is here taking a commanding, autocratic position, not a subordinate one.

Indeed, David Gottlieb, a top analyst in the Office of Economic Opportunity's Plans and Programs division in the mid-Sixties, generalized this point in a paradoxical fashion. The corporate-run Job Corps camps had, he said, a 'garment of approval,' for the conservatives in Congress who were always ready to attack the inadequacies of a Federal project run by Harvard, Columbia or Berkeley would not question the operations of a good, down-to-earth businessman. Therefore, Gottlieb continued, the corporate undertakings had a greater freedom from governmental supervision than, say, a Peace Corps training institute directed by a university. Precisely because social program administrators always try to get industry support, he concludes, they are less able to bring industry under public control when they do get it involved.

Gottlieb does not think that the companies abused this curious freedom. Yet it is clearly a dangerous trend when, at the very inception of the knowledge industry, private entrepreneurs achieve a certain immunity from democratic criticism which is denied to non-profit professors. In the field of education the presumption, one would think, should favor the scholar, not the money-maker.

In his Farewell Address, President Eisenhower had been particularly alarmed by the possibility that the military-industrial complex would come to control American education. He was concerned about 'the prospect of domination of the nation's scholars by Federal employment' and the possibility that 'public policy could itself become the captive of a scientific, technological elite.' In part, Eisenhower's fears have been justified. As Clark Kerr testified – perhaps too candidly from the point of view of his own career – in *The Uses of the Multiversity*, Federal grants and big-business needs are playing an ever-increasing role in determining the shape and quality of higher education in America. But now, with the social-industrial complex, the danger becomes more pervasive, for it extends to the kindergarten and the Job Corps camp as well as to the graduate seminar. There are those, like Keppel, who would make the knowledge industry the servant of the educators. But there seem to be many more who follow the jubilant philosophy expressed in the *Wall Street Journal* articles: that schools shall now be designed to fit machines rather than the other way around.

3

But then the social-industrial complex is not simply concerned with how Americans think. It may well attempt to decide how the nation lives as well.

During the hearings on the urban crisis chaired by Senator Abraham Ribicoff in 1966, the country got some idea of the enormous dimensions of the problem. It is necessary, in President Johnson's phrase, to build a 'second America' – i.e., between 1966 and 2000 the United States must construct more new housing units than it now possesses. The official estimates call for two million additional units a year, with at least 500,000 of them designed for low-income families. The AFL-CIO says we need 2.5 million new units a year; Walter Reuther's figure is three million. And these things can only be done, businessmen like David Rockefeller told Ribicoff, if there is a Federal subsidy to attract the social conscience of profit-makers. So a huge, new, tax-supported market may well be in the making.

This is at least one of the reasons why the backers of the Demonstration Cities (now Model Cities) Act in the fall of 1966 included Rockefeller, Henry Ford, Thomas Gates of Morgan Guaranty Trust, Alfred Perlman of New York Central, and R. Gwin Follis of Standard Oil of California. It also helps explain why General Electric is now interested in building a city of 200,000 people from the ground up – using GE products where possible, of course – and why U.S. Gypsum is demonstrating its skills in publicly supported slum rehabilitation and hopes to make an eventual 8 to 10 percent profit from such work. What was considered 'socialism' only yesterday is turning into a sound business investment.

There is a modest precedent for this pattern in the activities of the 'civic' executives who appeared in many major American cities in the Fifties and Sixties. These men were primarily bankers, department-store owners, office-building landlords and others with a strong business stake in the central city. They mobilized the entire community, used both Federal and local funds, and improved the downtown areas according to the needs of banks, department stores and office buildings rather than those of the black and white poor. In 1967 the New York *Times* reported that Mr Lewis Kitchen, president of the City Reconstruction Company, was preparing to spend half a billion Wall Street and insurance-company dollars in repeating this tragic, profitable error. He proposed to attract the upper and middle classes back to the city by creating 'an entire neighborhood screened from the blighted areas by wide parks and landscaping. . . .'

However, the real danger posed by the social industrialists in the city industry is not a repetition of the civic-development and urban-renewal patterns of the past. And, with a few exceptions, it is not simply a case of profiteering or of some kind of conspiracy against the common good. The issue goes deeper than that. For when business methods are sincerely and honestly applied to urban problems with every good intention, they still inevitably lead to anti-social results. In this area, as in education, only the primacy of the democratic political authority over economic values and interests will make possible the creation of new communities.

There are, of course, some fairly vulgar instances of groups simply placing their goals over and above those of the people. When the National Association of Real

Estate Boards, a group not noted for its social conscience and with much to answer for in the area of civil rights, comes out in favor of rent subsidies in order to kill public housing, there is no need for complicated analysis. The major banks and businesses in Pittsburgh which have also approved the rent-subsidy approach must be aware that they will eventually capture a good portion of the Federal grant. And the number of utility presidents, department-store owners and bankers who have backed the Model Cities program are, like the civic executives of recent times, determined that any urban renaissance be shaped in accord with their particular needs.

But it is precisely when such crass concerns are not paramount that the real problem – the inapplicability of business methods and priorities to the crisis of the cities – emerges most clearly. The testimony of David Rockefeller of Chase Manhattan before the Ribicoff subcommittee is an excellent case in point.

Rockefeller is an enlightened, and liberal, banker. Urban problems, he quite rightly told the Senators, 'are so closely interrelated they call for the establishment of over-all goals and guidance. Housing, schools, transport and pollution are all part of the same organic system. Public agencies, in most cases, must set the over-all goals, then provide assistance and incentives to private enterprise to carry out as much of the program as possible.' In order to accomplish this, it is necessary to 'take steps to make investment in urban redevelopment more appealing in comparison with other opportunities . . .' – i.e., for tax subsidies to lure social industrialists into a slum rehabilitation market which, in and of itself, is not attractive to money-seekers. (Senator Charles Percy's original home-ownership plan was most blunt on this point and candid about real motives. His program, he said, 'would be attractive to leaders because it promises a *competitive yield and no risk* in addition to its social and philanthropic appeal.') (Italics added.)

In theory, the Rockefeller approach subordinates the

businessman to the 'over-all goals' of the community which are determined by democratic process. But – and this is the crucial point – with all the good will in the world, Mr Rockefeller proposes in practice to interpret those goals according to an economic calculus that can only have anti-social consequences. And since he is talking in terms of five business dollars to every Federal dollar (Ribicoff hopes for a ratio of $7 to $1), the fact that he will allocate resources and order his design on the basis of tried, true and disastrous priorities is of some moment.

'Economic logic,' Mr Rockefeller says, 'dictates that the use of real estate be in some meaningful relationship to its value. The projects we have mapped for lower Manhattan are *massive, and generally of commercial, taxpaying nature.*' (Italics added.) This is the very approach that contributed so much to creating the present problem. As the 1966 Council of Economic Advisers Report analyzed the strain the commuters are placing on city transportation systems: 'Compounding this problem has been the increase in urban land values which encourages taller buildings with dense occupancy.'

In the Fifties and Sixties the Rockefeller conception of land use prevailed dramatically in Manhattan. The builders made quite sure that real estate had a meaningful relation to its 'value' as narrowly and commercially defined. Huge office buildings were constructed in the center of Manhattan without any regard for other possible locations in the city (Harlem, Bedford-Stuyvesant) or to alternative use of the resources for abolishing ghettos. An intolerable load was placed on already crowded and grim transit facilities. And there was, of course, a total lack of concern for history, beauty and civility.

So, a task force told Mayor Lindsay in 1966, 'Few stores, theatres or hotels can compete with the arithmetic of office buildings. Those sites which have become legendary, surrounded by character and convenience, often are just the ones the office builders want.' If this situation continues, the task force said, buildings which give New York much of its distinctive style, such as the Plaza Hotel, are doomed. The 'massive,' 'commercial' and 'taxpaying' structures that will go up in their place can be easily imagined. And if stores, theatres and even the Plaza Hotel cannot compete with office buildings, it is naïve to think that the poor of the central city will be able to do so.

Less than a year after Mr Rockefeller testified before the Ribicoff committee there was an excellent illustration of what his words really meant. Eighteen Congressmen asked Governor Rockefeller and Comptroller Arthur Levitt not to put state offices in the World Trade Center but to locate them in Harlem, the South Bronx and Bedford-Stuyvesant instead. As the New York *Times* reported the story, Levitt's refusal to accept this suggestion was on David Rockefeller's grounds: 'Mr Levitt, whose approval is required on contracts exceeding $1,000, said that his final decision would be based on economic factors, not on purported sociological advantages of locating in poor neighborhoods.'

But taking such 'sociological advantages' into account is precisely what is desperately needed if America is to emerge from its present crisis. It was both scandalous and utterly logical for the FHA to wait until just after the Detroit rising to decide to give mortgage insurance to blighted and 'economically unsound' neighborhoods. The insurance companies which pledged $1 billion in ghetto rehabilitation delayed, of course, until the FHA got around to thus insuring their investment. Their funds were to be directed toward rent-subsidy housing, which would mean further Government support and rents beyond the reach of the most poor. And finally, if the entire billion were devoted to creating new dwelling units (which is doubtful), the effort would create only 80,000 new units, or less than 20 percent of the annual need as defined by the Government itself. In short, the society cannot really look to business for the massive investments which it needs, for, even in the best of Federally subsidized and insured circumstances, the catastrophes of the other America do not yield commercial rates of interest.

Because of the pre-1967 FHA policy, Charles Abrams has reported, Negroes who fought their way into the home-buying class generally had to pay as much as two times the mortgage cost as compared to whites, and this involved good homes. This extraordinary pattern of Federal racism led Abrams to conclude that the hoopla over the insurance-company investment in ghetto housing, which is to be accomplished with FHA assistance, may well be one more noble exercise in rhetoric. At the FHA, Abrams remarked, the 'statement writers and the underwriters' do not always agree and the Administration 'has still to demonstrate that it will issue more than a token number of mortgages to low-income families.'

What the cities need are 'uneconomic' allocations of resources. Money must be 'wasted' on such uncommercial values as racial and class integration, beauty and privacy. And this is not simply a matter of some gigantic master plan, for it concerns individual trees in front of individual houses as well. 'Neighborhoods,' the New York Chapter of the American Institute of Architects has said, 'must be planned to create environments which offer more than mere Spartan utility, which have character, and provide pleasure for those who live there.' Businessmen, even at their most idealistic, are not prepared to act in the systematically unbusinesslike way that such amenities require. Take, for example, the 'turnkey' program announced for public housing in August 1967 (the word comes from the construction industry, not the prison system, although its use in the area of public housing is, to put it mildly, stupid). Under this experiment, private companies are going to contract – not simply to build but to manage – public housing projects.

In discussing this idea Joseph Califano of the White House staff was quoted as saying that 'once a contract had been made under the turnkey process for a fixed amount, developers were free to make whatever profit they could within the framework of the contract.' In such circumstances any honest and intelligent businessman would opt for the cheapest standards acceptable within the terms of the contract, and that could have profoundly anti-social consequences. For it was precisely such a Congressional insistence on minimum amenities in public housing that, as Charles Abrams has documented, led to the (economical) practice of building segregated, high-rise monsters.

But perhaps the most striking illustration of what commercial values do to social and aesthetic considerations is provided by the fate of the new town of Reston, Virginia. This project was initiated by Robert E. Simon and it originally envisioned architectural innovation and even a certain amount of social class integration. These goals could not be accommodated on a businesslike basis, and Simon was eventually forced to turn his dream over to the biggest investor, the Gulf Oil Corporation. Gulf's man, Robert H. Ryan, was quite blunt about the changes he intended to make: 'Economic feasibility must be a part of good planning and design,' he said. And therefore in building a new town 'you have to listen to the market.'

What Ryan heard on the market was to abandon even the ultimate aim of any kind of integration and to make the architecture much more conventional.

So businessmen are understandably loath to make anti-profitable and pro-social decisions on their own initiative. It does not pay. But even if they were willing to do so, they really do not have the right. The uneconomic values of community are, or should be, in the public domain and must be subject to democratic determination. In this area, even more than in education, the social industrialists must be subordinated to popular planning institutions.

There are those who get around this problem by ignoring it. Their magic, mythological word is 'rehabilitation.' A great many of the social-industrial complex proposals on housing – ranging from HEW's Urban Development Corporation to Senator Percy's home-ownership plan – pretend that the problem can be dealt with by refurbishing existing slums. In this way one is absolved from exercising any imagination in creating the second America, for all that is necessary is to spruce up the first America. The only difficulty with this solution is that it will not work.

There are, to be sure, neighborhoods in big cities that could be rehabilitated and thus preserve variety and sometimes even beauty (Georgetown in Washington, D.C., is a former slum). But in almost every case this could be done only by removing about three quarters of the present residents. In an area like Harlem, for instance, the problem is not just that people pay exorbitant rents for dilapidated quarters; it is that three, four and five human beings have been crammed into a space adequate to the needs of a single individual.

So rehabilitation will work only if it is part of a program to build millions of new housing units for the poor and the deprived (Senator Ribicoff estimates that, in reality, it takes a family income of about $8,000 a year to qualify for current Federal subsidies for housing – which omits the majority of the American people). And secondly, if the nation is going to pay more than lip service to its goal of integration, then even the most prettied-up but racially segregated ghetto will not do. Finally, both the problems of density and integration obviously require massive planning at the Federal, regional and local level if they are to be solved.

It is from this perspective that I would criticize the late Senator Robert F. Kennedy's anti-slum program. Kennedy was, of course, one of the most compassionate and conscientious of men with regard to the ghettos. He understood that decent housing is utterly central to both the war on poverty and the struggle for civil rights. Yet his $1.5 billion of tax incentives to lure investors into the slums would produce only 400,000 units in seven years – or 100,000 fewer than the *yearly* quota advocated by the 1966 White House Conference on Civil Rights. Indeed, none of the various proposals to get business into the low-cost-housing field which were being circulated during 1967 was designed to help the poor. In Kennedy's scheme, as in the suggestions of Senators Percy, Clark and Mondale, the units are intended to rent to families with incomes between $4,000 and $6,000. Now it is certainly true that this group has been effectively excluded from the postwar Federal subsidies and has a right to governmental help. But it is a matter of some moment that these plans offer nothing to the poor (the poverty 'line' in 1967 was set at $3,200 for an urban family of four) and therefore would not even touch the majority of Negroes in the United States.

Moreover, the Kennedy approach could result in subdividing the design of a neighborhood into 100-unit parcels. Even if, as the Senator proposed, the Federal Government insisted on minimum standards, that is hardly a substitute for the creative planning of a new urban environment.

The values that private business could well bring to the anti-slum task were well expressed by John Notter of the American-Hawaiian Land Company, an enterprise spun off by the American-Hawaiian Steamship Line, which creates new towns. As *Fortune* quotes Notter: ' "The secret," he says, "is getting other people to spend their money instead of you spending yours. Most of our office space is devoted to bookkeepers. In new town developments that's the real name of the game." ' And *Fortune* added admiringly, 'As American-Hawaiian and Humble [Humble Oil] are proving, that's one game large corporations can understand.' Where bookkeeping is the name of the game, what kind of a new urban civilization will it produce?

In short, even the most good-hearted social industrialism will aggravate rather than resolve the urban crisis. It is precisely the *de facto* planning authority that has been conferred on commercial interests which has brought us to our present plight. Business cannot play the dominant role in the attempt to rescue the cities from the mess which business methods and priorities have created. And it is impossible to get around this embarrassing fact by talking about rehabilitation. There is simply no substitute for a creative exercise of the social imagination and massive public investment.

4

At this point it is possible to synthesize various aspects of the social-industrial complex and to identify a new, and dangerous, American philosophy. It is the ideology of anti-ideology.

The notion that Western society is coming to an 'end of ideology' was first articulated by academics, most of them liberals, some of them socialists. As Daniel Bell developed the idea, the advanced economies had achieved such material affluence and political consensus that 'the old politico-economic radicalism (preoccupied with such matters as the socialization of industry) has lost its meaning....' The result was a 'post-industrial' society in which the 'new men are the scientists, the mathematicians, the economists and the engineers of the new computer technology.'

This theory was adapted to corporate purpose by business philosophers like Max Ways. For the proclamation of the end of ideology provided an excellent rationale for the social-industrial complex (Bell and his colleagues had not, of course, intended this use of their thesis). If the public market were still a Thirties-like battleground where antagonistic classes and groups fought for dominance, then business, as a minority special interest, could hardly be trusted with the social fate of the majority. But if, as Ways argued, 'U.S. politics is making a major turn from the politics of issues to the politics of problems,' then all is changed. The old ideological debate over

'issues' in which the radicals proposed to take from the
rich and give to the poor is no more. Problem-solving is
the order of the day. And the corporation, as a neutral
association of qualified experts, will, for a reasonable fee,
promote the public good in an absolutely impartial and
scientific way.

The evidence assembled here indicates that Ways and
the other philosophers of the social-industrial complex
are wrong. In producing a knowledge technology, running Job Corps camps, improving downtown areas, proposing priorities for revitalizing entire cities or suggesting
panaceas of slum rehabilitation, the social industrialists
are, at every point, pursuing a private interest and ideology. What is at stake is nothing less than how the Americans of the twenty-first century are going to think and
live. And how tragic this new and profitable business
conscience might be can be seen in the actual history
of one of the first industries to adopt the pretense of un-
selfishness and anti-ideology.

In the mid-Thirties William Paley of CBS appeared
before the Federal Communications Commission. He was
a sort of premature social industrialist. His company, he
said, was not primarily a 'business organization, except
to the extent that economics are a necessary means to
social ends. Surely any stress on economics as an end in
themselves would betray a lack of understanding of the
role which broadcasting plays in every plane of American life.' A generation later, after broadcasting had become totally commercialized, Newton Minow of the FCC
described the 'wasteland' that had resulted. The Kennedy
Administration then exhorted the broadcasters to live up
to their social responsibility. In March 1965, after four
years of this concentration on ethics, the FCC reported
that public-service hours had declined by 15 percent.

Walter Lippmann summed up the implications of this
particular experience, and his words apply to the social-
industrial complex as a whole. 'The regulatory method,'
he wrote, 'runs counter to the facts of life. It supposes

that broadcasters can function permanently as schizo-phrenics, one part of the brain intent on profits and an-other part of that same brain based on public service and the arts.'

In the debate over public television, the Ford Foun-dation corroborated Lippman's point. It had proposed a non-profit corporation which would utilize the revenues from domestic communications satellite service to finance an uncommercial network. The big companies in the field were, of course, opposed. But then Ford charged that in the case of Comsat, a public-private corporation, the private interest had a disturbing habit of prevailing (six of the fifteen members of the board are nominated by the commercial carriers, and the majority of the rest of the directors comes from business). Comsat, the Foun-dation said, had delayed orbiting facilities in the sky be-cause such progress might 'jeopardize existing, and highly profitable, relay functions on the ground.'

Ford made a succinct statement of why it opposed a private corporation in this particular part of the public domain. It told the Federal Communications Commission that such an enterprise 'would be bound by law to serve the interests of its stockholders – which may not be that of the nation at large.' The point is well made and not at all confined to television.

The knowledge and the city industries – and the entire social-industrial complex – suffer from the schizophrenia that results from the antagonism between profit and public service. And they are quite capable of making wastelands of the schools and cities. Like CBS in the Thirties, their ceremonial rhetoric disdains the 'stress of economics' even while their daily practice is based on a self-interest. So America, whether it likes it or not, cannot sell its social conscience to the highest corporate bidder. It must build new institutions of democratic planning which can make the uneconomic, commer-cially wasteful and humane decisions about education and urban living this society so desperately needs.

CHAPTER FIVE

TENTATIVE PROPOSALS FOR
A NEW CIVILIZATION

So the pragmatic, anti-ideological United States of America is in the embarrassing position of having to take some steps toward a new civilization, or else.

Washington has meticulously defined intolerable problems and then officially proposed inadequate solutions to them. The New Deal has, in many ways, become conservative, and business is incapable of resolving a public crisis in which it has a vested interest. Obviously, there is no individual or movement with finished answers to these complex challenges. Yet it is possible to suggest the broad outlines of a hope which, if it is vaguer than blueprint, is much more precise than the rhetoric of the Great Society.

Even in a society based on private economic power, the Government can be an agency of social, rather than corporate, purpose – if a vast popular mobilization forces it to do so. This does not require a fundamental transformation of the system which, unfortunately, the people will probably not want during the next twenty years in any case. It does, however, mean that the society will democratically plan 'uneconomic' allocations of significant resources. This should shake up the *status quo* even if it doesn't revolutionize it.

Under such conditions it would be possible to realize full – and meaningful – employment for all those ready and able to work. Going beyond the quantities of the New Deal, the economy could be stimulated by promoting the affluence of the public sector rather than by tax cuts, and in the process millions of creative jobs can be designed to better the nation's education, health, leisure and the like. Within twenty years such a policy of social investments should end all poverty, eradicate the slums and erode the economic and social basis of racism. And those people who are unable to work could be provided with a guaranteed annual income instead of shoddy, uncoordinated and inadequate welfare payments.

Now it is obvious that the accomplishment of these goals requires important structural changes in the system even if they do not demand a totally new society. Yet it is wrong to think that this can be done technocratically, by the very best intentioned of experts. Democracy, it must be emphasized, is a practical necessity and not just a philosophic value. For the people cannot possibly take charge of their own destiny unless there is a political revolution in knowledge and government is forced to let the governed know what is going on.

It will even be necessary to take America's most cherished conservative myth seriously: that the 'grass roots' should be a spontaneous, natural locus of political life. To make this old saw come true will take a radical reorganization of local and regional government in America – and therefore a frontal attack on a bastion of undemocratic, conservative power.

I

In his book *The New Industrial State,* John Kenneth Galbraith brilliantly analyzes some of the macro-economic forces that subordinate the common good to corporate purpose. His argument is masterful and persuasive, but in a brief, speculative section at the very end he becomes too sanguine. I am quite convinced by most of what Galbraith says, and I harp on my rather narrow disagreements for the very specific purpose of putting one of my own most basic premises into sharp relief: that in the most pragmatic and crass perspective, a vast expansion of the democratic principle is necessary to end poverty, solve the crisis of the cities, raise the quality of the national life, and so on. The most benign elites will not simply rob people of the civil liberties in a subtle way. They will also make a mess of things.

Planning can be used for just about every conceivable end, from the totalitarian statist to the private corporate. In every case, the content of a planning decision will reflect the way in which it is made. The shamefaced allocation of resources under Smith-Keynesianism favors business because it is largely determined by businessmen. The heavy-industry priority of the Stalin era expanded the power and privilege of the Stalinist bureaucracy which decided on it. Even in an affluent society where the passions of ideology have been moderated (but where, as will be seen, the clash of interests goes on) this pattern persists. Consequently, it is not populist sentimentality to insist on democratic participation in the planning process.

Galbraith and Robert Heilbroner, another perceptive writer, both have a qualified, but excessive, optimism about the democratic evolutionary potential of science and scientists, intelligence and the intelligentsia. They are not indifferent to mass politics and I share almost all of their values. Yet I do not think that they assign popular involvement a crucial enough role in the future.

The very character of modern technology, Galbraith says, renders the old market mechanisms obsolete. Now, enormous investments in sophisticated machines are needed over long periods of time. Where the first Henry Ford could have changed the design of his car in a few hours, the second, corporate Henry Ford has to commit himself to a new model eighteen months in advance. In these circumstances planning is obligatory. The state must manage the economy in order to guarantee sufficient purchasing power to buy the products of the industrial system. The labor force is no longer a great mass of blue-collar workers selling their muscle power in a shape-up.

So multiversities must be created to machine the intricate human parts which the times demand. Giant enterprises generate their own future capital and are no longer so dependent on the vagaries of the money market. And, last but not least, the Cold War provides the political rationale that allows the Government to assume most (roughly two thirds) of the risks of research and development.

Washington has a role to play at every part in this process. Since it would be political suicide to admit that the state is thus accommodating itself to the goals of the corporations, the exact opposite is proclaimed. This is done by defining the society's purpose so as to make it identical with that of the big firms. It is therefore a national article of faith that any increase in the Gross National Product is good, even if it takes the form of carcinogenic cigarettes or noisome automobiles. This creed provides ample justification for Federal support of just about anything the private sector desires, but it does so in the name of the nation rather than of business.

Up to this point in his analysis (which covers, in sketchy outline, the bulk of his penetrating book) I am obviously in agreement with Galbraith. Indeed, he provides an excellent theoretical context in which the various individual scandals I have chronicled appear as the moments of an historic process which fuses the corporations and the Government.

But then Galbraith becomes just a bit too hopeful. The industrial system he describes requires more and more organized intelligence in order to maintain and improve its technology. So a scientific and technical estate appears and takes on increasing functional importance. Since these physical and social scientists are prone to critical thought and sensitive to non-pecuniary motives, perhaps the system thus 'brings into existence ... that community that, hopefully, will reject its monopoly of social purpose.'

In *The Limits of American Capitalism* Robert L. Heilbroner put a parallel point into sweeping perspective. Feudalism, he wrote, 'gave way to capitalism as part of a subversive process of historical change in which a newly emerging attribute of daily life proved to be as irresistibly attractive to the privileged orders as it was ultimately destructive of them. This subversive influence was the gradual infiltration of commercial relations and cash exchange into the very daily round of feudal existence. . . .' Heilbroner then asks a question which he answers much as one suspects Galbraith would: 'Could there be an equivalent of that powerfully disintegrative and yet constructive force in our day . . . ? I think there is such a force. . . . This revolutionary power is the veritable explosion of organized knowledge and its applied counterpart, scientific technology, in modern times.'

Heilbroner shares with Galbraith the conviction that, because of its increasing dependency on intelligence, there are positive evolutionary tendencies in the economy (Daniel Bell has made a similar prognosis in his writings on the 'post-industrial' society). As Galbraith writes the scenario for this trend, the people will become more and more aware of the degree to which the productive system is planned, privately collectivized and state-supported. As this consciousness grows, the free-enterprise fantasies will lose their political force. Meanwhile, business will be corrupted from within. For management will be concerned with long-run stability rather than with robberbaron profits; and the technicians at Hughes and Lockheed in California work in the same scientific spirit as those at the non-profit Jet Propulsion Lab run by Cal Tech. Enterprises which have become public corporations in fact will more and more become public corporations in political and legal theory and thus be subjected to democratic control.

I disagree. There must most certainly be democratic control of a state machinery which is more and more under corporate dominion. Yet I do not believe that one can rely much on the benevolence of social evolution in this regard. Capitalism could develop incrementally within feudalism, for the revolutionists did not have to know they were making a revolution. An utterly personal desire to make more money turned a merchant into an agent of a new economic and social order whether he knew it or not.

But when one suggests that the society dictate to the Gross National Product rather than the other way around, the change must be conscious and democratic. New elites and underlying trends are not enough for such a transformation. If the scientific and educational estate were to make more and more decisions, but in the absence of a dynamic political movement asserting its own democratic priorities, these refined and sincere men would turn out to be the servants of the old values refurbished rather than the creators of new values. For the corporation, even as it 'socializes' itself by generating its own capital, meshing with the state and ignoring the functionless stockholders, remains powerfully self-interested and, when necessary, anti-social. There are economic, sociological and even psychological reasons for this institutional perversity.

John Maynard Keynes is helpful in understanding the economic basis for corporate egotism in the age of the experts.

Keynes was, in one part of his mind, quite optimistic about the corporation (so was Marx, who viewed the joint stock company as 'the abolition of capital as private property within the boundaries of capitalist production itself' and therefore a transitional form to socialism). In 1926 Keynes wrote that 'one of the most interesting and unnoticed developments of recent decades has been the tendency of big enterprise to socialize itself.' This could eventually result, he thought, 'in the growth and recognition of semi-autonomous bodies within the State – bodies whose criteria of action within their own field is solely the public good as they understand it, and from whose deliberations motives of private advantage are excluded.'

Keynes was an aristocrat by temperament, a partisan of the middle class by conviction, and he believed, like so many good government reformers, that 'moderate planning will be safe if those carrying it out are rightly oriented in their own minds and hearts to the moral issue ...' (as he wrote in 1944 to the conservative economist F. A. Hayek). But he also knew that the very policies he himself proposed required that the state accommodate itself to businessmen. He said of the executives that 'if you work them into that surly, obstinate, terrified mood, of which domestic animals, wrongly handled, are so capable, the nation's burdens will not get carried to market.'

In *The Age of Keynes* Robert Lekachman spelled this point out in some detail: 'If a government is resolved to operate through the mechanisms of private capitalism, that government should refrain from upsetting the delicate state of confidence of businessmen, large and small. On the business state of confidence depends the marginal efficiency of capital, the level of investment, the direction of change of national income and employment. If an administration wishes to substitute state for private direction of investment, the case is very different, but such was never the intention of the Roosevelt administration.'

In other words, there is a tendency within Keynesianism to strengthen the business system and its values. The national planning function is, in effect, delegated to the various private producers and the state action is directed toward enhancing their prospects and *through them* the good of the society as a whole. In the American, Adam Smithian reading of this theory, each corporation is given the familiar instructions to serve the country by enriching itself. So there is an old-fashioned motivation which is subsidized by the Government, and this is true even when the managers of industry belong to the scientific and educational estate.

Galbraith has consistently been one of the most brilliant analysts of this trend, yet I do not think he gives sufficient emphasis to the way in which it can corrupt his own hopes for the economy of organized intelligence. He has called this coddling of business 'reactionary Keynesianism' (Lekachman's term is 'commercial' Keynesianism). In John Kennedy's Administration, Galbraith championed the cause of public investments in the social sector as against the tax cuts. Kennedy rejected this advice on the grounds that his electoral margin was slender, the Dixiecrat-Republican coalition powerful in the Congress and that it was therefore necessary to conciliate business.

Once the Kennedy-Johnson policies managed to get a boom in motion, the corporations scrambled in a Victorian and irresponsible way to get an unjust share of the socially induced gains. Between 1960 and 1965 after-tax profits went up 52 percent, dividends 43 percent and take-home pay for factory workers 21 percent. It was only in 1965-66, when a tighter labor market put the unions in a better bargaining position, that wages went up enough to increase unit labor costs. At this point the companies acted in a decidedly self-interested way. They had already received magnificent incentives in the form of tax cuts, new formulas for computing depreciation and an investment tax credit; they had succeeded in obtaining an inequitable share of the prosperity that followed; and then, the moment problems arose, they advised the nation to cut down on social spending. The rich benefited from the good times and the poor were supposed to pay for inflation and the war in Vietnam.

Joseph Pechman has documented such patterns over a forty-year period. In the late Twenties corporate taxes were extremely low. Since then America has repeatedly made the democratic decision that big business should make a larger contribution to the common good. Yet, despite all the paper increases in corporate tax, the after-tax returns of the Sixties were as high as those of four decades ago. This was sometimes done by raising prices and passing the tax on to the public (a technique that made the companies, in Kenneth Boulding's terms, tax collectors rather than taxpayers). Sometimes it was accomplished in a more sophisticated and stealthy fashion. As the Council of Economic Advisers sadly recognized in 1967, the corporations were not sharing their decline in costs with the public. In the circumstances, keeping prices stable was really an invisible way of raising them.

And there are social as well as economic reasons why the old greed continues to operate in the new setting. Corporate traditions, the method of recruitment and the process of promotion all help to preserve the vestigial prejudices. Paradoxically, these tendencies may well be reinforced by the fact that so many of the most talented of the educated young are now turning their backs on the private sector. The executive suites of the next generation may, therefore, be occupied by the less bright, phlegmatic children of privilege.

But even more importantly, there is a distinct psychology at work within the corporation, a sort of managerial id. Even when an enterprise is concerned with long-range stability rather than maximum profit, even when its leaders are cultivated men, it remains a center of power. And, as Ralf Dahrendorf put it, 'If a person occupies a position of domination in an enterprise, it is irrelevant on principle whether his authority is based on property, election by a board of directors, or appointment by a government agency.' There is, in short, a drive which leads salaried experts to behave something like vulgar entrepreneurs.

The conglomerate enterprise is a perfect case in point of this atavism. Textron is one of the best examples of the breed. It makes cologne, rolling mills, pencils, helicopters, rocket engines, bathroom towel racks, chain saws, eyeglass frames – and broiler chickens. 'And how can any group of executives,' the *Wall Street Journal* asked, 'maintain control over such dizzyingly varied businesses in most of which they can have had no experience? The answer to the ... question, say Textron men, is simple. The company has acquired unrelated businesses to make money.' The individual scientists in, say, Textron's rocket-engine division are moved by many non-pecuniary considerations. But as an institutional entity, as a whole, the corporation acts like a throwback.

One cannot, in short, put much confidence in evolution as an agency of democratic change. For even if the private sector comes to be peopled by the most cultured managers history has known, the economics of Smith-Keynesianism, the sociology of the business world and the psychology of power will still encourage an anti-social egotism in the most mature and sophisticated corporations. This will mean a further expropriation of popular autonomy, but, even more than that, the elite will not even accomplish its stated aim of dealing with various social problems. The abolition of poverty and racism, the reconstruction of urban life, and all the rest simply do not make economic sense within the corporate calculus. And therefore these fine and educated people will unwittingly perpetuate the very chaos which offends their sensibilities.

The only way to get resources allocated to satisfy the people's needs is to let the people determine what these needs are.

2

If the people are thus going to impose their own priorities on the political spending of their money, there must be new institutions. To begin with, there must be a political revolution in knowledge so that society is actually provided with intelligible information about the basic choices before it.

There are those who think that it is impossible to translate the technical components of modern governmental decision into English plain enough for Congressmen, much less the voters, to understand. Reform, Daniel Patrick Moynihan says, has become professionalized; the parliaments which preside over European indicative planning, Andrew Shonfeld writes, do not even understand the language of their own technical experts. And Galbraith emphasizes that in 1945 the British Labor Government gave the nationalized industries great autonomy and did not require them to be under the constant supervision of the Commons because the managers needed the freedom to act on data the politicians could not even comprehend.

It is obvious enough that the people are incompetent to deal with the details of economic policy. But if they have the information, they are quite capable of making the underlying value judgments which precede, and inform, the expertise. Since Washington is designed to make the most important options before the society obscure to the Government as well as to the people, this is a crucial area for innovation.

Let me be quite blunt. It is conceivable that, had the American people been asked whether Federal housing policy should favor the white middle class and rich and discriminate against the poor and the Negroes, they would have said yes. In the absence of a dynamic political movement with democratic values, the electorate can use magnificent institutions to make inhumane decisions. But had the society known what was going on in the area of housing, it is much more likely that it would have rejected the systematic injustice to be found there. And, in any case, the facts would have made the task of a democratic political movement much easier. There is, then, no automatic procedure for the popular determination of Truth. All that is proposed here is that the people be given a fighting chance to govern themselves.

So the process of social and economic decision must be made transparent where it is now opaque.

The Federal Government currently bases itself, to quote Andrew Shonfeld again, on an 'anti-planning' principle which is defined in 'the pluralist formula: if you can't lick it, atomize it.' There are some eighty departments that report directly to the President; and in the 1965 Budget, funds for education were to be found in forty different agencies. In these circumstances, the White House often finds it difficult to discover what its own Administration is doing. In my own experience in 1965 quite a few members of the initial anti-poverty task force under Sargent Shriver concluded that there must be a general staff which, relying on a close relationship to the President, would give some coherence and coordination to the social programs scattered all over Washington. But the special relationship never developed, the various agencies defended their baronial rights, and the Republicans attacked Shriver as a 'czar.'

Moreover, two of the most important planning institutions under Presidents Kennedy and Johnson were, as Walter Heller notes in his *New Dimensions of Political Economy*, informal: the 'troika' of the Secretary of the Treasury, the Director of the Budget and the Chairman of the Council of Economic Advisers; and the 'quadriad,' which is the troika plus the chairman of the Federal Reserve Board. Now, it is certainly true, as Heller argues, that the President must have the right to try out economic and social ideas in private. But then there must be some institution which protects the people's right to information. Under Mr Johnson the social-problem task forces often did their studies as if they were the CIA. This undoubtedly enhanced the President's freedom of political maneuver, but at the expense of depriving the society of a look at the choices before it.

There is, however, one main locus of comprehensive planning: the Bureau of the Budget. All of the various programs must compete with one another for available funds, and there is, therefore, cost-oriented overview of the Government. The decisions of the Budget Director on the legislative shopping list are, as Andrew Shonfeld put it, the 'closest that any member of an American Government gets to the power exercised by the leader of the House of Commons in England.'

The Government must certainly be limited by the

availability of resources. But if it also looked at the economy from the grand perspective of need – if it kept social, and not just cost, accounts – it could carry out its budgeting function more humanely and probably more efficiently. There is even a place for visionary planning that would look into the far distance and estimate what *should* be done in the name of imponderables like justice. Once the $1 trillion GNP is reached in the Seventies and begins to compound, there could well develop a gap between the nation's ability to spend money speedily, effectively and ingeniously and the fiscal drag created by the automatic increase in Federal revenue from taxing higher and higher incomes. It would be too bad if the shape of a new civilization were mainly debated in the Bureau of the Budget.

And yet, even though Washington thus seems geared to anti-planning, it does plan. The day-to-day decisions eventually add up to historical trends such as providing transportation and homes for the rich instead of the poor and thereby encouraging riots. Only now this Hegelian process of quantity turning into quality is quickening like everything else in the world. In 1965 President Johnson himself calmly asked his Automation Commission to consider 'appropriate periods of work – daily, weekly, annually and over a lifetime.' Once the rising and setting of the sun defined the time for labor, and then a factory whistle. Now man is in a position to write his own calendar. As I noted earlier, the Commission replied to the President that, if all productivity gains from 1965 to 1985 were taken in the form of leisure, the nation could choose between a twenty-two-hour week, a twenty-seven-week year, or retirement at thirty-eight years of age.

It is perfectly clear that the country is not going to invest all of its advances in free time rather than in wages, and the final resolution of the issue will come through a series of settlements in the spheres of collective bargaining, social security, education and the like. Yet there is this underlying and historic choice and Washington has even identified it. If it is made covertly and according to the priorities of economic power it will probably be made badly. Or the society, alerted to the alternatives before it, could consciously make up its own mind.

In recent years Washington has come to concede at least part of the case stated here but for administrative, rather than democratic, reasons. As far back as 1949 the Hoover Commission advocated a 'performance budget' that would define the Government's role according to functions, activities and projects. Then in 1961 Mr McNamara arrived at the Pentagon with a 'systems' approach developed, in large measure, by Air Force intellectuals at the Rand Corporation. By 1966 every department of the Government was required to use this method (Planning-Programming-Budgeting System, or PPBS) in which specific appropriations are plotted within the context of an over-all plan. This should certainly aid the Government in finding out what it is doing. Now the people need similar information.

The following scenario should illustrate the kind of reforms that are needed. The imagined law is not presented as a guidepost for legislative draftsmen, and none of its details is sacred. It simply dramatizes a principle. For I am convinced that if there is a democratic will to action, a way will be found to act.

To some, this proposal might seem implausibly futuristic. Yet the French National Assembly already takes an overview of the economy and debates long-range priorities. The French system is, thus far, quite technocratic and there are many suggestions for reform (the last time around, a socialist party presented a 'Counter-Plan' to that of the Government). But the debates in the Palais Bourbon do demonstrate at least the possibility of popular intervention into basic economic decisions. In what follows there is a very brief outline of an American, and more democratic, approach to the same problem.

The President shall be obliged to make to the nation a periodic Report on the Future.

The report shall project the basic choices and different futures before the country and estimate both the economic and the social costs of alternate programs. It shall specify what groups stand to make particular gains from the various possible courses of action.

The report shall state a Social Consumption Criterion which will clearly measure the impact of every department of public expenditure on the social standard of living.* In particular, it shall explain exactly how the major areas of spending are contributing toward the abolition of poverty and racial discrimination.

The report shall be presented to a Joint Congressional Committee on the Future, which shall hold public hearings on it. Staff funds will be provided to any significant group of legislators, whether they are on the committee or not, so that they can write a substitute report or propose major amendments to the President's draft.

The House and Senate will then debate, and vote on, the general economic and social orientation of the American Government during the next period. (I am deliberately vague about the time span. Whether it should be geared to a four-year Presidential political cycle or to a period determined by economic considerations hardly need be settled now. The important point is that the report's horizon be set in the middle distance where the historic options begin to take shape.)

3

The focal point of the Report on the Future is the Office of the President. Yet truly democratic planning obviously

*This concept is borrowed from John Kenneth Galbraith's proposal that planners in developing countries adopt a Popular Consumption Criterion. They should, he argued, choose those ways of increasing GNP that will also better the life of the people immediately and directly. American planners, with their enormous technical sophistication, should be able to work out formulas that show whether Government spending promotes Government aims.

cannot be simply centralized in Washington, in the White House or even on Capitol Hill. The decisions to be made are not technical and cannot be determined by the most idealistic expert. They will, among other things, inevitably provoke conflict. Moreover, if there is even a hope that the people will have a meaningful role to play, the democratic Left will have to take the conservative myth of the grass roots much more seriously than conservatives have ever done.

To begin with, then, the Government must encourage difference at least as much as it seeks consensus.

Everyone knows that social accounts are not a matter of dollars and cents in the same way as a report of the Council of Economic Advisers. Yet there are many who would see a Report on the Future in the domain of computerized philosopher-kings who use the latest social-science techniques to decide what is really good for the public: the people shall like strawberries and cream or else. In fact, definitions of social good and evil depend on the vantage point of self-interest and are a most contentious matter. The private-car producers estimate the utility of mass-transit investments in a somewhat different fashion than the ghetto dweller without an automobile; and the cancer research financed by cigarette companies tends to have a distinctive, 'scientific' view of the pathology of the lung.

Examples abound in Washington of academic debates over statistics which are the façade of group conflict. The AFL-CIO definitions of unemployment usually yield higher percentages than the department of Labor, which, in turn, takes a grimmer view of joblessness than the National Association of Manufacturers. The scholars involved in this fight are not dishonest, but they do have special angles of vision. (As I wrote in *The Other America*, in 1959 *Fortune* magazine and I used the same income figures and they were happy about how many Americans were rich and I was outraged about the number who were poor.)

There is a distinct danger that this antagonistic reality will be ignored and social accounting and planning turned into social engineering. This is particularly the case, since the New Economics has convinced some that government can be turned into a semi-science. Walter Heller, one of the most thoughtful of the governmental experts, succumbed to this temptation in his *New Dimensions of Political Economy*. He describes how the liberal Democrats (in his terms, the Kennedy Administration) moved in the early Sixties from a consumption to an investment stress, from public spending to tax cutting, from expanding demand to achieving cost and price stability. Did this mean, he asks, 'that a major political party has moved from left to right . . . ? On the contrary, it is an escape from dogma. It is a realization that, in President Kennedy's words, "What is at stake in our economic discussion today is, not some grand warfare of rival ideologies which will sweep the country with passion, but the practical management of a modern economy." '

And yet, every one of the decisions that Heller enumerates was taken, in part at least, because of Kennedy's political position and, more precisely, because of the strength of conservative forces in the Congress. The labor movement was defeated when it proposed public spending rather than a tax cut, not because the President made an academic judgment in economics but because of the relative strength of the Left and the Right in America. There was, in short, a conflict of social class interest even though it did not take the form of passionate ideological struggle. President Kennedy, despite his talk of managing an economy 'practically,' certainly was aware of his position. For, as Heller himself recounts, he intended to place a much greater emphasis on the social sector as soon as he could.

Rather than deploring this fact of conflict, it should be brought out into the full light of day. Concealing it in the name of consensus rhetoric does not end the power struggle but simply drives it underground, which is where the democratic forces are at a disadvantage and money talks so persuasively. That is why the scenario of the Report on the Future contains positive encouragement for minority statement of opinion. And even more to the point, the Government must subsidize dissent at every level of American life.

At this point, then, one of the most dialectical aspects of a modern society comes to the fore: that it will take resolute Federal action in order to make it possible for the grass roots to grow.

According to the national romance, Washington is a distant, inhuman and bureaucratic place which has somehow usurped the rights of the folks in the towns and neighborhoods. In point of political fact, the poor, the workers, the Negroes and even significant sections of the middle class have found that the Federal Government is closer to them than City Hall or the State House. And even while Rightists argued for decentralization they understood this reality. This explains the irony, noted by Edward C. Banfield and James Q. Wilson in *City Politics*, of conservative insistence on planning in the housing programs of the Fifties. Banfield and Wilson write that the conservatives 'thought that local planning commissions, which in most cities had always been closely allied with real estate, and other business interests, would afford some kind of check on the liberals who (as it seemed to the conservatives) dominated the housing and urban renewal programs.'

There are many reasons for this undemocratic conservative strength at the so-called grass roots. The energies of the liberal-labor movement have been directed toward Washington, where they have the greatest impact; municipal reliance on property taxes has given the small property owners a passionate interest in city politics; and the incredible fragmentation of local government, with its 80,000 separate units, has created a bewildering network of vested bureaucratic interests. Whatever was the case on the frontier or in the town meeting, the seemingly libertarian demand to return power to the people is often a disguised way of proposing minority rule.

It was precisely this structural conservatism of local and state government that forced the nationalization of so many government functions in Washington. As the business-oriented Committee for Economic Development put the paradox in a 1966 policy report, either there will be 'a revolutionary readjustment' at the lower levels of politics or else the Federal power will grow even greater. This would mean, the CED said, an 80 percent reduction in the number of local governing bodies and a consolidation of jumbled sovereignties into metropolitan and county units large enough to provide a functional economic basis for their tasks. This rather radical perception on the part of sophisticated executives is clearly relevant to the central problem of this chapter: how to get democratic participation in national economic planning.

Indeed, one of the CED proposals is an excellent point of departure for structuring dissent and debate into the nation's political life. There should be, the CED report said, neighborhood units of about 50,000 people throughout the society. These would be excellent places to focus the political revolution in knowledge. In New York City in the fall of 1967 the report of a commission on school decentralization headed by McGeorge Bundy provoked vigorous controversy on all sides. But, with the exception of the central education bureaucracy itself, every party in the dispute – Bundy, parents' organizations, civil-rights groups and the teachers' union – recognized that local control would be possible only if the people involved could ask their own questions, make their own studies and check their own statistics. Earlier, in 1966, Albert Shanker, president of the United Federation of Teachers, was one of the first to argue that a community school board would have to have its own, independent research funds in order to interpret, and even controvert, the facts as represented by the Board of Education.

This idea should be generalized. No group in a modern society can play a serious political role unless it has access to expert information. In France, for instance, trade-unionists told me that they often did not even take the seats assigned to them on various planning commissions because they did not have the technical competence to deal with the issues (the labor federations in that country are, of course, much less centralized than in America, a fact which doubled this particular disadvantage). And, as a rule in this technological civilization, policies are deduced from data and the data are profoundly influenced by the questions that are asked. Boards of education and national economic planners in Washington want to ask their questions and get their answers. They should have the right to do so. And the grass roots, if they are to be taken seriously and even have the chance to be democratic, should have the same right.

So these creative suggestions from capital and labor should be merged. The Federal Government should provide research funds for neighborhood institutions and functionally organized metropolitan areas. And, so that the consequent agony of officials being forced to pay their critics may not become intolerable, this should be done under automatic, objective formulas and not through administrative discretion. In addition a Federal trust should be established – a sort of National Institute of Social and Economic Health parallel to the present Institutes of Health – to grant money to private, voluntary organizations and individuals.

However, Federal action to make neighborhood political life possible is only a first step in making planning democratic. In addition, new, unheard-of governmental units must be created.

Economic and social problems do not conform to the state and municipal lines the nation inherited from the accidents of its history. The Tennessee Valley Authority constituted an isolated, enormously successful recognition of this fact, which now must become a norm rather than an exception. It seemed for a while in 1964 that anti-poverty sentiment would lead to the creation of a second, multistate region called Appalachia. That did happen on paper, but the new structure was primarily devoted to the ancient rites of highway building, which was hardly an exercise in democratic creativity. And while *ad hoc* crises, like the Northeastern drought, periodically force governors to cooperate, nothing really fundamental is changed by the event.

The problems of BosWash, ChiPitts and San San (the nicknames, respectively, of the Northeastern, Midwestern and West Coast megalopolises of the next generation) require regional authorities even more than those of the Tennessee Valley did in the Thirties. This is obviously true in functional, economic terms, but it is also relevant to the issue of democracy. For, once again, the problem is to make the decision process as transparent as possible, and this can be done only when political units stand in some reasonable relationship to social reality.

Building new structures of regional government will, like practically every other proposal in this book, occasion conflict. Suburbia was Balkanized as a conscious strategy of a white middle class which wanted to flee big-city problems. This tactic allowed the suburbs to build comfortable, Federally financed and lily-white Shangri-las. The situation had become so extreme by 1966 that the United States Conference of Mayors asked the Federal Government to withhold grants to these principalities unless they agreed to provide a 'reasonable share' of low-income housing in their areas. In 1967 Model City planners in St Louis and Baltimore had already been forced to find ways to move poor people out of the central city. As A. Donald Bourgeois of the St Louis agency put it, '. . . the problems of the inner city cannot be solved unless we think of them in terms of the entire metropolitan area.'

There is a marvelous Federal instrument for persuading all these autonomous political authorities to consent to their own regionalization: money. As part of the Social Consumption Criterion for Government programs described earlier, Washington should insist on the creation of functional units to receive funds. In his tax-sharing proposal for assigning a specified portion of Federal revenue to local government, Walter Heller admitted that the problem was so acute that he had thought of putting strings on the grants to force the establishment of area-wide bodies. But he turned down the idea on the grounds that keeping the whole program flexible was a paramount consideration. I do not think that one should thus so easily surrender so persuasive an argument for convincing the middle class of its basic responsibility.

However, recent events have demonstrated that there is a fraudulent, and perhaps even racist, regionalism which must not be confused with the real thing. In the Sixties, Washington was driven to recognize that the old political jurisdictions were regularly irrelevant to the new problems, but it did so in a conservative way. The Federal Highway Act of 1962, the Housing and Urban Development Act of 1965 and the Demonstration Cities Act of 1966 all had provisions insisting on metropolitan and regional coordination of spending. This was usually accomplished through 'councils of government' established on the reactionary principle that each mayor had one vote – i.e., that the middle-class and white suburb of 40,000 or 50,000 was 'equal' to the central city with its hundreds of thousands of black and white poor.

Such a formula can obviously be used to expropriate the political power of the people in the central city. It would be a sophisticated, technocratic gerrymander which would allow a minority of well-off whites to dictate to the people of an area. Since this change would occur at precisely the moment that Negroes are achieving some kind of political power at city hall, black Americans would rightly regard the move as a cynical, anti-democratic trick. For this reason, metropolitan and regional planning institutions must be structured so as to give a proportionate and democratic voice to the people involved. However the details are worked out, the guiding principle cannot be 'one mayor, one vote'; it must be 'one man, one vote.'

So the case for new regions in the United States should not be put primarily in terms of establishing a more rational system. It must emphasize the liberation of democratic creativity as well. In the state of Washington, the *Wall Street Journal* reported, there are twenty-two Public Utility Districts serving 287,000 customers at costs less than half the national average. And Harry Caudill, the author of *Night Comes to the Cumberlands* (one of the most perceptive books on poverty ever written), and the Congress of Appalachian Development have advocated the nationalization of the mineral resources of the entire area and their development through local public enterprise.

In summary, then, democratic economic planning on a national level cannot take place unless there is a political revolution in knowledge as well as new structures for regional, metropolitan and neighborhood government. This will make our implicit conflicts explicit, which will be a great gain in the direction of making social choice transparent for all to see. It would also provide forums in which the people can absorb information, argue over values and modify or reject proposals from Washington. It is, as one can see, a very radical thing to take a conservative myth seriously.

4

In the fall of 1965, when Washington was still talking the bold language of the Great Society, A. Philip Randolph, the chairman of the White House Conference on Civil Rights, urged the delegates at a planning session – and the President – to adopt a Freedom Budget. In this perspective, the Government would publish a budgetary timetable for the abolition of poverty for all citizens, white as well as black, over a period of ten years. There was silence from the White House, and the proposal never came to a vote at the conference.

Then, in the fall of 1966, Randolph published a model of the Freedom Budget, complete with precise figures and quantified goals. It was endorsed by major figures in the civil-rights, religious, labor and liberal movements and, among others, by internationally known economists like Gunnar Myrdal, John Kenneth Galbraith and Leon Keyserling. Randolph estimated that, if the Administration would make a serious effort to end poverty, the resultant full employment would add between 2.3 and 2.4 trillion dollars to the GNP compared to what it would be if the 1965 rates prevailed over the next decade. In terms of this unprecedented generation of wealth, the $185 billion of Federal expenditures which the Budget assigned to various social tasks was a modest practicable percentage of the increment. Justice would, so to speak, finance itself.

A. Philip Randolph's Budget is not, of course, a final and finished answer to all the problems of America, nor was it intended as such. But it is a dramatic illustration of the fact that, once the basic political value judgment is made to go ahead, America has the intellectual and financial ability to remake the nation. Moreover, it is highly significant that the support of the Freedom Budget came from precisely those movements and institutions which form an incipient new domestic political majority in the United States (more on this point in Chapter 10).

So the broad orientation of a Report on the Future can be expressed in the quantities and target dates of a Freedom Budget. But there is yet another crucial moment in the democratic planning process: the design phase. It is generally admitted that the way in which public housing has been constructed – high-rise and concentrated in limited, segregated areas – is inadequate. It is not so generally noted that this fact is largely a function of the diversion of so much money to the housing of the middle class and the rich and the puritan determination of the Congress that the homes of the poor be built to minimal standards. In any case, there clearly must be a dialogue between architects, planners and other experts and the people on exactly how the moneys should be spent. It is a paradox of the times that it is simpler to devise ways of raising money than it is to determine how to spend it imaginatively.

Therefore, one of the very first public investments should be for research and discussion of the kinds of cities the nation wants. Such an appropriation need not wait on acceptance of some of the more radical reforms urged in this chapter, since it can easily be justified in terms of our present commitments. In January 1967, for instance, Senator Abraham Ribicoff made the excellent suggestion that all the funds then budgeted for 'model cities' – $924 million over three years – be immediately spent on planning. For, as this book should have made clear by now, the way in which a city is built or rebuilt is not a matter of economics in the narrow sense of the term but of political choice.

For instance, quite a few scholars in the mid-Sixties argued that it would be foolish to seek both decent housing *and* racial and class integration for the poor. Yet, as Herbert Gans demonstrated in his study *The Levittowners*, integration not only can be but has been planned and carried out in a suburban community. This is not to say that there is some overnight program which will disperse some twenty-five million black Americans throughout the land. For one thing, a great many Negroes, like other ethnic and racial groups before them, prefer their 'own' neighborhoods. Therefore, the choices in the foreseeable future are not a simple either-or of better ghettos as opposed to black entry into the suburbs. Both policies have their simultaneous use.

And yet integration must remain as a basic national goal of the United States. Black America simply cannot solve its economic and social problems on its own, not because the Negro is incapable of vigorous, creative action but because no 12 percent minority of any kind could independently deal with the massive, monstrous indignities that have been imposed by American whites on blacks. Therefore a top priority should be given to the Federal initiation of Model Cities. If the social industrialists can build communities from the ground up for profit, so can the democratic society, but with a social purpose. No one, white or black, would be required to live in such new cities; and no one who did not live in them would receive the tax subsidies which would be provided for them. In such circumstances it would be possible to provide a living example of the feasibility of integration. It is this kind of democratic experiment and innovation which must be sought.

But this is not to say that the private sector has no role to play in dealing with these problems. The danger, as it was described in the chapter on the social-industrial complex, is that businessmen would use the criteria of profit to make decisions which are essentially 'uneconomic' and a matter for democratic determination. However, as long as the companies simply execute the contracts drawn up through the political process, instead of dictating them, the $1.3 trillion of corporate assets in the United States are obviously quite relevant to what must be done.

Here the basic tactic is not direct Federal spending but indirect, though often not very subtle, Federal persuasion. In Europe it is called 'indicative' planning.

There are many ways in which government can motivate industry to act in a given way. A national economic plan is, from a businessman's point of view, a free piece of market research, a sophisticated guide for his investments in the future. As it is now, American executives are extremely sensitive to shifts in the 'public market.'

If they had a really developed perspective—a ten-year projection in a Freedom Budget, an even more speculative description of trends and priorities in a Report on the Future – their self-interest could be directed toward the common good. In this case, unlike that of the social-industrial complex, that self-interest would not determine the common good but be subordinated to it.

One of the most important means of government persuasion is, of course, tax policy. This is true even though it is precisely in this area that so many discreetly antisocial subsidies have been made. Suburban middle-class home building has been encouraged to the detriment of people in the slums; the Kennedy-Johnson cuts reduced the most progressive levy in the land, the Federal income tax, but increased regressive deductions for Social Security; and, as Philip Stern documented in *The Great Treasury Raid*, an incredible series of loopholes has been bored into the law so that there are actually millionaires who pay no tax at all. Indeed, the very concept of taxable income in the United States has been rigged so as to exclude a great deal of the money taken in by the middle class and the rich. The organized workers and the working poor, on the other hand, pay as they go and have no such benefits.

And yet, tax policy could be a powerful weapon for accomplishing justice. As Joseph Pechman described the extraordinary range of policy alternatives it can serve, 'The tax structure may encourage consumption or saving, help to raise or lower private investment in general or in particular industries, stimulate or restrain the outflow of investment funds to foreign countries, and subsidize or discourage particular expenditures by individuals and business firms.' If this enormous power were utilized to further the democratically determined goals of America's future, it could help to motivate business to make a social contribution.

Indeed, there is probably no better example in all of

government of the need for transparency in administration. Tax laws have served so many clandestine reactionary purposes precisely because they have been the work of experts and special pleaders. And a major function of the President's Report on the Future – and, even before such a planning perspective is adopted, of the Presidency with its present values – should be to translate the hidden social priorities of the tax system into plain English. All of the subsidies to particular groups in the name of the common good should be clearly labeled so that the laymen can understand them. Congress should mandate the Executive to do this, but private-sector foundations and universities might seek to make an even more candid statement of the situation.

Eventually, I suspect it would be well to think of an America in which there would be only a progressive income tax and no other. There is an immediate case for financing Social Security out of general revenues in this fashion and doing away with the actuarial fictions which allow that system to redistribute income from the poor to the rich (a married man with four children and $5,000 a year pays a 3.9 percent tax. A $50,000-a-year bachelor pays .5 percent of his income). Moreover, the Federal Government might make various grants contingent on the reduction, or abolition, of state sales taxes, which are also reactionary in effect. It must be remembered that, particularly if military spending were to level off, this society is going to have to work hard to spend money in the future. As Walter Heller computes it, there will be a 'fiscal drag' (the revenues automatically generated by a fast growing GNP even without an increase in taxes) of $20 billion in 1970, assuming that defense expenditures stay at the 1967 level. Heller makes out an excellent case for returning a portion of this bonanza to the states and cities but, as I noted earlier, is much too rigid about making these grants without any strings.

If there were a basic national economic and social orientation, Federal tax sharing could be a means of creating viable local and regional governments and promoting the social goals of the entire society.

Government purchases are another important Federal lever for moving the corporations to action. In 1964, as Leonard Lecht of the National Planning Association estimated the figures, Washington bought more than 19 percent of GNP and local governments paid for about 11 percent. With allowances for double counting, the combined governmental expenditure at all levels amounted to 28 percent of GNP. That makes the nation its own biggest customer. And the 1967 Manpower Report computed that no less than 21 million jobs were directly or indirectly dependent on Federal spending, a figure which extended to approximately a third of the non-agricultural work force.

During the 1960 Presidential campaign John F. Kennedy promised to use this enormous Federal bargaining power as a major weapon against racism in the economy. By a stroke of the Executive pen, he said, he could accomplish a quiet revolution. That was true then and it is true now. Kennedy never acted boldly, probably because he felt his political position so precarious. Yet if there were a dynamic democratic Left, the Government could write compulsory social specifications into every one of its contracts. In such circumstances it would be remarkable how much conscience the private sector would suddenly discover.

5

This chapter has moved from the more to the less visionary, from the need for democracy in planning and the Report on the Future to the immediate possibilities of a Freedom Budget, tax reform and the progressive use of Government contracts.

I have proceeded in this fashion for two reasons. First of all, the democratic Left can hardly adopt an all-or-nothing program geared to what should be twenty years hence while the poor suffer and the cities fester in the meantime. A proposal like the Freedom Budget provides a current, quantified demand for a ten-year program to abolish the slums and achieve full employment. Its adoption would require a move to the Left in American society but not the radical kind of change which would have to precede national economic planning. The strategy of massive public investments and of governmental persuasion of the private sector can be put into effect at once. They already command the support of a potential new majority in the civil-rights, labor, liberal and religious movements.

But, secondly, these urgently needed ameliorations should not be artificially separated from the larger, more distant goals. The function of the democratic Left is not technocratic and rationalistic, though it certainly must propose concrete solutions to specific problems. Above all the democratic Left must incarnate a vision of the future. America's unplanned planning has been rigorously guided by commercial priorities. Unless there is conscious movement in a new direction, this society will continue publicly to fund its catastrophes, though in the next period it will do so more in the name of social industrialism than in that of Adam Smith.

But if this country were to become aware of the basic and fundamental choices which lie just beneath the immediate options, it actually has the power to redeem some of the bold promises that it has made. So the democratic Left must balance both the visionary and the practical. It must propose, in short, the first steps toward a new civilization.

CHAPTER SIX

SOCIAL STRUCTURE AND
SPIRITUAL LIFE

The proposals in this book might help stultify personal freedom and contribute to the rise of a well-intentioned, genteel totalitarianism. They also provide the only realistic alternative to such a tragedy.

In the conservative myth, the dangers of depersonalization are a result of liberal and radical experimentation, and if only the reformers had left the economy alone, autonomous individuality would have flourished. In fact, as I documented at some length in *The Accidental Century*, this threat is a tendency of modern life, and conservatives, by pretending that it is the conspiratorial work of the Left, disarm society in the face of it. Advanced technology requires scientific calculation which gives rise to bureaucracy, and this is true under all present social systems. On the one hand, the world cannot feed, clothe and shelter itself, much less think of liberty, unless it rationalizes production; on the other hand, the spirit cannot survive if it is subjected to such calibrations. It is therefore always possible in these times that external progress will be purchased at the price of interior freedom.

The American businessman thinks that he defends the individual against these evils just because he opposes those Federal investments that are not profitable to him. But, as a humorous fantasy in the *Wall Street Journal* recently made clear, the reality is somewhat more complex than that. The wags of high finance, it related, were saying that, in the not too distant future, the ultimate conglomerate corporation, American International Consolidated Everything, would finally buy out General Motors and thus acquire title to the whole economy (Karl Marx considered such a possibility in *Das Capital*, but he was not amused). This joke realistically expresses the contribution of the private sector to the centralization and bureaucratization of America.

It is not entirely clear whether the Right thus subverts its preclaimed principles out of innocence or Machiavellianism. In any case, the Left cannot tolerate such a contradiction between its own theory and its practice. It must candidly realize that its solutions are themselves problematic, that a mere rational society could well be less vital. Therefore it must be concerned with the intimate effects of macro-economics.

Unfortunately, such commitments to the quality of life are usually vague and airy. The crude and vulgar priorities are supposed to come first, the higher values second: the flower arrangements wait upon the completion of the construction work. In fact, the qualities and quantities of social life are inseparable. This interdependence has always held true – the spiritual potential of starvation has never been very great, to take one example – but it is particularly important today. Modern production and administration seem to imbue organizations with a mind of their own, and technical decisions become the ultimate ends of the society rather than the means of liberation. Yet, the reform of political and economic structures can still be made to serve the inner self; the gross proposals can be designed so that they create more space for the private person. What follows are a few, very brief examples of what this might mean. Social structure cannot create spiritual life. It can help make it possible.

I

Bureaucracy is the only way to coordinate the complex functions of a modern economy and society and therefore cannot be dismissed with a curse. Yet it is also an enormous potential source of arbitrary, impersonal power which folds, bends, spindles and mutilates individuals but keeps IBM cards immaculate. It is in this specific, and dehumanizing, sense that it is challenged here.

For many people bureaucracy is more a matter of humdrum humiliations than of Kafka-like tragedies. The Internal Revenue Service contacts a citizen and informs him that his income-tax returns are being audited but refuses to say why. A private corporation terminates an automobile insurance policy without giving any reason. A credit-card company denies an application on the basis of private information which may well include rumor, spite and even mistaken identities. A university administration refuses to allow students to hear a speaker of their choice.

For some, however, bureaucracy is a matter of life and death. In New York City perhaps half the people qualified to receive welfare benefits do not receive this desperately needed aid, many because they do not know how or are afraid to apply. In the slums the fact that police forces investigate and adjudicate complaints of police brutality is an incitement to riot. Private security checks have destroyed careers in industry and entertainment, and Federal procedures have allowed faceless accusers to do irreparable harm to those whom they attack. And with the technology of electronic surveillance becoming more and more sophisticated, these trends are becoming more dangerous by the day.

Finally, in a case that should particularly disturb the democratic Left, the Social Security number which was initially a technical detail for the administration of a major (and inadequate) social reform now identifies the citizen for the tax collector and will probably eventually code his entry in a socialized data bank.

So it is obvious enough that the relationship of the individual to bureaucracy – be it public or private – has to be redefined. To be specific, at any point at which a corporate or government employee – or even the elected official of a voluntary association – has the power to say yes or no in a way that substantially affects an individual's life, there must be speedy appeal from the decision. There is one important precedent for this approach already in existence: the Public Review Board of the United Automobile Workers union. Its principles should be extended to every large-scale organization in America.

The UAW Review Board was voluntarily created by the union leadership to protect the members from bureaucratic practices on the part of their own officers. The board is composed of prominent citizens who have no relationship with the UAW. When a member feels that his rights have been denied, he can prosecute his grievance through the regular union channels up to the International Executive Board. Then he can choose to carry his case either to the Convention or to the Review Board. The union has voluntarily surrendered part of its sovereignty to an independent authority, and there are cases in which the latter has overruled the Executive Board and found for the rank-and-filer. But more important than the mandatory decisions of the board is the voluntary compliance with union due process which it has fostered. Local and regional officers know that there is an independent agency that might be called to check on them, so they become much more scrupulous in respecting members' rights in the first place.

There should be a similar independent appeal from every important bureaucratic decision in the society, both public and private. Administrators should be required to make a clear, open statement of the reasons for any ruling, and the testimony of unnamed informers should be deemed worthless. Putting such a program into effect obviously requires innovation at every level of government (and it would be enormously facilitated by a program aimed at making the grass roots meaningful). To avoid creating a new bureaucracy to supervise the old, the law could establish minimum standards, and any organization which voluntarily set up procedures that met this norm would be subject to only a periodic check. Such a freedom from bureaucratic control would, one suspects, inspire many a bureaucrat to libertarianism.

One intimation of this proposal is already appearing at various levels of government: the institution of the ombudsman, which is being urged for states and municipalities. But many of the ombudsman suggestions limit the power of the office to publicizing the wrongdoings of bureaucracy. That is certainly a step in the right direction, but what is eventually needed is an independent tribunal with the authority to command bureaucrats. And, more importantly, the ombudsman is generally confined to attacking the evils of public bureaucracy, and the individual is left defenseless in the presence of corporate hierarchies which often affect his life more profoundly than government agencies.

For instance, in 1967 Irving Baldinger, the Community Relations Director of Group Health Insurance in New York, called for a Medical Ombudsman. Health care, like everything else in the society, is becoming bureaucratized. There are public bureaucracies like Medicare, non-profit bureaucracies like Blue Shield and Group Health Insurance, and private bureaucracies in hospitals and clinics. People are often bewildered by these structures and they must have a center for information about them and, I would add, a tribunal to which they can quickly appeal decisions they consider to be unfair. Baldinger focused his suggestion on the poor neighborhoods, relating it to one of the most creative experiments of the War on Poverty, the provision of free legal services for the other America through neighborhood law offices in the slums. The greatest need for such an approach is certainly to be found among the poor, yet the middle class and even the rich need protection against arbitrary bureaucracies too.

But then both the idea of the ombudsman and that of the review board are really anticipations of a much broader principle. For it should be a matter of public policy that wherever a group of people have a continuing relationship with a bureaucracy, they should help fix its rules. And even though, as will be seen in a moment, it is too early to talk about details, it is time to think about a National Bureaucratic Relations Act similar to the National Labor Relations Act (the 'Wagner Act') of the Thirties.

During the New Deal the nation committed itself to the principle of collective bargaining in the economy and thus limited the previously absolute rights of private property. As a result, American labor introduced some minimal civil liberties in the factory. Under the old dispensation, the conditions of work were under the sovereign control of the company. With unionization, workers won a say in such vital matters as the speed of the assembly line and time for washing up as well as wages. Now, as Chapter 10 will detail, the collective-bargaining principle is moving from the plant to the office and even into the schoolroom.

The Federal Government did not impose unionism on the nation in the Thirties. But it did make it a matter of national policy that unions, which are private, voluntary associations, have certain public rights in their relationships with corporations. There are now many antibureaucratic insurgencies emerging in America. They do not yet have the sweep and power of labor consciousness during the Depression, yet they are already making both history and law. And in the not so long run, it may well be necessary for Washington to establish certain defined prerogatives for any group of citizens that wants to democratize authority.

The most successful anti-authoritarian impetus in recent times has come from American students. On a broad front they have challenged the rationale of *in loco parentis* according to which the college administration is given a power over the student somewhat like that exercised by a Victorian parent over a small child. Because the organized Free Speech Movement, which led the Berkeley revolt of 1964–65, disintegrated there are those who think that the effort failed. In fact, colleges across the nation have made significant concessions to their students in response to, or out of fear of, mass pressure.

Negroes have, of course, made the control of ghetto institutions a central demand. As a means of black liberation this tactic has the limitations described in Chapter 3; but it also has a great practical, moral and psychological value in and of itself. In New York, for instance, the authorities, acting with the worst possible grace and the least imagination, have allowed the establishment of some community boards of education, largely because of the dedicated perseverance of slum parents. School policy is thus now the concern of organized parents, teachers and community leaders as well as of professional administrators. This will not produce pedagogic miracles – the heavenly hosts would be unable to provide decent education with the resources now available to the poor – but it has already succeeded in establishing new relations between people and bureaucrats.

And there have been other insurgencies. Poor communities have organized with the assistance of Federal and foundation money. Welfare clients have rebelled against the humiliations to which they are so often subjected. In the West Village section of Manhattan, a resilient neighborhood fought city hall and stopped a bulldozed 'renewal.' One of the reasons that this particular group of citizens won is of special significance. The West Village contains writers, lawyers, social scientists and other highly trained people, and it was led in this instance by a prominent, articulate urbanist, Jane Jacobs. Most communities are not so rich in human resources. And this is why there must be governmental funds to enable rebels to become as expert as the authorities.

Public policy has already begun to respond to these democratic pressures. The Supreme Court decisions in the sit-in cases in effect recognized that there was a public relationship between the consumer and the private luncheonette, and the direct actionists were seen as agents of the entire society rather than as trespassers. There are also measures which allow tenement strikers to pay their rent into escrow so long as landlords refuse to live up to their minimal obligations. And every single proposal of the democratic Left to federalize an economic or social function must contain specific provisions detailing the rights of those who are being helped to challenge the helpers. It is, for instance, scandalous that public housing in the United States has so often been organized so as to discourage the tenants from forming committees and bargaining collectively with the administration. In the future, local officials should not be allowed to take advantage of any Federal money in this area unless they can prove, among other things, that such democratic rights are being positively encouraged.

In the long run, which happens fairly quickly in this century, the problem of bureaucrat and citizen will be seen as just as important for the common good of the country as the clash of management and labor in the Thirties. When that moment does come, a national policy establishing legal rights for those who challenge impersonal authority might well accomplish as vast an increase in individual freedom as that achieved and maintained by the trade-unionists.

This analysis should not, however, be taken to imply that all problems can be solved at the grass roots. It is necessary to stress this point because, as the Sixties come to an end, many people are disillusioned by the contrast between the soaring rhetoric and timid accomplishments of the Johnson Administration and looking for panaceas on the local level. This is true of Black Power advocates and of some of the young New Leftists with their vision of semi-anarchist communes. But there are also New Frontiersmen like Richard Goodwin and Daniel Patrick Moynihan who have been caught up in the same mystique for quite different reasons. It is an irony of the times that both the young radicals and Moynihan, who tend to be bitter critics of each other, have talked of allying with the conservatives in a united front against bureaucracy. Neither has understood one of the most important paradoxes of the time: that bureaucracy is itself a weapon to be used against bureaucracy.

The disenchantment with the Federal role has a basis in reality, as will be seen. It is also middle-class nostalgia. When Richard Goodwin writes that the 'growth in central power' affects the individual by 'transforming him from a wielder into an object of authority,' he cannot possibly be talking about industrial workers, Negroes, or the poor, all of whom have gained in autonomy by the centralization of functions in Washington. The middle class, on the other hand, has indeed seen some of its power, and much of its confidence, expropriated by public and private bureaucracies.

Yet there is substance in Goodwin's position too. It is true that people do not trust 'in the capacities of local structures to modify the political conditions of existence' (but it is not true that the poor and the Negroes have therefore 'lost' confidence in these institutions; they never had it in the first place). And Goodwin is quite right to insist that the Federal Government work toward the rejuvenation of these local structures 'by assisting and compelling states, communities and private groups to assume a great share of responsibility for collective action.' He does not go as far as the revitalization of local rule proposed in the last chapter, but his thinking tends in this direction. Still, Goodwin and other liberal critics of Federal failures sometimes simplify the way in which national and local power impinge on each other.

On the whole, the recent bureaucratic failures of Washington are not a consequence of doing too much but of not doing enough.

Washington has talked big and acted small and thus there is a vulgar, quantitative reason for its lack of accomplishment. When the Administration acknowledges

that it must build 500,000 units of low-cost housing in a
year and then constructs around 30,000, it has discovered
a sure road to unsuccess. In such circumstances it is
hardly necessary to argue, as Daniel Patrick Moynihan
told the national board of the ADA, that the urban
crisis derives in part from 'the notion that the nation,
especially the cities of the nation, can be run from agencies in Washington.' The agencies might have boasted
that they were going to remake metropolis, but they most
certainly did not even try. Moreover, it is suicidal to conclude, as Moynihan did, that liberals should therefore
bloc with conservatives in the struggle for democracy.
For the penny-pinching of the American Right did more
to promote the problems of the Sixties than any bureaucrat in Washington or any liberal with illusions about
Federal omnipotence. And, a further sobering thought on
united fronts of reformers and conservatives, the Right
used the myth of grass-roots democracy in efforts like
urban renewal in order to establish the dictatorship of
real-estate interests.

Secondly, because of the Madisonian, anti-planning
structure of the Government, meager resources were
often channeled in the least effective way, or even coun-
terproductively. It was only with the creation of the
Office of Economic Opportunity in 1964 that a domestic
agency of government undertook a systematic examina-
tion of the actual consequences of Washington's social
programs.

But if sufficient sums were appropriated to fulfill
specified needs and the money were allocated through a
democratic planning process, many of these 'inherent'
deficiencies of Federal action would disappear. For, as
Gunnar Myrdal pointed out in *Beyond the Welfare State*,
decentralization often spawns bureaucracy and centralization can help to eliminate it. The 80,000 units of local
government in the United States are, as the sophisticated
businessmen of the Committee for Economic Development realized, a threat to democracy. Making these units

large enough to be functional and rational – bureaucrat-
izing them, if you will – would actually give the citizen
a greater sense of participation in and control of the
political process, and a greater reality as well.

Many welfare and housing programs provide other
cases in point. It is precisely because relief payments are
utterly inadequate and often administered according to
the (conservative) philosophy that the point is to catch
'chiselers' rather than to help people that there is such
a proliferation of bureaucracy in this area. In New York
City in 1967 officials moved to eliminate much of this
social detective work on grounds of efficiency as well as
humanity and accepted affidavits from applicants. Were
there a guaranteed annual income, the decisive Federal
act would eliminate the need for all kinds of supervision
(it would not, as Rightist thinkers claim, substitute for
all the rest of the social programs). Similarly in public
housing, much of the rule-making and policing derives
from the fact that the authorities are rationing an extremely scarce resource. If there were an oversupply of
low-cost housing, many of these problems would take
care of themselves.

The experimentation of the Great Society programs in
1964 and 1965 does not prove, as many assume, that the
Government failed because it tried so much. Rather it
illustrates the penny wisdom and pound foolishness of
getting everyone excited about an imminent utopia and
then investing funds that, by official definition, are not
enough for a modest reform. But if, instead of trying to
make a black ghetto a more livable, educable, workable
place, one first built new, decent and integrated housing
for the people and then tore the old slums down, the
massive, multi-billion-dollar social investment made here
and now could well eliminate the need for the next
generation of social workers. (The chronology suggested
in the last sentence is important: no slum dweller should
ever be moved until there is new housing waiting for
him.)

But, and this is the crucial point, there is no amount of institutional tinkering which will ultimately guarantee the freedom of the individual against the public or private bureaucrat. The proposals in this chapter obviously depend on the existence of dynamic, local groups capable of taking advantages of new openings. There have been notable cases of such popular vitality in recent years but, were there a mass movement of the democratic Left, these insurgencies would multiply by geometric leaps and bounds.

There is an anecdote which John Cort tells of the Thirties. During the great surge of labor consciousness, the phone rang in a union office and a woman's voice said, 'This is Mary Jones at the drugstore. We've just kicked the manager out and started a sit-down strike. What do we do next?' A generation later the same wild-fire spirit was touched off when four young Negroes sat down and demanded a cup of coffee at a Jim Crow lunch counter in North Carolina. If in the next period there were a movement which would play the role of the CIO in 1937 or the civil-rights organizations of 1960, there would be an enormous gain for both the individual and the society. In short, all the reforms urged throughout this book can take on their proper meaning only when people are in motion.

2

'As the university becomes tied to the work of work, the professor – at least in the natural and some of the social sciences – takes on the characteristics of an entrepreneur.' – Clark Kerr

It would be intolerable if society succeeded in banishing dog-eat-dog competition from the economy only to introduce it into the academy.

In the old days practical men did not bother much about education since it was largely irrelevant to their affairs. A degree was a mark of social prestige, if it were not taken too seriously; businessmen sat on college boards of trustees both out of civic duty and to see to it that long-haired professors did not corrupt the young by preaching socialism. The institutions of higher learning turned out gentlemen, engineers, lawyers and socialized agricultural research.

Now, of course, all this has changed. There is a knowledge revolution creating new industries, and, as Galbraith has pointed out, organized intelligence is becoming a more decisive resource in modern society than capital itself. So science, and even social science, departments are subsidized and the class struggle has been transferred to the campus.

Parents now understand clearly that their children's academic careers are rough forecasts of future earnings. This has led to sharp battles between groups: Negro mothers fight valiantly to upgrade the quality of schooling in their neighborhoods so that their young can catch up; and suburban parents devote just as much energy, and more money, in seeing that their offspring stay ahead. In 1966 the White House Conference on Civil Rights reported that the per-capita expenditure for pupils in rural Georgia was $265 a year; in Cleveland, $447; and in rich, suburban Scarsdale, $1,211. But it is within the middle class that competition is perhaps the most bitter, for there is a greater consciousness among the elders of what is at stake.

Middle-class children begin to prepare for admission to the better colleges and graduate schools at the nursery level. In New York City, entry into the good pre-school classes requires interviews and recommendations, for this is the first step in a screening process which Harvard will complete. The competitiveness intensifies at each higher rung of the educational ladder, since success in the exams for a first-rate academic high school will lead to greater opportunities for the best college, which in turn will guarantee access to the top-ranking professional and graduate faculties.

The pressure on young people running this educational obstacle course is extreme – and this might explain why the brightest students at the finest schools so often rebel against their parents' values and turn to the Peace Corps, community organizing or some other form of social service, or even drop out. By the time they have reached Berkeley, Ann Arbor or Cambridge, they have received bitter lessons in the anatomy of status-seeking as well as formal instruction in traditional disciplines. The first moment they have the independence to do so, they vent the emotions which were repressed during the years of scholastic combat. Others, whose cases are less dramatic but more poignant, fail; and, worst of all, there are those who internalize the competitive ethic and are thus narrowed by the experience of an education.

So the intellectual life is corrupted. Higher learning is carried out by multiversities, the trade schools of the technological society. The concept of a liberal education is lost (even though that ideal was often put forward by gentlemen-amateurs who disdained the vulgarity of relevance, it expressed some of the most important Western values concerning the pursuit of truth and the humanizing role of the life of the spirit). Now, as Clark Kerr rightly observes, the professor becomes less scholar and more entrepreneur. And, one might add, he does so at exactly the ironic moment in history when the entrepreneur has finally learned to admire the professor.

It should be frankly admitted that these things are not the work of malevolent technocrats. They are, among other things, a way of responding to unprecedented problems. America is the first nation to seek genuine mass higher education, and the attempt was bound to strain the old categories and institutions. The technology does require extraordinary specialization, and it is out of the productivity which is thus achieved that the society creates an abundance that allows it to contemplate daring innovations. But even with these complexities, it is unconscionable that the nation's ability to think deeply and independently is seriously impaired just when it is most needed.

In addition to this irreparable social loss, there is an individual anguish in these trends. The United States could be building a full-fledged meritocracy in which intellectual ability and competitive drive determine a person's social and economic position. If that is the case, then there is a grim future in store for the winners and the losers. Those who achieve will do so by turning their brains into a salable commodity. Those who fall behind – and they will be disproportionately recruited from the black and white poor, through no fault of their own – will have greater feelings of resentment and inferiority than those at the bottom of past societies. Their humiliating plight will be theoretically a consequence of their innate deficiencies and not of the structure of the economy. In fact, as Chapter 3 showed, their educational and cultural deficiencies will have been cruelly imposed on them by the white and well-off. But the hurt will be done so discreetly that even the victims will think it their fault.

The most immediate tactic for countering these tendencies is to raise the intelligence of the entire society. What is called intelligence is, in any case, to a considerable degree, a social product. At the most brutal level, starvation during a child's early years will physically affect his brain and maim his mind for life, a savaging of the human spirit which was documented in Mississippi as recently as 1967 and which certainly persists to this moment. Providing a decent diet for everyone in the society would, among other things, put an end to this tragedy. More subtly, increasing the levels of health and the standard of living and widening the range of experience have already made the IQs of middle-class schools higher than those located in the slums. Thus, one consequence of programs for full employment and decent housing will be to make people, and particularly those who are now systematically denied the decencies of life, smarter.

Other gains would not occur so automatically. It is one of the abiding wrongs in America that those most desperately in need of the very best education are subjected to the worst. Both the Coleman Report and the investigations of Kenneth Clark have shown that ghetto schools regularly succeed in lowering the IQs and intellectual curiosity of their pupils. Conversely, there are intensive, quality programs which have already increased the IQs of poor students. So it is obvious that one of the major areas for social spending is on the education of these young people. And if this were done, not simply in a pleasant school but in a livable neighborhood, there is no way of estimating how much wasted talent, and even genius, society would recover.

Yet these reforms, important as they are, still evade the heart of the problem posed here. They would equalize the conditions under which the educational rat race is conducted, but they would not eliminate the competition. To do that requires more than an unprecedented expenditure of money in traditional programs. It means that society must redefine intelligence.

I am not here speaking of the utopian possibilities that will be forced on man in the middle distance but of much more immediate changes. I assume that the Protestant ethic and the central social and psychological role of work in the society will continue to dominate the nation for the next two decades. (Eventually, technology is going to destroy utterly that cherished Western and bourgeois conviction that it is through sweaty, miserable labor that a man establishes his identity and his relationship to both his neighbor and to God.) And therefore introducing a new definition of intelligence means changing the meaning of work.

There is, of course, a sweeping revolution in the concept of work which is already taking place. Almost half of the eligible age group are now delaying their full entry into the labor force until they have some college training; there is a constant shift in the economy to higher levels of intellect; and the transition from the primary and secondary occupations in field, mines and factories to the tertiary employments in the office and eventually to the research institute is proceeding apace. These enormous alterations in the way in which people spend their lives are, for the most part, the side effects of technological change, and, like everything else in the society, they mainly benefit the better off. But it is not necessary simply to submit to all these changes. They can be shaped as well.

One of the most significant accomplishments of the War on Poverty has been to prove that 'sub-professional' work is of tremendous value both to individuals and to the society. There are poor people today working as teachers' aides, research assistants, social-work aides and as staff members of various anti-poverty projects. The nation has learned that a person who is lacking in formal education and skills may possess other talents which the conventional wisdom is too rigid and obtuse to recognize. Slum dwellers knew the argot of the street and the socio-logical structure of the neighborhood more profoundly than social workers or graduate researchers. They have already made singular contributions to the nation as communicators, data gatherers and community leaders. And theorists like Frank Reisman rightly argue that those jobs should be turned into careers with possibilities for growth, learning and advancement.

The National Commission on Technology, Automa-tion and Economic Growth was a sober, responsible group located at the Johnsonian center of the political spectrum. Yet it noted that there were over five million jobs, primarily in various forms of public service, that could be filled by poor people without taking any further training. At about the same time that the commission made this inventive suggestion, the Government was more concerned in creating tragic occupations in Viet-nam than in mobilizing the squandered potential of the slums in a serious war on poverty. Yet the fact remains

that society has at least glimpsed the possibility of designing, rather than accepting, work.

Such innovations have already demonstrated a great
value in and of themselves. But they also have a great
bearing on an effort to save the realm of the spirit from
the vices of the market place, for they show that human
intelligence is much more varied and vital than has been
thought.

In the postwar years, one of the most imaginative
social investments ever made in the United States, the
GI Bill, actualized the collegiate potential of a great
number of veterans who would have been denied a
higher education a few years before. This was one more
proof of the fact that society had been wasting talent all
along. But there was an unintended and typical evil that
also resulted from this excellent program. As so often
happens when a subsidy is made available to 'everyone,'
Negroes and poor whites were unable to take advantage
of it to the same degree as others, the former because
they had been denied access to the military on racist
grounds, the latter because they were unprepared for the
opportunity when it came. Those who did avail themselves of the chance leaped farther ahead – and the rest
fell farther behind.

So what is needed now is an approach to education
which will not be strait-jacketed in the old scholastic
categories. There should be a peacetime GI Bill in which
anyone who has talent – and I use the term in its broadest sense and not in that formal academic framework
which favors the middle-class young – should be paid to
develop it without being first required to risk his life in
battle. There should also be, as Kingman Brewster of
Yale has proposed, an ROTC for social service which
would grant the same financial support to those willing
to live for their country as has been given to those ready
to die for it. But here again the important thing is that
such a subsidy should not be restricted to the classroom.
It should be available to the sub-professional who can-

not pass a written exam as well as to the conventional student.

In the mid-Sixties, educational theorists concerned with the disastrous failures of slum schools to teach reading (and therefore to provide the most minimal preparation for life in modern society) focused on the rote, impersonal methods used to introduce pupils to the written word. Yet before these very same children had even reached school, they had achieved the enormous intellectual accomplishment of learning to speak a language. That feat was accomplished 'naturally': it was part of the spontaneous, fascinating process of life itself. Middle-class children are exposed to books and newspapers in much the same way that they are to speech. But the young poor must rely on the compartmentalized routines of their inferior schools if they are going to learn to read, and, as a result, many of them fail. A mere investment of even billions of dollars will not solve this problem. For in addition to the appropriations and the new buildings and all the rest, contact must be made with that impetuous intellectual vitality which was capable of learning to speak but which does not conform to the middle-class categories.

Such an undertaking would benefit the entire nation, for the contributions of these people would improve the life of the society at every level. But it would also be a way of attacking commercialization of education. First of all, it would stress the importance of social service (this revision of the status order which has already been begun by Peace Corpsmen, Vista Volunteers and college students working in the slums). Secondly, it would burst asunder the technocratic definitions of intelligence by giving formal recognition, material rewards and prestige to unorthodox forms of ability. And thirdly, it would even help the country to begin to prepare for that not too remote moment when the work ethic will no longer be relevant to an economy in which machines produce abundance on their own.

At that point it will be necessary to regard activities which have been thought of as hobbies, pleasures and avocations as the serious business of the society. Then the arts and sports and even philosophy will take on a new meaning. For now, it is possible, in the course of making a real war on poverty, to begin to redefine what intelligence is. The sub-professional experiment has opened up exciting possibilities in this regard, and they are only a beginning.

In the mid-Sixties, for instance, a volunteer group called the Free Southern Theatre toured the Mississippi backwoods and presented *Waiting for Godot* as well as *In White America*. Their audiences were composed of black Southern farm laborers, perhaps the most culturally deprived group in the land. But the response was enthusiastic, even to the *avant-garde* play, and they discussed the drama with the actors after the performance. Indeed, the cast felt that the people brought an unsophisticated but strongly religious sensibility to the theatre and, in some ways because of their lacking a cultural veneer, directed the attention of the professionals to new meanings in the play. This was, in the best sense of the word, an educational experience for everyone who was involved in it. It deserved the support of the society at least as much as, if not more than, the preparation of an engineer.

3

There must be public planning to insure individual privacy.

A handful of people might set up a remote Shangri-la somewhere and opt out of human society. More probably, and worse, the white middle class could continue to purchase its suburban quiet with Government funds at the expense of the central-city poor. But, as Chapter 2 argues, this strategy will not really guarantee peace to these civic dropouts. They are morally, economically and politically implicated in the metropolitan crisis and simply will not be able to remain spectators while the big cities disintegrate.

So it is obvious enough that the inner self cannot really find haven in a tense and torn land. But – and this is less obvious – there is also a threat from a random, heedless affluence. Supposing that the United States would accomplish the minimal, quite practical, justice of abolishing poverty in the next ten years, that modest achievement would in some ways make it even more difficult for the citizen to find a space of his own.

In *The Medium Is the Massage*, Marshall McLuhan and Quentin Fiore summarized one consequence of man's technological ingenuity: 'Electric circuitry has overthrown the regime of "time" and "space" and pours upon us instantly and continuously the concerns of all other men. It has reconstituted dialogue on a global scale. Its message is Total Change, ending psychic, social, economic and political parochialism. The old civic, state and national groupings have become unworkable. Nothing can be further from the spirit of the new technology than "a place for everything and everything in its place." You can't *go* home again.'

Now this is both quite hyperbolic and quite true. In general, McLuhan subscribes to an overdeterminism in which the media of communications shape the totality of man's life rather than being one important element – as cause and effect – in the dialectic play of economy and society. Yet he has also perceived an important, frenzied reality. The problem is that, in keeping with his premise, he takes the trends he describes as inevitable. It has certainly become much more difficult for urban man to 'go home,' but that need not be a permanent fate.

The main human agents of the electronic revolution are the affluent young. Teen-agers are, as I pointed out in *The Accidental Century*, an authentic, unprecedented social type – more so, for instance, than the 'new Soviet Man' – which was invented in the United States and then exported all over the world. They are not just an agglomeration of youth between twelve and twenty, but relatively moneyed, mobile participants in a subculture and consumers in a multi-billion-dollar market. Suddenly they seem to be everywhere in the society, literally crowding the streets in some cases, or else ubiquitously impinging on the eye and ear through the various media which transmit their values. Sometimes their taste is surprisingly perceptive, as in the early recognition they accorded the Beatles; and sometimes they stir up a din as a way of asserting themselves against stuffy elders.

Perhaps one of the most perceptive summaries of the meaning of teen-age is to be found in, of all places, the 1967 report of the President's Commission on Law Enforcement and the Administration of Justice (occasionally, but only occasionally, Federal social science actually has style). 'In America in the 1960s, to perhaps a greater extent than in any time or place, adolescents live in a distinct society of their own. It is not an easy society to understand, to describe, or, for that matter, to live in. In some ways, it is an intensely materialistic society; its members, perhaps in unconscious imitation of their elders, are preoccupied with physical objects like clothes and cars and indeed have been encouraged in this preoccupation by manufacturers and merchants who have discovered how profitable the adolescent market is. In some ways it is an intensely sensual society; its members are preoccupied with sensations they can obtain from surfing or drag racing or music or drugs. In some ways, it is an intensely moralistic society; its members are preoccupied with independence and honesty and equality and courage. On the whole it is a rebellious, oppositional society, dedicated to the proposition that the grownup world is a sham. At the same time it is a conforming society; being inexperienced, unsure of themselves and, in fact, relatively powerless as individuals, adolescents to a far greater extent than their elders conform to common standards of dress and hair style and speech, and act jointly in groups – or gangs.'

To some of the recent commentators on the 'generation gap' all this is one more expression of the immemorial tensions between fathers and sons, mothers and daughters. That is not true. For science and technology – and not just the media – have been revising the meaning of age: biology has been socialized. There are now more elderly people alive than in any society man has known; middle age has become less debilitating and more active; and the youths have taken on this autonomy on their own (or is it rather, as Erik Erikson has said, 'A collective style of individual isolation'?). The generations have never lived in such close contact, and there have never been as many opportunities for hostility between them.

In a sense the teen-agers, who are quite literally the children of affluence, are one example of a much larger trend. For as society becomes richer, and particularly if it achieves some justice in its economic and social relations, there are more and more people with a claim to resources which were once aristocratic. The problem, as the case of the teen-agers demonstrates, is not simply that the population is increasing but that the increasing numbers of people are more and more able to make themselves seen and heard. So there is a fierce fight for good schools, the airports and beaches are crowded and even the exotic islands are invaded (it takes less than ten years for a faraway place to proceed from its discovery by artists, writers and remittance men to its commercialization by tourist managers).

By current Government standards (which understate the problem radically) almost a fifth of the society is poor and another fifth lives at levels below the 'modest but adequate' budget worked out by the Bureau of Labor Statistics. If simple justice were done to these people, one consequence would be to double the number of citizens who would be bidding for pleasures and luxuries. Economic progress, which has already created the teen-ager, would probably once again turn up the volume of the entire society.

So there are also economic and social sources for the din McLuhan celebrates. But it could well be that the human organism is incapable of absorbing all these external stimuli without serious psychological consequences. Daniel Bell is quite right to suggest that we are probably approaching a state of communications overload in which the individual will be unable to deal with all the messages with which he is bombarded. This being the case, I propose that the democratic Left not simply raise the living standards but seek ways to permit men to 'go home' again if they choose. In saying this, however, I do not want to underestimate the trend which McLuhan describes. It is a profound and frenetic tendency of the age and it will be reversed not by a conservative nostalgia but only by an even more dynamic futurism.

There are, to be sure, immediate, conventional ameliorations which will defend the people against the stridency of one another's new affluence. Laws can insist that builders meet 'uneconomic' standards of soundproofing in city buildings. A rational transportation policy would limit the sovereign authority of the car to pollute the air with fumes and give priority to the noiseless motor. An imaginative public servant, like Thomas Hoving, the former Parks Commissioner of New York City, can even take a park away from the automobile and give it back to the people.

On a more complex level, the advanced economies must begin to think about a population policy. In the less developed countries a high birth rate subtracts from the resources desperately needed for investments which will break the cycle of poverty. That is so obvious that almost everyone now recognizes that family planning must be a matter of determined public policy in these areas. It is then often assumed that the number of people can increase moderately and indefinitely in the richer lands, that America can move from 200 million to 300 million inhabitants. But even if this is economically quite feasible (it is), it has profound psychological, cultural and social consequences. Affluent hordes could drive the individual crazy, which is an unprecedented but quite real problem.

So the issue which McLuhan, Bell and others have raised demands frank discussion of a tabooed subject: a population policy based on spiritual, as distinguished from economic, overcrowding. I do not suggest that I have the answer to the questions thus posed – it is conceivable that space exploration will open up new areas so vast that there will be an interstellar manpower shortage and there are even demographers who predict a zero rate of population growth by the year 2000 – but I do know that they must be confronted.

In a somewhat less apocalyptic but still quite radical vein, America must plan for leisure as carefully as it does for work. For if a growing and ever more affluent population tries to cram itself into the old facilities for amusement and rest, no one will be able to hear himself think above the roar of the crowd. That will intensify the hostilities between the generations, the summer people and the winter people, the natives and the tourists. A relatively minor incident in the Greenwich Village section of Manhattan might make this analysis more precise.

The Village is, of course, an historic seacoast of the American Bohemia, and it has long been one of the major sightseeing attractions in New York. Until quite recently that was a fact of manageable proportions: there were crowds on weekends and in the summer, but the area managed to retain much of its charm and individuality. With the rising standards of living in the entire society, however, real-estate developers began to tear down the old houses and replace them with luxury apartments; and the numbers of teen-agers who could afford to patronize the shops and hang around the streets increased radically.

Eventually, the MacDougal Street area of the Village became a kind of teeny-boppers' Coney Island. The people who lived there, most of them Italian Americans, organized in self-defense against the racket. The young viewed this effort as an attack on them by the square and authoritarian society; the elders could not understand why their peace and quiet had been expropriated by hordes of 'outsiders.'

In the midst of the ruckus a young planner, David Gurin, wrote an article in the *Village Voice* which urged a simple solution to the problem. A few blocks to the east of the disputed block, but still within the Village, were some commercial streets without sleeping tenants. If the City had used its licensing power, and other incentives, in a creative way, much of the action could have been moved in that direction. This would have deprived the youth of some of their more exhibitionistic joys – scandalizing the residents was, after all, part of the fun – but it would have left most of the lures which brought them to MacDougal Street intact.

During the MacDougal Street controversy, the president of the Democratic Party club in the Village, Martin Berger ingeniously generalized the approach advocated by Gurin. He proposed that business areas of the city which operated for only eight or nine hours a day be turned into amusement and entertainment centers the rest of the time. Wall Street is deserted, wasted space for almost sixteen hours. In addition to acting as the financial center of the United States it could also swing. To accomplish this would not require much more than a little judicious exercise of the muncipal licensing power within the context of an over-all plan.

There are, then, new generations as well as new media, and cities have to be designed to contain both in something less than a state of war. McLuhan rightly says that if the society tries to confront these unprecedented communications systems with its old categories and institutions, it will be helpless before the future. And, I would add, the same is true if it tries to react in that way to its historically unheard-of children, adults and elderly. Then affluent crowds will dispute among themselves for the scarce resources for pleasure, no one will be truly enriched, and everyone will be profoundly angered.

So there must be social investments, not simply in housing, education and transportation but in pleasure as well. Once upon a time economics kept youth quiescent, biology killed off most people before they became old and a tiny elite could find plenty of quiet and recreation and good food and wine. Now the age mix of society is becoming unprecedented, and affluence has already vastly increased the number of people competing for leisure time and space. The accomplishment of a modicum of social justice would rapidly step up all these pressures. Beaches, parks, ski areas, quiet streets, fresh air, privacy – these things must be multiplied; they cannot, in the circumstances, be expected to multiply by themselves.

So the misallocation of resources structured into American society does not simply affect the gross quantities of the national life but its qualities as well. We have known for some time that poverty is an environment of spiritual as well as physical torment with the incidence of psychosis so much greater than anywhere else in the nation. We are now learning that affluence has created utterly new problems for family life, the relationship between the generations, and the like. Clearly, this chapter is not a catalogue of these issues, much less an exhaustive analysis of them. It provides only a few illustrative examples of how the intimate self in these times is the victim, and could be the beneficiary, of public action.

Whether it is a case of making aristocratic quality possible in a truly democratic society, or saving education from the spirit of the market place, or of countering bureaucratic tendencies, the social imagination is at least as important as the social investment.

CHAPTER SEVEN

THE CREATION OF THE WORLD

The democratic Left must complete the creation of the world.

The world – and I borrow here from Peter Worsley's imaginative way of speaking – is scarcely begun. The globe has, of course, existed for eons; and humans project their various histories more than four thousand years into the past. But those daily interrelationships which transcend tribe, nation and empire, uniting the people of the earth in a common destiny, whether they like it or not, are only a century or so old. The first day of this creation took place when economics, science and warfare put the planet together. The second day is now, and there might not be a third.

Such portentous, biblical imagery applied to politics would strike most Americans as grandiose. The people leave the world-to-come to the preachers while they pragmatically reconstruct the reality that is. Until the Second World War the Pacific and the Atlantic oceans allowed them to disdain foreign entanglements on principle. And being an anti-imperialist imperialism, a power which usually dominated other lands through the subtlety of money rather than the brutality of force, America burdened its people with an excessively good conscience. For all of these reasons, it is particularly important to insist within the United States that the day-to-day decisions of foreign policy involve the choice of a new order of things in the twenty-first century.

And, so far, though it need not be so, America is creating the world very badly.

America is imperialist. To the average citizen this statement is a patent slander. If the nation has erred, he would say, its fault has been its generosity, and only a Communist could deny the charity and the anti-colonialism of its historic record. And yet, as these chapters will show, the United States has been profoundly imperialist in the decades after World War II (and before – but that is another story). This does not mean that the devil theses suggested first by Moscow and then by Peking are true. On the contrary, America has organized the world so as to maximize its own profit and perpetuate injustice with the very best and most sincere intentions. What is required is not propaganda, Communist or otherwise, but a careful unraveling of this paradox.

The United States need not be imperialist. This notion would strike most of the revolutionists of this globe, and not just the Communists, as unpardonably tender-minded. To them, fat, prosperous, capitalist America cannot possibly ally itself with the downtrodden and against the international *status quo*. It is fated to be reactionary, the very headquarters of the world counter-revolution. This trust in the country's inherent evil is, however, almost as naïve as the patriotic faith in its goodness. For it is possible, given a turn to the democratic Left, that this nation could play a crucial and positive role in finishing the creation of the world.

We have one foot in genesis and the other in apocalypse, and annihilation is always one immediate option. Or the future might even turn out according to a half-truth found in the fantasies of Mao Tse-tung. The advanced Communist societies benefit from international injustice every bit as much as the corporations. This could lead to a deal between well-heeled commissars and executives to end the old-fashioned conflict between East and West so that the industrialized North can get on with the serious business of exploiting the backward South without regard to race, class or political creed.

Indeed, anti-utopia is more probable than a better

world, as will be seen. There are tremendous social, political and economic forces urging the United States, the West generally, and the rich Communist East to do wrong. And yet there is a hope. For there is still a practical possibility that this country can take the lead in making a democratic revolution, which is to say, in finishing the creation of the world in a humane fashion.

This fragile hope is my point of departure.

I

'For unto every one that hath shall be given, and he shall have abundance; but from him that hath not shall be taken away even that which he hath.'
– Matthew 25 : 29

It has been said so often that the rich nations are getting richer and the poor nations poorer that the very enormity of the fact is lost in the cliché.

In the middle of the 'Development Decade' proclaimed by the United Nations, the Food and Agricultural Organization (FAO) announced that the developing lands were more ill-nourished in 1965 than they had been before the Second World War, and the Organization for Economic Cooperation and Development (OECD) estimated in 1966 that the nourishment needs in these countries would grow twice as fast as the supply in the remaining years of the century. Also in 1966 the UN World Economic Survey stated that the purchasing power of the Third World had declined while the net outflow of interest and profit from them to the wealthy powers – the tribute the poor pay to the rich – had increased by 10 percent. In 1967 the Secretary General of the UN Conference on Trade and Development told the Council of that organization that the 'decade of development' was in reality a 'decade of frustration and disappointment.' This outrage has been repeatedly denounced by the Secretaries General of the UN, various Popes, the World Council of Churches and, for that matter, by the Secretary of Defense of the United States of America.

As Robert McNamara summarized the anguished prospect in a Montreal speech in 1966, in the year 2000 half of the developing nations will have achieved a per-capita income of $170 a year, assuming a continuation of present trends. The American figure would be $4,500.

This tragedy is utterly rational according to the economic 'laws' of the world which the West carefully created in the last century.

When capitalism conquered the planet, it first destroyed or corrupted all the indigenous achievements it encountered. 'Beside the Delhi of the Moguls,' John Strachey has observed, 'the London of 1715 must have seemed in many respects a country town. . . .' Native industry was broken up either by force or because it could not compete with cheap, manufactured goods; direct tribute, and sometimes slave labor, was required; and the 'mother' country entered into an alliance with the most reactionary of the local leaders. And yet these cruelties were much more sophisticated than those of the pirates and freebooters, for the triumphant entrepreneurs proposed not simply to steal from their subjects but to integrate them into a coherent world economic system as well.

'You cannot continue to inundate a country with your manufactures,' Karl Marx shrewdly observed at the time, 'unless you enable it to give some produce in return.' So a new economy was created. The colony exported primary products from its fields and mines according to the needs of the metropolitan economy (the profits were shipped out, too). Then, with whatever pittance was left to them, the natives were allowed to buy manufactured goods from their own exploiters and thus provide them with still another profit. In the process there was, to be sure, some economic progress, some modernization, and this was proclaimed in most noble terms: the French thought they were engaged in '*la mission civilisatrice*.'

But the main result of this development was the fabrication of an international division of labor that reserved technology and progress to the capitalist West and assigned the rest of the world to manual labor. According to the rationalizations of the time, the various countries were simply doing what they could do 'best' and therefore submitting to the impersonal laws of economics. People somehow failed to note that these 'laws' were the artificial construction of Western power. Asia, Africa and Latin America were carefully and systematically denied the benefits of the new industrialism. They had been designated the hewers of wood and the drawers of water.

Moreover, the poor countries helped to finance their own backwardness. In *The Economics of Poverty*, Thomas Balogh gives a striking illustration of how this was done. The big companies funded their colonial undertakings out of profits or by selling shares back home. In the metropolitan country itself, at least some of the surplus sweated out of the people was channeled by the banks into economic development. But in the colonies the bank was an agency of underdevelopment. Whatever surplus the native elite had been able to retain was exported to the money markets of the rich rather than being invested in the modernization of the colony. The banking function was therefore taken over by moneylenders. So the industrial powers paid between 3 and 8 percent a year for the money they needed in foreign trade, and anyone foolish enough to invest in anything except the export sector of the colony borrowed at rates between 12 percent and 48 percent. In this way the profits produced by colonial peoples did not even have the indirect effect of transforming their society, as the labor of workers did in Europe and America.

After World War II there was a new indignity in store for the Third World. Paradoxically, the new nations suffered in the postwar period because the advanced lands were no longer as interested in exploiting them as they had once been.

The new, mid-century technology was less and less dependent on the service of the ex-colonials. It did not require such great quantities of the traditional raw materials; synthetics substituted for some of the old imports; and subsidized, protected agricultural sectors took care of about 80 percent of the need for primary products. And then, ironically, the very success of the Western welfare state, and particularly of government policies to promote full employment, made profiteering in the backward areas less attractive. For now the wealthy powers discovered that they had created such stable and enormous markets that they could make more money producing for one another's affluence than by investing in underdevelopment.

In short, mid-twentieth-century capitalism was making it increasingly difficult for the new nations to carry out even the humiliating, inferior role in the international division of labor which had been forced on them by nineteenth-century capitalism. On the world market the demand for manufactured goods zoomed while that for primary products declined. The result, as reported by the First Committee of the UN Trade and Development Conference in 1964, was that between 1950 and 1962 the prices paid for the exports of the impoverished peoples went down by 7 percent and the prices they paid for their imports from the industrialized countries went up by 27 percent. And when, as will be seen in greater detail, the Third World managed to attract some public or private capital from the great powers, they paid cash on the barrelhead. The result of these trends has been, in the words of Raul Prebisch, 'a regressive redistribution of income ... between the developed and developing countries.' And thus, while the UN General Assembly has passed excellent resolutions, the world's poor increasingly support the living standards of its rich.*

*The figures on the shift in the composition of international trade and the declining importance of exploiting the ex-colonies can be found in Andrew Shonfeld's *Modern Capitalism*,

This outrage, of course, makes perfectly good business sense.

It was Gunnar Myrdal who realized that the bitter quotation from St Matthew which heads this section is an accurate description of the world market. For, Myrdal has pointed out, everyone knows that money is invested in safe projects rather than in risky ones – i.e., in European and American affluence, not in Third World poverty. And given the political and social outlook of private business, it is also understandable that the available funds go to private rather than to public enterprises and to undertakings in the ex-colonies only when they promote a quick profit rather than a balanced growth of the whole society. In short, the priorities which were so skilfully built into the very structure of the international economy are often a more efficient and subtle way of keeping the poor of the planet in their unhappy place than the gunboats and troops of the earlier imperialism. In order to do incalculable harm to the masses of the Third World it is not at all necessary that the Western politician or businessman be evil. He has only to be reasonable and realistic.

Indeed, so compelling is the man-made logic of the international division of labor that it even directs the developing country to embrace the misfortune that has been visited on it. And this is precisely what the Committee on Economic Development (CED), one of the

Appendix I, and in the UN *World Economic Survey* for 1965. There are scholarly arguments over the exact dimensions of the unfavorable terms of trade between rich and poor nations and how long they have been in effect. Arguments on both sides are to be found in Chapter 11 of *Leading Issues in Development Economics*, edited by Gerald M. Meier. Gunnar Myrdal's *International Economy* also contains very important data and analyses. *After Imperialism*, by Michael Barret Brown, is a fascinating study of these issues from a British socialist point of view. In any case, whatever the various disputes may be, there is no doubt that the developing nations have fared quite badly in the postwar period. The poor are paying the rich. The debate is over how much.

most sophisticated and liberal of the business organizations in the United States, advocated in a 1966 policy statement.

The new nations, the CED said, must invest 'where the increment in value of product promises to be greatest.' This sounds quite sensible, as does the conclusion that priority should therefore be given to those export industries 'that can earn substantial foreign exchange if they can compete with effective industries in other countries. . . .' But it soon becomes obvious that fledgling societies cannot possibly compete with the giant and advanced industries of Europe and America. Therefore, it would be a waste to allocate their resources to a modern technological sector which would, after all, only duplicate the achievements of Western factories but at a much higher, and non-competitive, cost. So it is only enlightened self-interest that tells the poor country to specialize in those economic activities the great powers don't bother with – i.e., in primary products.

In other words, the new nation is to volunteer for the status forced upon it when it was a colony. It is to do so not at the point of a gun, as in the old days, but in obedience to the 'laws' of the world market. These dictate that the developing country find some export specialty which suits the needs of the big powers, for that is the only rational thing to do in a system created by, and for, those big powers. And this logic can easily override any considerations of the needs of the people or the requirements for building a balanced, modern economy.

But even if a country somehow manages to escape these inexorabilities of the international economy and invests in an advanced enterprise, it is still victimized by the way in which the world is organized. Celso Furtado, a brilliant Latin American economist, vividly analyzed what this means.

Technology developed 'organically' in the West. When the first factories needed semiskilled and unskilled operative, peasants were expropriated and a working class created. As mechanical ingenuity advanced, the workers were progressively withdrawn from primary and secondary occupations (agriculture, mining and mass production) and channeled into the service and white-collar sector. At times these transitions were accomplished by brute force; at times, mass action won concessions and ameliorations. But in either case the economy and the society grew up side by side with the machines and the organization of work.

Thus, Furtado points out, the corporation develops according to the needs of profit-making in an advanced economy. But when one tries to transplant its technology to impoverished, developing lands, furious contradictions result. The newest machines save on manpower, which is a blessing in the United States and a curse in a country with rampant underemployment. Mass production requires a huge market, and this, of course, simply does not exist when the overwhelming majority of the population still lives in an archaic agricultural society. So, Furtado concludes, the very structure of economic life in the new nations – a structure forced on them in the last century – makes it difficult for them to absorb the benefits of scientific and technical progress even on those rare occasions when they have the opportunity to do so.

It is, then, written in the contemporary order of things that the rich nations shall specialize in those activities which make work easier, goods more abundant, leisure more widespread and living standards higher. The poor nations are left with the grubby tasks of primary production and faced with a stagnant or declining market. They must, therefore, sell cheap and buy dear from the booming factories. In such a world it is absolutely inevitable that the gap separating the impoverished from the affluent will grow no matter what resolutions are passed in the UN General Assembly.

2

*'It seemed to me that if we could encourage stabilized
governments in underdeveloped countries in Africa,
South America and Asia, we could encourage the
use for the development of these areas of some of
the capital which had accumulated in the United
States. If the investment of capital from the United
States could be protected and not confiscated, and
if we could persuade the capitalists that they were
not working in foreign countries to exploit them, it
would be to the mutual benefit of everybody concerned.'*
– Harry Truman on the Point Four Program

The automatic workings of the international economy
guarantee the profits of the rich nation and the poverty
of the poor, as has been seen. And yet the big powers, like
the United States, did not simply put their trust in the
happy working of economic 'laws.' Their foreign policies
operate in such a way as to reinforce the logic of injustice
which had been structured into the world the nineteenth-
century West created. Thus statesmanship has played a
significant role in increasing the distance between the
haves and the have-nots of the globe.

To the average American, burdened as he is with his
excessively good conscience, the previous paragraph is
either gibberish or Communist propaganda. It is well
known that the United States possesses no colonies, that
it has spent tremendous sums in the military defense of
freedom around the earth and that it has literally given
away billions of dollars to the unfortunate nations. In
return for all of this idealism and largess, many citizens
would conclude, the country has received little but in-
gratitude. How can the recipients of all this charity persist in calling the United States imperialist?

This perplexed and even angry view is not transcribed
here for purposes of ridicule. There is no doubt that a
very real generosity is a peculiarity of the American
national character and that it was this excellent emotion
which provided the political basis for foreign aid from

the Marshall Plan to the present. Yet it is precisely because the results of this effort have been so much at variance with the spirit that often motivated it that it is so important to understand how the United States, even when it acts out of its best instincts, has intensified the very social and economic miseries it honestly deplores. When the nation acts out of its worst instincts – hysterical anti-communism, oil diplomacy and the like – there is nothing very subtle that needs explaining.

The quotation from Harry Truman which heads this section sounds like a parody of Lenin's *Imperialism*, for it justifies a foreign policy in terms of its usefulness for the profitable export of capital. To a certain extent, the self-interested cynicism of these remarks has to be discounted. There is a deep American political tradition which holds that a man who gives away something for nothing is probably effeminate and certainly not fit for public office. Therefore, it is often necessary for the politician to disguise his most noble impulses in the rhetoric of the counting house. To a considerable extent, then, Mr Truman's Leninism was probably verbiage designed to win support from a dubious business community for the do-gooding conceptions of Point Four.

And yet there is very real substance in Truman's statement. From his Presidency down to the present, it has indeed been the policy of the United States to proceed according to his scenario: to discover some reasonable ex-colonials committed to a capitalist development of their lands; to instill some social purpose in American businessmen; and to have the American Government provide the financial framework within which these two groups can make a free-enterprise idyll of peaceful progress. But there were contradictory elements in this vision, and they guaranteed its self-defeat. For on the one hand the United States honestly felt itself committed to a democratic alternative to Communist industrialization, to an abolition of the inequities of the globe by means of freedom rather than dictatorship. Yet this fine aspiration was to be accomplished according to the traditional rules of world capitalism – rules that were precisely a major source of the misery which was supposed to be abolished.

Concretely, American foreign-aid and military programs, private investment and tariff policy were permeated and guided by the principles of the old order they were intended to challenge. While trying to be noble the United States thus unwittingly, but inevitably, made money for itself and, more often than not, worsened the plight of those whom it wanted to help.

Quite early in the Cold War, Dean Acheson gave an important speech in Cleveland, Mississippi, on the direct orders of President Truman. He noted that American exports were twice as great as the imports and that the balance of trade was therefore *too* favorable. Therefore, he concluded, there must be American funds for Europe. Now it is clear that the Marshall Plan was not simply designed in order to give businessmen a stable market in the old world. There were political, military and even cultural considerations in the decision to defend the Continent from what was seen as the imminent threat of Communist insurrection and/or invasion. But it is also true that American generosity and anti-communism did have the effect of priming the European pump, that it was a type of international Keynesianism creating an effective demand for U.S. products overseas and consequently leading to higher profits.

This self-interest rationale for foreign aid persists to this day. The CED policy statement quoted earlier made this argument for helping foreign people out of poverty: 'Improved incomes in these countries will bring them into fuller participation in the world economy. . . . These changes will contribute to the economic growth of other nations, including the United States.' And in lobbying for the Administration's 1967 program, AID told the Congress, 'In the less developed world today, the AID program is introducing American products and performance standards to some of the great potential markets of the future.' And then came the clincher: 'The goods and services go overseas, the dollar stays here to pay for them.'

In part, this is dishonest cynicism, as when Harry Truman used Leninist tough talk to conceal his decent motives. But it also has a deadly serious aspect. For when there is a conflict between the needs of the American corporation and those of the impoverished whom we are supposedly helping, the domestic dollar comes first. In March 1966 a Buenos Aires meeting was convened to consider what gains had been made by the Alliance for Progress. There was an immediate uproar when the Latin Americans attacked the policy of 'tied' aid – of requiring the beneficiary to spend his gift or loan in the United States ('The goods and services go overseas, the dollar stays here to pay for them'). The delegates pointed out that they could often get cheaper goods in Europe or Japan. Lincoln Gordon of the State Department replied for America. His nation, he said, was interested in world-wide trade liberalization, but 'considerations of national security and structural problems within our own economy have led to the imposition of import restrictions.' In plainer English, this meant that the Latin American developers were to subordinate their needs to those of the American commitment in Vietnam, the balance-of-payments problem and the alleged threat of domestic inflation.

India provides an even better example of the profitable uses of American generosity. This particular case grows out of the fact that there is money to be made in the starvation market. *Forbes* magazine – which advertises itself as a 'capitalist tool' – headlined the cover story in the March 1, 1966, issue 'Feeding the World's Hungry Millions: How It Will Mean Billions for U.S. Business.' The American oil companies, *Forbes* said in its article, had got the message and were embarking on fertilizer production. Then there came this frank and revealing anecdote: 'For a long time, India insisted that it handle all the distribution of fertilizer produced in that country by U.S. companies and that it also set the price. Standard of Indiana understandably refused to accept these conditions. AID put food shipments to India on a month-to-month basis until the Indian government let Standard of Indiana market its fertilizer at its own price.' And so it was that, in the 1967 AID proposals, the request for $50 million for fertilizer to India was a 'tied' grant and had the stated goal of encouraging private enterprise – which is to say American oil corporations – in this area. Oil is, after all, more sovereign than India.

Thus foreign aid has been an immensely profitable undertaking for the American economy, and whenever it shows any sign of becoming a real gift – i.e., of requiring more giving than getting – it is cut back. Given this conservative and essentially business-oriented underpinning to American charity, the allocation of aid also tends to follow the priorities described by Gunnar Myrdal and St Matthew. Here, too, the 'rational' approach is to give the largest amount of help to the richest rather than to the poorest nations. Once again this is quite logical in terms of the international division of labor and the world market. Europe is, after all, more able to absorb capital than Asia, Africa or Latin America and so, as St Matthew so well put it, 'unto every one that hath shall be given . . .'

So of the $40 billion spent by the Agency for International Development and its predecessors between 1946 and 1965, $18.5 billion went to restore capitalism in Europe ($13 billion during the brief Marshall Plan period, an extra $2.7 billion for Greece and Turkey, $2.8 billion to Europe after the Marshall Plan). Chiang's 'China,' Vietnam and South Korea received another $6 billion. India received more money in the years after the Communist attack in 1962 than in the fifteen previous (and largely neutralist) years ($1.4 billion as against $1.022 billion). The funds for Europe were mainly grants, for the poor countries mainly loans. The priorities involved in these allocations were, with one major exception, of the same kind that would motivate the investment of a private corporation. That is, the aid was directed to the areas of the greatest pay-off. So even benevolence increased the gap between the rich and the poor.

There was, and is, however, a major exception to this rule. In certain cases the non-profit logic of military need prevailed over the calculus of the market in the American aid effort. Then a very poor nation could obtain huge sums of money for nothing – although there was usually an unspoken interest rate computed in the numbers of the dead and maimed. For better or for worse, and usually for worse, this exception proved that it was possible, where there was a real political will, to defy the rationalities of the artificial world in which we live and to favor principles over balance sheets. It is, of course, only one more irony imposed on the impoverished of the world that this burst of idealism took place for purposes of destruction rather than construction.

As a result, the military defiance of economic law accentuated rather than reversed the reactionary priorities at work in the rest of the American aid program. To qualify for this exceptional support a regime had to be impeccably and fanatically anti-Communist, which almost always meant opposed to any real democratic social progress as well. Inefficiency, corruption and instability were tolerated, as in the various governments in Vietnam in the Sixties. But a genuine program for social justice smacked too much of communism as far as the American military was concerned. Indeed, in the postwar period, American military funds for the avowed and practising opponents of decent change in Asia and Latin America were much more generous than the moneys given to the modernizers.

But, to return to that familiar and vicious world the nineteenth-century West made for us, one cannot talk too loosely of 'giving' with regard to foreign aid. It is not just, as has been seen, that these grants are often an indirect and subtle subsidy to American businessmen. More than that, the hungry of the globe have been paying a larger and larger tribute each year in order to be helped.

The UN Economic Survey of the world during 1965 put the matter quite succinctly. In that year the self-help efforts of the Third World resulted in an increase in saving (that is to say, of the surplus they were able to deduct from their meager, sometimes starving, consumption) of 6 percent. But at the same time there was an outflow to the advanced countries in interest and profit which went up by 10 percent. As a result, the UN concluded, the developing countries were sending back more than half of the funds they received! The external debt of these nations in 1964 was 'on the order of' $40 billion, or roughly equal to the entire postwar American aid program up to 1965.

But these figures cover a wide range of societies at different levels of development. The London *Economist* reported in October 1966: 'The poorest among them, a former World Bank official has estimated, are now paying more interest and principle on World Bank loans than they are receiving from the World Bank in new loans.' To take some random cases in point of this kind of fantastic situation: the New York *Times* reported in 1965 that Latin American 'debt payments were as high as the total of all public development loans and grants during the year'; the interest due on past loans to India in 1966, to quote the *Times* again, was equal to 35 percent of the foreign exchange required for the next five-year plan; and perhaps the most summary and cruel statement of this phenomenon was made by Jacques Ferrandi, director of the Fonds Européen du Développement: 'We can say without exaggeration that certain recently contracted loans [for 'development'] are being used to pay old debts.'

Indeed, this trend is so powerful that it overwhelmed the little progress which the developing nations have achieved in recent years. Since 1964 Third World exports grew at an average annual rate of 6 percent, as compared to 4 percent in the five previous years. In theory, this should have meant that these countries would have more money to spend on imports for modernization. In fact, their imports declined. The reason for this paradox, the *Economist* pointed out, was the increased cost of 'invisibles' such as transport charges, the outflow of dividends and other investment income. 'But it was also caused by the need to switch increasing sums of money into the service of past loans. In Latin America, debt servicing absorbed 15 percent of export earnings in 1964 compared with only 6 percent in 1955. . . . The annual increase in bilateral aid in the last few years has been swallowed up by the repayments on past loans.' This pattern appears at a time when the advanced nations are more and more switching from free grants to tied aid and to loans. In other words, this particular injustice has a promising future.

So it is that some of the poorest countries on the globe have done more to raise the standards of living of the affluent than to help their own people. But this monstrous subsidy from the miserable to the fat is, after all, quite logical. With the enormous amounts of money being invested in Europe and America, it is only reasonable that risky, emergent societies should pay dear for whatever they receive. In October of 1966 there was a neutralist 'summit' at New Delhi, and there were reports that Tito, Nasser and Madam Gandhi were going to protest this tragedy and call for a 'freezing' of the debt of all the developing countries. However, the London *Economist* reported, both India and Yugoslavia were fearful that the advocacy of such a radical step would bring the wrath of the United States down on their heads. And so, in order to protect what financial support they do receive, they refrained from complaining.

But then the backward economies export more than money to the industrialized resource – trained human beings. An Iranian sociologist has reported that Togo sent more physicians and professors to France than vice versa and that, between mid-1950 and mid-1964, Argentina sent 13,800 engineers to the United States. The president of Cornell University has estimated that in a twelve-year postwar period, some 43,000 scientists and engineers, 'many' of them from developing countries, have migrated to America. As a result, in 1964–65, 28 percent of the internships and 26 percent of the residencies in United States hospitals were filled by foreigners – and 90 percent of the students from Asia who came to study in America didn't go home.

But perhaps the single most revealing example of how American policy reinforces the systematic injustices of our artificial economic world is found in the area of tariffs.

I am not referring now to the straightforward evils of protectionism. These were honestly designed to do harm to the poor and good to the rich. Thus, for example, the 'differential' tariff raises the duty on an import according to the degree to which it has been industrially processed. So if the backward country contents itself with the simple – and impoverishing – extraction of raw materials, it is rewarded, but if it develops itself and sends out most sophisticated products, it is penalized. And while the United States is forever lecturing other nations on the importance of free trade and the test of international competition (in the 1960s India was particularly favored with such lectures), it scrupulously ignores these pieties where its own corporate interests are involved. Domestic agriculture is subsidized, world oil prices are rigged to suit the needs of Texas millionaires, and so on. And, in fairness, it must be added that the Common Market agriculturists are especially adept at the same games.

As far as the Third World was concerned, the Kennedy Round changed little. The various tariff reductions were designed to benefit the advanced economies, but the concessions the poor lands have been demanding since the Geneva Conference of 1964 were denied them. Each of the big powers has its own special deals – the United States with Latin America, France with its ex-colonies in Africa, England with the Commonwealth – and none wanted to sacrifice their privileges. So it was that Raul Prebisch told the Council of the UN Conference on Trade and Development in 1967 that there was a danger of a 'vertical division of the world' in which the Common Market, the Americans – and, one should add, the fat Communists – would all stake out their own preserves.

The failure of the Kennedy Round to do anything about economic development was bad enough. But in its wake, significant elements of American business from the textile, oil and meat industries fought to make the situation even worse. They were opposed to the relatively modest reforms of the Kennedy Round and were trying, in the words of the chief Administration spokesman on the subject, 'to turn the clock back ... all the way to the Smoot-Hawley Tariff Act of 1930' (which was the most protectionist law the nation ever had).

But there are cases that are much more interesting than these routine and self-interested betrayals by us of our own cherished principles. These occur when the United States does wrong in the name of virtue. They are justified by a denial of the very existence of an international order of economic inequity; they prove the contrary.

Shortly after the Second World War rules and regulations for world trade were drawn up at a meeting in Havana (they were partially embodied in the General Agreement on Tariffs and Trade, or GATT). To most Americans, the principles thus enunciated are the essence of fairness and common sense. They proclaimed that the nations would exchange with one another on a reciprocal basis. The advanced country would lower its duties on raw materials in response to a reduction of charges on industrial imports in the poor lands. In this way all the nations would obtain a larger market for whatever they happened to sell, and each one would thus be encouraged to specialize in the area of its particular genius. This was a practical expression of the classic economic faith in free trade and the benevolent workings of the (world) market.

This marvelous symmetrical theory assumed that there could be a free economic exchange among the equals of this globe. Only there were no equals. On the one hand, the advanced countries were making brilliant use of the advantages they had secured for themselves by force during the previous two centuries. They were moving into the spheres of super-industrialization, automation and affluence, and they were making so much money off one another that they were a bit less interested in even exploiting their ex-colonies. They were, to borrow an irony from George Orwell, becoming 'more equal' than ever before. And on the other hand the impoverished lands were, as described earlier, suffering more and more from their inherited, imposed disadvantages. The demand for their raw materials was stagnant, or shrinking, at the very moment that they needed to increase their imports in order to feed an expanding population and/or to industrialize. They were becoming 'less equal' than before.

In this setting, the principles of 'fairness' laid down at Havana allowed Western capital to increase international economic unfairness. For 'reciprocity', as the Secretary General of the UN Trade and Development Conference reported in 1964, had actually widened the gap between the rich and the poor. In a world of pure mathematical logic, all nations would indeed gain by making equivalent concessions to one another. In the impure world fashioned in the nineteenth century, and persisting to this day, reciprocal deals required the impoverished lands to give up the possibility of protecting their new industries during the first, hesitant phase of development. That could be a matter of economic life and death. In return, the advanced economies were merely obliged to make a reduction in duty, which was, at most, a minor annoyance to them.

In such circumstances justice would paradoxically require, as Gunnar Myrdal has phrased it, a double standard of international economic morality. The 'more equal' big powers and the 'less equal' developing nations cannot be treated as if they were one another's peers. In order to compensate for the tremendous disadvantages that have been imposed on the poor lands for well over a hundred years, they must, in strictest equity, now be given special advantages. But this notion was decisively rejected by the Kennedy Round.

In any case, the disastrous results of America's seemingly fair policy of tariff reciprocity can stand as a sort of summary symbol of the way in which this nation made money and harmed the poor of the Third World even when it was sincerely and honestly trying to do good. For foreign aid, military aid, grants and loans and tariffs were all organized according to the irrational rationality of the world market. And by far and large, postwar American policy reinforced the vicious economic 'laws' from which the country benefits so profoundly and made St Matthew's parable of the rich getting richer and the poor poorer come true on a global scale.

3

'The prices for which the socialist countries sell their goods are influenced mostly by the conditions of production in the capitalist lands, and for this reason the exchange proportions are not always commensurate with the proportion of the expenditure of socially necessary labour within the framework of the socialist world economy.' – 'Cost Accounting in Economic Relations Between Socialist Countries,' *World Marxist Review*, October 1966

This turgid piece of prose in the international organ of the pro-Moscow Communists is a clumsy expression of an extraordinary potential which exists in the world of the late 1960s. For it is possible that the struggle between East and West, communism and capitalism, which has dominated international politics since the end of World War II, could come to an end – and be replaced by a conflict between the North, both Communist and capitalist, and the South, which is poor.

Che Guevara made the same point in blunter language than the Russians of *World Marxist Review*. In a 1965 speech Guevara said, 'We should not speak any more about developing mutually beneficial trade based on prices which are really disadvantageous to the underdeveloped countries because of the law of value and the unequal relations of international trade caused by that law. How can "mutual benefit" mean the selling at world market prices of raw materials that cost the underdeveloped countries unlimited sweat and suffering and the buying at world market prices of machines produced in large, modern automatic factories?' There is no way of evading this point. For world prices reflect, precisely, the cheapness of primary products and the expensiveness of industrial goods, and if the fat Communists use these prices in their relations with the impoverished Communists, then they are getting the same kind of unjust advantage as the capitalists.

Indeed, Guevara followed his logic to its conclusion: 'If we establish that type of relationship between two groups of nations, we must argue that the socialist countries are to a certain extent accomplices of imperialist exploitation.' And this is exactly what is being admitted in the convoluted phrases of the *World Marxist Review*. After conceding that the trade between 'socialist' countries is run on capitalist principles, the authors of the article delicately comment that the system 'does not yet fully satisfy all the socialist countries.'

This strange notion of a non- and even anti-capitalist imperialism was first put forward by one of the most brilliant of the Bolshevik economists, E. Preobrazhensky, during the 1920s. I recall his analysis here not as a scholarly footnote but because it casts a very revealing light on the present relations between the Communists and the Third World.*

The essence of trade between a capitalist power and a colony, Preobrazhensky said, was that 'the figures will always show an inequality in the expenditure of labor on the two masses of goods exchanged as equivalents' – i.e., in Guevara's terms, sweat is cheap and machines are costly. But, Preobrazhensky continued, this 'non-equivalence of exchange' would go on even *after* the victory of socialism in the capitalist countries, for it was, in part at least, a function of the backwardness of peasant economies as compared to *any* industrialized economy, capitalist or socialist. Preobrazhensky was for abolishing this inequity as fast as possible, but he believed that the main way to do so was through the modernization of the retrograde societies.

As it turned out, Preobrazhensky's anticipation of a victorious socialist revolution in the 'capitalist countries' – that socialism based on the European working class and technology which all of the original Bolsheviks looked toward – never came to pass, and his hypothesis was never tested in the form in which he made it. Yet it is clear from the record of Communist totalitarianism (a system which is neither capitalist nor Communist) that the Bolshevik theorist had divined one of the most important truths of the second half of the twentieth century: that the division between the rich and the poor, industrialized and backward, North and South, can transcend social systems. As the *World Marxist Review* admitted shamefacedly and Guevara boldly asserted, both the fat Communist and the capitalist can benefit

The New Economics, by E. Preobrazhensky, translated by Brian Pearce, Clarendon Press, Oxford, 1965. Marx himself glimpsed Preobrazhensky's insight in the 'fourth volume' of *Das Capital*, the posthumously published *Theories of Surplus Value*. (Theorien über den Mehrwert, Teil 2, p. 493, East Berlin, 1959.)

from the 'non-equivalence of exchange' on the world market.

This fact has not escaped the notice of the Third World. Here is how Julius Nyerere expressed it: 'Socialist countries, no less than capitalist countries, are prepared to behave like the millionaire – to use millions to destroy the other "millionaire," and it need not be a capitalist millionaire – it is just as likely to be a socialist "millionaire." In other words socialist wealth now tolerates poverty, which is an even more unforgivable crime ... don't forget that rich countries ... may be found on either side of the division between the capitalist and socialist countries.'

But this imperialist process on the Communist side was not restricted to profiteering from world market prices; it was political as well. Thus, the pro-Castro editors of the *Monthly Review* in the United States rightly noted that Cuba, by specializing in sugar production for the 'socialist' market, had become politically dependent on the Russians. There can be little doubt that this client relationship helped initially cause Fidel to opt for Moscow against Peking in the Sino-Soviet ideological dispute and still makes it difficult for him to be as independent as he wants. And, on the other hand, the East European Communist countries have been openly fighting since 1956 to reject the 'socialist' division of labor proposed by the Russians, which suggested that some of the East European states play the classic role of raw materials and agricultural supplier to the industrialized big brother in the Soviet Union.

And, again acting in a classic capitalist fashion, the Russians were quite willing to subordinate their own ideology in order to make a killing on the international market. In the summer of 1966, for instance, Fidel Castro was outraged at the 'criminal' idea that Moscow was going to sign a commercial pact with Brazil. Nikolai Patolichev replied for the Soviet Union in the pragmatic phrases of a good businessman who will let nothing interfere with a good deal: 'We believe that foreign trade cannot, and should not, acknowledge frontiers or ideology. My government attributes the utmost importance to commercial relations with countries in the course of economic development, like Brazil. . . . The continuous increase of production in the Soviet economy permits us to accelerate the rhythm and volume of our exports. . . .' In this last sentence the Russian spokesman sounded very much like Harry Truman imitating Lenin. And the clear implication of his point is that, as his country becomes more industrialized, it will more and more take advantage of the exploitative relationships which have been so carefully and conveniently designed by world capitalism.

Thus Russian penchant for subordinating Communist principles to profitable deals was a major issue at the Latin American Solidarity Conference in Havana in 1967. The insurrectionary, Castro-oriented revolutionists considered such actions a betrayal of fundamental principle; the more reformist, Moscow-oriented groups did not want to make a fuss. The Fidelistas won, and Guevara's individual insight about Communist imperialism became a platform plank for a tendency in the world Communist movement. 'How can this be?' Castro asked at the conference. 'This is absurd! Dollar loans to an oligarchic government that is repressing the guerrillas, that is persecuting and assassinating guerrillas!' But this is exactly what happens in a standard Soviet commercial treaty.

It is at this point that one encounters the element of truth in the Maoist fantasy of international politics and Russian Communist perfidy. There are practical reasons that have already impelled the United States and Russia toward a measure of *détente*. The armaments race has appeared to both powers as an endless, Sisyphian process; the threat of nuclear holocaust frightens both of them; and as Russia has become more modernized, the two social systems have seemed to some of the proponents to be less at odds, less hostile, than was thought in the old days. If these trends were to continue, it is not unthinkable that the old antagonists of the Cold War might make a *de facto*, world-wide gentleman's agreement in which each would tacitly respect the right of the other to exploitation in its own economic and political sphere. (This notion, as will be seen in the next chapter, was actually proposed by an influential Cabinet member of the Roosevelt Administration toward the end of World War II.)

Therefore, there is a serious possibility of a development like the one described by the Algerian delegate to the UN Economic and Social Council meeting in Geneva in July 1966: 'Even as the *détente* in the Cold War has permitted an attenuation of the conflict between blocs with different social systems, one must fear that the East-West opposition will revolve on its axis and become an antagonism of North against South.'

4

'In all such particulars the employer and the employee have equality of right, and any legislation that disturbs that equality is an arbitrary interference with the liberty of contract which no government can justify in a free land.' – Mr Justice Harlan, *Adair v. United States*

It might seem strange to conclude an analysis of the international economy in the late 1960s with a quotation from a Supreme Court opinion of 1908. Yet the current American wisdom about the world is strikingly similar to a reactionary idea which ruled domestic life more than half a century ago. Though it has been abandoned within the United States, the nation has the mentality of the 'yellow dog contract' when it comes to the globe.

The 'yellow dog contract' was one of the main features of the 'American Plan,' a concerted business attempt to destroy the labor movement. Employees, it was said, were absolutely free to join, or not to join, a trade union. But then employers were also free to ask a job applicant to sign an agreement – the 'yellow dog contract' – not to sign up in the union. The court held, with strict logic and marvelous ignorance of reality, that management and the individual worker met as equals in the market place and were free to make any deal. In fact, of course, corporate power was becoming more massive and concentrated and strikes were being broken by the armed force of both private and public armies. No matter, the two sides were officially declared to be 'equal.' The worker could, after all, refuse to work.

It took decades of bitter struggle to shatter the Court's abstractions and force judicial notice of bitter truths which every laborer knew (the 'yellow dog contract' was finally made unenforceable by the Norris–La Guardia Act of 1932). In the process, an allegedly eternal, immutable principle of economic life was easily discarded, to the enormous benefit of the nation as a whole. The mythic freedom of contract was seen as a formula for the domination of money and economic power over men, and it was realized that the active intervention of the state was required if there was to be the most minimal 'equality' between the employer and the employee.

Now it is necessary to transcend the mentality of the 'yellow dog contract' on a world scale.

By far and large, the big powers still act as if one need only lift the barriers that impede trade and then there will be happiness and efficiency. They persist in instructing developing lands to submit to the test of competition on a market which was scientifically designed to favor the rich against the poor. And the reactionary priorities inherent in this market system even come to corrupt the advanced economies when they think they are being benevolent through foreign aid or tariff reciprocity. The myth which justifies all this injustice, the yellow-dog theory of the second half of the century, is the notion that equals, having voluntarily decided to specialize in this or that aspect of production, are trading with one another.

The reality is an artfully designed, self-reinforcing in-equality.

There are a few hesitant signs of hopeful change. Some of the theoretical justifications of the Kennedy Round recognized that tariff reciprocity was profoundly un-reciprocal in practice; and the Third World emerged as a cohesive bloc at the UN Conference on Trade and Development. But as the grim figures of failure and even retrogression during the first half of the Development Decade show, the basic anti-human trends distributing more wealth to the rich and more poverty to the poor remain very much in force.

Therefore the problem is not one of simply changing this or that aspect of American, and Western, policy. A fundamental reorientation is required. The cherished – and man-made – 'laws' of the world market must be re-pealed much as the 'yellow dog contract' was abolished. As it is now, the relationship between the rich and the poor countries is as unequal and unjust as that between the American worker and businessman of the turn of the century. It is therefore the 'natural' tendency of the present international economy to perpetuate, and deepen, the gap between the starving and the fat.

The improbable, but only, hope is to create a new world to replace the inadequate one in which we now live.

CHAPTER EIGHT

THE ALMOST-IMPERIALISM

The revolutionists and modernizers of the Third World and the Communists of all varieties would take the horror stories in the last chapter as proof that the world is indeed an orderly place. To them America is inexorably fated to play the role of global counter-revolutionary. They would not be shocked by a recital of evils but by the notion that the most advanced capitalist power could ever serve the ends of justice.

In one way or another these people argue that America's very social structure impels it toward worldwide reaction. It is said that there are domestic contradictions that must be exported or super-profits that have to be made. In either case, the fat, affluent United States benefits enormously from the systematic injustices of the international order. It therefore regards any threat to the *status quo*, whether Communist or non-Communist, as a challenge to its own privileged position. Consequently, it often acts as an unwitting recruiting sergeant for the Communists by stigmatizing every proponent of social change as an agent of Moscow or Peking and thus making it impossible to build democratic and revolutionary alternatives to the Russian and Chinese movements.

The implications of this view within the United States lead to an intransigent and most radical quietism. For it is asserted that there can be no real change in American policy without a thoroughgoing transformation of its basic social system – and that thoroughgoing transformation is not imminent. So the militant (usually young and middle class) who takes this view seriously finds himself condemned to wait, like a secular Anabaptist, for a mystical, revolutionary Day on which history will end and America will finally be able to behave decently.

More seriously, the theory that the advanced powers are inevitably committed to reaction implies that there is no hope of democracy in the new nations. For, as will be seen in greater detail, if these countries cannot expect any effective aid from the affluent economies, if they are forced to modernize on the basis of their own impoverished resources, then they will be forced to exploit the one thing they have in abundance: human beings. This can hardly be done with the freely given consent of the people, and democracy will therefore be seen as hostile to economic development and real political independence. Indeed, there are more than a few theorists, both within and without the Third World, who describe these terrible necessities as if they were the finest flowering of civilization itself. Their word for the brutal and forced accumulation of capital is 'socialism.'

And yet it would be wrong to reject a theory just because its conclusions are pessimistic from the point of view of justice and freedom. The basic question to ask about these tragic projections of America's evil function in the world is not whether they are sad but whether they are true.

At the present moment the answer is ambiguous. The various formulations of the American (or, more precisely, capitalist) fate from Lenin to Mao have obvious deficiencies, and these have even given rise to a small, scholarly industry in the United States. Yet it is a fact that the country does have a vested interest in at least some of the misery and poverty of the globe. The defense of these ill-gotten gains could be (and in the past has been) the basis of a world view and foreign policy. That is the tragic possibility in the present situation and it would have America continue to promote the gap between the rich and poor nations. But, on the other hand, it can be shown that the exploitation of impoverished peoples is not a matter of life and death for the American economy but only a cruel convenience. So the nation could make new international departures even though it had not undergone a sweeping domestic transformation. There would be many conceivable motives for such a change, among them the enlightened self-interest which even a Defense Secretary acknowledges (the present trends hurry toward more instability and violence that could be disastrous for the wealthy and hungry alike) as well as democratic idealism.

So I would conclude that the United States is an almost-imperialism. It has palpable, material reasons for shoring up the injustices of the international economy and society, but it is not inevitably forced to do so. It has the possibility of positive change in the direction of creating a new world, yet that would require a considerable radicalization of political life. If, as Aldous Huxley once said pessimistically, a 99 percent pacifist is a 100 percent militarist, then perhaps one can hope that an almost-imperialism will become anti-imperialist.

I

*'To the numerous "old" motives of colonial policy,
finance capital has added the struggle for the sources
of raw material, for the export of capital, and for
"spheres of influence," i.e. for spheres of profitable
deals.'* – Lenin, *Imperialism*

V. I. Lenin believed that capitalism's inability to resolve its own internal contradiction drove it to seek imperium over the entire world. This is one of the most influential ideas of the twentieth century.

It is not just that all those who submit to Communist orthodoxy give lip service to this analysis (and, as will be seen, in the case of the Chinese Communists, it is only lip service, for they have made the most sweeping revisions of doctrine, albeit in a spirit of fanatic fundamentalism).

Beyond that, almost all the nationalists, non-Communist revolutionists and reformers of the ex-colonial world have affirmed one or another version of the Leninist thesis. And even in the advanced countries Lenin's idea has had a profound effect on intellectual life.

On the whole, the postwar experience violates the letter of the Leninist argument at almost every point – and leaves much of its spirit quite intact.

Following Marx, Lenin held that capitalism was not simply interested in plunder and booty abroad. For now the struggle between the various Western powers 'for the sources of raw materials ... and for "spheres of influence"' was also a fight to avoid crisis at home. Since 1945 and with the single but glaring exception of oil, this assertion has been less true with every passing day. For, as noted in the last chapter, advances in technology, synthetics, the organization of the market and a whole host of factors have reduced the importance of the ex-colonies as far as the big powers are concerned. Paradoxically, in the short run, the Third World would perhaps be a bit better off if the capitalists were more interested in exploiting it.*

But then the heart of Lenin's argument was not the simple assertion that there was a greedy scramble for resources and markets. More profoundly, he believed that capitalism was forced to export its capital because it could not be profitably (or profitably enough) invested within the limits of the metropolitan economy itself. As the system became mature and overorganized, the rate of profit fell and business was driven overseas in a search for capital outlets. Thus imperialism was the distinctive and last historical stage of capitalism itself, a final, desperate attempt to postpone the crisis of the system. However, the very same maturity which forced the capitalists

*The relevant figures for the trends in international trade are to be found in *Modern Capitalism* by Andrew Shonfield, Appendix I, pp. 428–29. The September 1966 *Survey of Current Business* gives some of the most recent Government figures.

to war among themselves over the division of global spoils also heightened the revolutionary consciousness of the working class. So World War I signaled the beginning of the epoch of 'imperialist war and proletarian revolution.'

There is no need here of going into the complex question of how much this analysis applied to the events before 1945. The relevant fact is that throughout the postwar period the trend in the export of capital has been to accentuate investment by the affluent powers in the affluent powers rather than competition among them for opportunities in the ex-colonial world. During this time American 'direct investment' abroad (where business sets up a plant in a foreign country rather than exporting American goods to it) more than doubled – and England and Canada absorbed more than 60 percent of the increase. At the same time, these capital movements, leaving the oil industry aside for a moment, accounted for less of a proportion of the national income than similar exports for Britain in the nineteenth century.*

At this point, Harry Truman's unwittingly Leninist hope that the Point Four development of the Third World 'would keep our industrial plant in business for untold generations' can be put into an ironic context. For the big powers in the postwar period profiteered off one another more than off the poor.

Indeed by the mid-Sixties this fact had become a key element in Gaullist economic thinking in France. The failure of the French computer industry had made that country dependent on American corporations – and allowed the American State Department to veto the sale of machines which would have facilitated the development of the *force de frappe*. As a result, the French Government launched a state subsidized merger movement in order to create a corporate base large enough to sustain

*Cf. *After Imperialism* by Michael Barret Brown, p. 206. This fascinating book makes more contemporary sense out of Lenin than anything I have read.

a modern computer technology. And in a series of articles in *Le Monde* during December 1966, Pierre Drouin actually concluded that '... now the Common Market profits American corporations more than European.' This was true, he said, because the companies from the United States were huge and therefore at an advantage in a big market and also because they had particular ability for creating new products.

There were those who criticized General de Gaulle from the Left for not having acted earlier and more decisively in this area. For instance, the socialist Gaston Deferre said, 'Europe will be colonized by the United States unless we decide to pool our resources in order to create industrial concerns comparable in size to the American ones and able to compete with them on an equal footing.' And the British Labour Government took much the same line when it reopened its bid for entry into the Common Market in 1966.

The most poignant statement of this postwar trend came at the end of 1966 from the Duke of Edinburgh. 'There is a great risk,' he said on a Paris visit, 'that Europe will become only an underdeveloped region by comparison with the immense technical potential which exists in the East and on the other side of the Atlantic.' In a 1967 speech to the New York Chamber of Commerce, Thomas J. Watson of IBM responded to such criticisms by arguing that it was in the 'enlightened self-interest' of American business to share its technological genius with the Europeans. Otherwise, he said, some nasty laws might get passed on the Continent.

Now all of this has a familiar, Leninist ring to it and hardly shows that the world market has been turned into a charitable trust. Gigantic corporations with the conscious political support of their governments are engaged in a fierce competition for markets. But then the setting is not at all Leninist, for the fight is not being conducted so much in Asia, Africa or Latin America as it is in Europe and America. Thus it is that Western business has preserved much of its old-fashioned Leninist spirit while it profoundly revised the letter of Lenin's law.

But there is a recalcitrant exception to these trends: oil.

For the economy as a whole, the raw materials and capital export markets of the Third World have become less and less important. In economic terms it is not *necessary* for the United States to promote international injustice in order to maintain domestic prosperity. But the huge and politically powerful oil industry thrives on all the inequities which have been described.

In 1964 there were $44.3 billion of U.S. direct investment overseas. In 1965 $49.2 billion. In both years, net foreign investment was only about 5 percent of gross private domestic investment (the percentage actually declined a bit from 1964 to 1965). And the distribution of this capital was about the same each year. In 1964, for instance, 31·2 percent of the American money had gone to Canada, 27·2 percent to Europe, 20·1 percent to Latin America, 6·9 percent to Asia and 3·5 percent to Africa. All of these figures support the thesis that exploiting the Third World is a diminishing and non-crucial department of the American economy.*

The petroleum and mining industries accounted for around 40 percent of this total, or about the same portion as manufacturing. More to the point, the income in 1964 on $14.3 billion of petroleum investment was more than *twice* as great as that realized on the $16.8 billion of investment in manufacturing ($1.9 billion as against $.876 billion). This is most obviously a super profit and it depends on arrangements with countries that are either poor or rich in a distorted way (Kuwait, which has the second highest per-capita income in the world, is a Balkanized fief for oil and not, as it should be, a source of wealth for Middle Eastern development generally).

In recent years successful pressure from the oil-producing countries for a larger share of the wealth they

* The figures are taken from the 1965 and 1966 reports on foreign investment of *The Survey of Current Business.*

produce has reduced the oil-company take. In 1966, according to a Chase Manhattan Bank report, the large U.S. oil corporations made more on their domestic investment than on foreign for the first time in twenty years. The overseas percentage (which includes the figures from Europe and Canada as well as from the Third World) declined from a 30 percent return in 1955 to 11·7 percent for 1966. But even with the new risks, the gains to be made from oil in the Middle East and Latin America are tremendous.

In the process of accumulating this enormous wealth, the oil industry works hand in glove with the United States Government, and vice versa. The companies benefit, of course, from direct production controls within America – the money made in this rigidly *dirigiste* sector of the economy paradoxically seems to create *laissez-faire* millionaires – and the princely benefits from the 27·5 percent depletion allowance. Import controls are also designed to support the (costly, non-competitive) American wells in the manner to which they have become accustomed. Indeed, world oil prices are such an ingenious and artificial creation that John Strachey once calculated that, were the Arabs to nationalize the petroleum operations in their countries and permit a 'market' price to emerge, the oil consumers in the West would be able to buy at a much cheaper price than now prevails. However, since a single decision of Royal Dutch Shell was reported by Elizabeth Jager to have affected the balance-of-payments position of both Britain and Italy, it is unlikely that any such experimentation is going to be allowed.

Thus, when the Arabs threatened nationalization during the war with Israel in 1967, there was considerable corporate unrest. But, as the London *Economist* pointed out, 'there is little doubt that the odds in a post-nationalization price battle would be heavily stacked in favour of the companies. Relieved of many of their capital commitments and of their major interest in production, they

would be in a good position to bargain for lower prices.'
One can safely assume that such a decrease in cost would
not, as in Strachey's hypothesis, be passed on to the consumer. It would be used to keep the empire of oil in the
super-profit style to which it has become accustomed.

And the maintenance of this privileged position for the
oil corporations has, of course, involved American
foreign policy.

The basic premise was stated in Harry Truman's
reminiscence of the 1945 Middle Eastern crisis: 'If the
Russians were to control Iran's oil, either directly or indirectly, the raw material balance of the world would
undergo a serious change and it would be a serious loss
for the economy of the Western world.' So, Mr Truman
disclosed, on this same basis the American military were
to oppose the independence of Israel since it would
offend the Arab oil producers. Some time later, in the
early Fifties, the Iranian fields were nationalized under
Mossadegh. As Robert Engler relates the cooperation
between the Government and the corporations: 'The
industry received full backing in its economic blockade of
Iran throughout the struggle. This meant government
sanction for the private pricing and marketing controls
governing the world supply. Oilmen had an assurance of
immunity from anti-trust action as the Petroleum Administration for Defense worked with companies in the
states to synchronize refining, storage and shipments to
compensate for the oil lost through the closedown. *The
chief threat to the order of oil was not so much shortages
or even nationalization, but rather the possibility of oil
flowing into the world markets outside the control system.*' (Italics added.)

The italicized passage is crucial. For the oil industry's
argument is, of course, that as the producer of a strategic
fuel its interests must be protected in the interest of the
common good of the United States. In fact, however, the
Iranian incident demonstrates that the real issue was not
access to oil but the system rigged to guarantee profits

to the private companies. More recently, in a Senate speech in May 1966, Senator Robert F. Kennedy gave another example of this kind of private self-interest dominating the policy of the nation. In Peru, Kennedy said, President Belaunde had asked for $16 million for a Domestic Peace Corps type of project. The State Department held up these funds in order to 'make the Peruvians more reasonable' in the negotiations they were then carrying on with American oil companies. Kennedy added, 'The same was true in Argentina.' And, it should be noted, when AID threatened to cut food shipments unless India accepted American price-fixing for fertilizer, it acted as the agent of oil companies.

The oil industry, then, acts according to the classic Leninist scenario. It profiteers in the Third World, supports local reaction, opposes democratic and modernizing movements and sometimes is able to treat the United States Government as if it were a hired plant security guard. At almost every point the result has been to make American foreign policy more reactionary. If the country's international actions were dedicated toward the creation of a world in which the gap between the rich and poor nations would be reduced, the oil industry would suffer. The resultant misery of various millionaires would be real, but it would not overturn the American economy. The catch is, of course, political. Oil is tremendously powerful in Washington, and therefore any hope of a truly democratic foreign policy would require the defeat of its domestic influence.

With this very important caveat about oil, the general and un-Leninist proposition of this section can be restated: the prosperity of the American economy need not depend on the exploitation of the Third World and, to a considerable measure, does not at this moment.* The

*Robert Heilbroner estimates total American capital in Asia, Africa and Latin America at $16 billion. The loss of this sum in an economy with total corporate assets of $1·3 trillion is, he says, manageable on the economic plane. Heilbroner doubts, how-

reactionary policies the country has followed in widening the international gap between the rich and the poor are thus not the inexorable expressions of economic and social structure. They are reasonable, businesslike but unnecessary evils perpetrated according to the rules of this world which was so carefully made for us. But these rules could be changed. And this possibility is something that is not to be found in the philosophy of V. I. Lenin or his followers.

2

'There is entirely too much truth in the repeated American assertions that we seek no advantage, no territory, no bases, no clients from this war. It might have been better if we did.'– Edmund Stillman and William Pfaff, *Power and Impotence: The Failure of America's Foreign Policy*

The late Paul Baran, a Marxist sympathetic to the more orthodox brand of communism, saw how these postwar economic trends turned the Cold War into a world-wide paradox. For America, he argued, was devoting enormous military and political means to the service of relatively modest material ends. (Baran's resolution of this paradox will be noted shortly.) A similar conclusion developed out of quite another point of view. In the mid-Sixties, Walter Lippmann and other moderate critics of the war in Vietnam held that there simply was not a discernible American self-interest that could possibly justify the commitment of hundreds of thousands of troops to Southeast Asia.

More generally, it can be said that the flag of American almost-imperialism usually did not, during the postwar period, follow the dollar, except in the case of oil. There-

ever, that America is politically able thus to adapt itself to a world in revolution. On this point, more later. *Cf.* 'Counter-revolutionary America,' *Commentary*, April 1967.

fore it is not only statistically possible for United States policy to escape from economic determinism. It is already a curious fact.

The Cold War began with a series of crises in Eastern Europe and the Middle East (Poland, Greece, Iran and Turkey). But the real struggle was over the future of Europe.* The American commitments were, of course, made in the revered name of centuries of historical, political and religious ties. But they rested on a very crass substratum of self-interest. I am not here suggesting anything subtle or Machiavellian – that, say, wily financiers realized, along with Dean Acheson, that the Marshall Plan would turn out to be profitable international pump-priming from the point of view of business. More simply, Communist domination of Western Europe or capitalist domination of Eastern Europe would have decisively tipped the international balance of power. Such a disequilibrium would have been intolerable enough according to the old-fashioned rules designed for nations within a single social system. But it became utterly and completely impossible when the contending powers represented alternate ways of organizing the very globe itself.

'In effect,' Stillman and Pfaff wrote, 'the early Cold War was a contest for the control of a prostrate, but fundamentally very rich, continent that had functioned as the center of world politics for three hundred years.' Here there is a very close correspondence between material self-interest and the political and military commitment on both sides. But once one leaves the initial, European period of the Cold War and turns to the Third World,

*Of all the classic Marxist theorists, Rosa Luxembourg would be the least surprised that a battle fought in Athens or on the border between Iran and Russia actually had to do with the fate of Paris or Berlin. She understood that economic determinism provides only the basic context in which various conflicts function. But the actual line-up of forces and the tangled course of events are then profoundly modified by 'accidents' of history, religion, geography, etc. See, for example, her *Junius Broschure*.

the disparity between economics and foreign policy becomes manifest.

The historians of the twenty-first century might well conclude that the Korean War was the strangest 'accident' of the entire postwar period. That country had been partitioned in desultory fashion on the basis of proposals made by General MacArthur and sanctioned by Stalin. The Russian-Korean treaty in 1949 did not even contain a mutual-assistance provision, and in January 1950 a speech by Dean Acheson suggested that both Korea and Formosa were outside the American defense perimeter. The Chinese Communists did not maintain an ambassador in North Korea and, as Robert Guillian speculated in *Le Monde* in 1966, may well have regarded the invasion of the South as a Stalinist adventure. There were even public-opinion polls in the United States that showed, in the late Forties, that there was no strong popular support for action against Mao. For that matter, in August 1946, five months after Winston Churchill's famous 'Iron Curtain' speech, President Truman was telling Chiang Kai-shek that, unless he liberalized a bit, 'it must be expected that American opinion will not continue its generous attitude toward your nation.'

But with the Korean war, the ideological hostility which was rooted in the serious conflict of interests in Europe began to take on a life of its own in Asia. The French were then able to involve the United States in their Indochinese debacle, and thus lay the basis for the tragic Vietnamese conflict of the Sixties. The issue of who 'lost' China began to play a role in American politics, and Chiang's pseudo-China on Taiwan became a centerpiece of the nation's Asian policy. So it was in the 1950s that Chiang, Syngman Rhee, Bao Dai and Diem received a vast outpouring of American aid – and Nehru relatively little. The former group had enlisted in the cause of the 'Free World'; Nehru was, of course, a neutralist.

It was John Foster Dulles who officially gave the Cold

War its most ideological, even theological, cast. The struggle between the United States and the Soviet Union was turned into a titanic conflict between good and evil in which any challenge, no matter how remote, had to be met. A far-flung network of alliances and treaty organizations was established which excluded the modernizers, non-Communist revolutionaries and neutralists and was based on conservative and reactionary powers. This approach was designed to accentuate the gap between the rich and the poor, for it meant that American donations were effectively militarized and almost always assigned to the indigenous friends, rather than the foes, of backwardness.

But if American policy in the post-European Cold War was hardly a reflex of economic interest, that hardly means that it was capricious. The nation in this period was ruled by domestic conservatism. A Republican, business-oriented Administration held office for two terms, the Dixiecrat-Republican coalition prevailed in the Congress, McCarthyism made it sometimes difficult even to have a debate. There were thus profound internal reasons for the nation's reactionary foreign policy. Unable to see the need even for reform at home, the American leadership was of course bewildered by a world in revolutionary transition. And since the Administration – and the people – genuinely and passionately believed themselves to be benevolent, the only possible explanation for nationalist and anti-American movements abroad was subversion, spying, infiltration. And these demons are fought with guns and counter-espionage, not with social programs.

In his brilliant account of John F. Kennedy's presidency, Arthur Schlesinger, Jr, illustrates how the Eisenhower Administration applied this methodology to Latin America. If democratic reformers came to power, the argument went, that would only create instability, a breakdown of order and conditions which would lead to a Communist take-over. Therefore the only true friends of the 'Free World' were on the Right. It was this logic that, in the Fifties, brought American support to Batista, Pérez Jiménez, Trujillo and their like.

However, this interpretation of Dulles' policies should not be taken as an attack on any and all value commitments which go beyond a narrow national self-interest. In 1945, as De Gaulle bitterly recounts the fantastic incident in his *Memoirs*, Roosevelt was in favor of independence for Indochina on the basis of the 'ideology' of democracy. Yet if the United States had persisted in a policy of cooperating with the nationalist revolutionary movement in that country, there would have been at least a chance of avoiding the more than two decades of bloodletting that followed on the return of French colonialism. Where Dulles erred was not in propounding a philosophy which transcended the dollar sign but in doing so in an oversimplified, reactionary way.

In any case, the main point remains: the history of the Cold War shows that American foreign policy need not be the puppet of economic interest because much of it has not been. It is, however, sad to remember also that most of our disinterested idealism has been reactionary, as in the case of Dulles. But even such an unfortunate example proves that our role in the world does not have to be determined by cost accountants.

3

'In the councils of Government, we must guard against the acquisition of unwarranted influence, whether sought or unsought, by the military-industrial complex. The potential for the disastrous rise of misplaced power exists and will persist.' – Dwight Eisenhower, January 17, 1961

Another important theory seeks to demonstrate that America's reactionary stance in foreign affairs, and particularly in the Third World, is an inevitable consequence of the very structure of the society. In this view, the society needs the Cold War not in order to protect its overseas profits but rather as a justification for a domestic war of economy which is the main defense against depression.

This was one of the ways in which the late Paul Baran resolved his paradox about the disparity of the enormous military means America deployed to protect its relatively modest international economic ends (at times Baran veered back toward the classic Leninist thesis, as in *Monopoly Capital*, which he wrote in collaboration with Paul Sweezy). But then it was hardly necessary to be a Marxist to understand the tremendous significance of the tens of billions of dollars of annual armament spending. In his farewell message President Eisenhower had said of the 'immense military establishment,' which was 'new in the American experience,' that its 'total influence – economic, political even spiritual – is felt in every city, every state house, every office of Federal Government.'

If America were to embark on a genuinely democratic foreign policy and seek to create a new world in which the gap between the rich and the poor nations would be abolished, this vested interest in death would be threatened. For an emphasis on international construction, massive investments of men and money in the Third World, and disarmament would reverse the priorities which have prevailed in the postwar period. Could the American economy tolerate such steps toward peace?

In theory, the answer is yes. In practice, everything depends on politics.

There is no question that building an arsenal of annihilation is an extrordinarily congenial activity for American society. The mass unemployment of the Depression, it must be remembered, was not ended by the social and economic policies of the New Deal. Indeed, as Richard Hofstadter pointed out in his *American Political Tradition*, by the end of the Thirties, Keynes himself wondered whether any peacetime (and capitalist) government would ever intervene on the scale required by his computations. And, in fact, the abolition of joblessness took place during the reign of Dr Win-the-War and not during that of Dr New Deal.

There are solid, conservative reasons for this high esteem which is conferred on spending for destruction. Government investment in socially useful projects tends to raise disturbing, ideological questions. There is, for example, always the danger that some reformer will suggest that moneys be appropriated for an undertaking like TVA which would actually redefine the lines between the public and private sectors. To the class-conscious executive (and it is often on the moneyed heights of American life that one finds the most convinced, albeit upside-down, Marxists) such an approach is a challenge to the system. And then, in a New Deal era, egalitarian and even radical political movements tend to arise and insist on even greater redistributions of wealth in favor of the mass of people.

A vast increase in war spending, on the other hand, is almost always accompanied by an end to social innovation. The emotion of patriotism unites the entire nation, and class differences are submerged in the common effort. In the case of a shooting conflict, the military obligingly dispenses with competitive principles and adopts uneconomic methods like cost-plus contracts (when it is necessary in a conservative cause, or in fighting a war, America is always ready to turn its back on the myths of the market economy, but such idealism is almost never applied to truly idealistic projects). In a cold war, particularly one run by a top executive from the Ford Motor Company, the old rules of efficiency are in force, but then military hardware has the marvelous quality of becoming obsolete almost on the day it becomes operational. The production possibilities are therefore almost infinite.

For these, and many other reasons the American Congress will enthusiastically vote $50, $60 or even $70 billions for defense while it haggles over a less than

$2 billion appropriation for fighting poverty. And it is dangerous to think that, as peace begins to break out, it would be simple enough to transfer funds from the work of destruction to that of construction. The socialization of death is, thus far at least, much more generally popular than the socialization of life. A shift of money from Defense to, say, Health, Education and Welfare would demand a basic turn toward the democratic Left within the society.

And yet, does this complexity amount to an iron law – is a huge military budget the only form of effective social spending to ward off a depression? If this were the case, then even though overseas profits are not decisive for the American economy, a Cold War policy would be a requirement of our domestic needs. This is precisely the position taken by the late Paul Baran and by Paul Sweezy in *Monopoly Capital*, an ambitious attempt to adapt Marxist theory to the realities of the mid-century. They are, I think, wrong.

For Baran and Sweezy, the corporate-dominated American economy tends to generate larger and larger surpluses since it operates not according to the laws of competition of Marx's day but within the framework of monopoly. Part of this surplus is systematically wasted in lavish advertising, packaging, 'planned obsolescence,' model changes, credit schemes, etc. Part is spent on civilian government, but there are crucial limitations to this expenditure (more on this point in a moment). Thus, the financing of militarism and imperialism have a fundamental internal function within the system by overcoming the innate tendencies toward stagnation. 'From which it follows,' they write, 'that if the military budget were reduced to 1939 proportions, unemployment would also revert to 1939 proportions.'*

---

* In their treatment of imperialism proper, Baran and Sweezy attempt to show that foreign trade plays an increasingly important role in the American economy and that Standard Oil is thus becoming a prototypical image of the corporation. In so

Now the crucial question here is whether or not it is possible, without a revolution of the system itself, to substitute social for armaments spending. Baran and Sweezy curiously treat this most fundamental issue in a footnote. Taking note of the liberals who 'postulate ... a substitution of welfare spending for military spending,' they comment: 'We must say of such liberals what Marx said of the bourgeois reformers of his day: "They want all the impossible, namely the conditions of the bourgeois existence without the necessary consequences of those conditions."' This argument from a Marxian generality (which arose out of a controversy with Proudhon) is hardly a convincing proof of the state and tendency of the American economy of the late Sixties and Seventies. It is necessary to consult reality as well as authority.

This point can be best made by examining the actual, living fate of a projection very similar to the one urged by Baran and Sweezy. The author was V. I. Lenin; the date, 1916; the text, *Imperialism*. 'It goes without saying,' Lenin wrote, 'that if capitalism could develop agriculture, which today lags far behind industry everywhere, if it could raise the standard of living of the masses, who are everywhere still poverty-stricken and underfed, in spite of the amazing advance in technical knowledge, there could be no talk of a superabundance of capital. ... But if capitalism did these things it would not be capitalism; for uneven development and wretched conditions of the masses are fundamental and inevitable conditions and premises of this mode of production.'

Lenin's prediction certainly held up from 1916 to 1945. In the Twenties the purchasing power of the masses of Americans was held down while the productive capa-

doing, they ignore the most significant international trend of the postwar period – the growth in investment among the big powers and the decline in the importance of the Third World. These developments have made Standard Oil the exception rather than the rule. A similar approach was suggested by Harry Magdoff in the analysis he made before the Socialist Scholars' Conference in New York in September 1966.

city of the society was vastly increased and there was an eventual collapse. In the Thirties the Rooseveltian attempts to follow Keynes and to inject effective demand into the economy were, as noted before, halfhearted and ultimately ineffective. But from 1945 on, every one of the advanced capitalist powers pursued some variant of a full-employment policy. These efforts hardly created Utopia, and they were consonant with the persistence of great poverty, increasing injustice in the distribution of wealth and, particularly in the United States, a chronic and scandalous level of unemployment (but not general joblessness of the Thirties type). Capitalism had remained capitalism, yet it had learned that improving the lot of the masses could be good business.

There is no point in picturing this development in idyllic terms. The version of Keynesianism embraced by the American businessman of the Sixties most certainly did not involve the notion that a reduction in defense spending would be compensated for by a corresponding, multi-billion-dollar rise in social investments. The 're-actionary Keynesians,' as I have already pointed out, favoured tax cuts which would disproportionately benefit the rich and would maximize private consumption and keep the public sector on starvation rations. If American society has come to a certain consensus that the Government must intervene to stave off depression and that intervention would certainly be needed in the case of peace, there is still a fierce debate as to how this shall be done. The conservatives propose to prime the pump by raising the living standards of the wealthy, the liberals and radicals by improving the lot of the poor and of the society as a whole.

So one cannot speak of an effortless substitution of social spending for defense outlays. As John Kenneth Galbraith showed in *The New Industrial State*, the billions for armament go to a very specific sector of the economy, one that requires extensive research and development for the creation of a sophisticated and advanced technology. Some of these machine and human skills could be converted to benevolent use – but some could not. There must therefore be, Galbraith argues, a public investment in a peacetime production which is technologically similar to the annihilation industry. Space exploration, he concludes, would meet this requirement.

There is a certain puritanism on the Left, however, whenever the question of space comes up. It is the fashion to denigrate spending money on heaven when earth is still so shoddy. But this view overlooks two important points. First, if peace were indeed to break out, a massive cutback in the billions for defense plus the normal growth of a full-employment economy would provide sufficient funds for rebuilding America *and* going to the stars. And secondly, space is not empty of social, scientific and even aesthetic significance. It could conceivably provide room for human beings, vast new resources for the development of the world and it will certainly incite a deeper knowledge of both man and the universe. Beyond these pragmatic considerations there is a moral imperative that requires that humanity live up to the fullness of its powers.

So there are considerable difficulties when one rejects the economics of disarmament. But whatever the complexities, the American economy does not correspond to the rigid simplicity of the Baran-Sweezy model. In 1916 Lenin had the excuse that he could not peer thirty years into the future, but we have now lived that future and cannot afford to ignore it. There is a general American commitment to government intervention against depressions and capitalism has developed agriculture, raised the living standard of the masses and remained capitalism. In Lenin's own terms such a society is not inevitably imperialist. There is a political possibility that, with a turn toward the democratic Left, government intervention could take the form of a vast social investment which would substitute for the armament sector. Here, as in the case of overseas exploitation, there are powerful vested interests in the prevailing order of injustice. These

will not be easily defeated – but they can be. And therefore, Cold War, imperialism, the accentuation of the
chasm between the rich and poor nations are deep trends
within both the national and the international economy
of the United States, but they are not inexorable fates.

4

*'Taking the entire globe, if North America and
Western Europe can be called "the cities of the
world," then Asia, Africa and Latin America constitute the "rural areas of the world"... In the final
analysis the whole cause of world revolution hinges
on the revolutionary struggles of the Asian, African
and Latin American peoples who make up the overwhelming majority of the world's population.'* – Lin
Piao, 'Long Live the Victory of People's War!'

Finally, no consideration of America's predispositions toward global good and evil would be complete without
reference to the thought of Mao Tse-tung.

It would be hard to imagine a more audacious revision
of Lenin than the one contained in Mao's version of
Leninist orthodoxy. Imperialism is, in effect, no longer
defined as the last stage of capitalism but as the united
front of the rich, whatever their social system. In his
famous essay on 'People's War,' Lin Piao delicately refrained from noting that Russia and Eastern Europe were
really part of the 'cities of the world,' but the Maoists of
the mid-Sixties were obviously working on the basis of
that deduction. And then where Marx and Lenin had
seen the working class as the historic agency of social
change, the Chinese Communist leader looked to the
peasantry – i.e., to that class which Marx had regarded
as being lumpish like so many potatoes in a sack.

It is easy to ridicule the fantasy elements in Mao's
vision – and it is more important to understand their profound relationship to reality. For, as noted earlier, there
is a basis for a theory of a conspiracy of the industrial

North, corporations and commissars alike, against the backward South. There are even American liberals who advocate such an arrangement as a way of ending the Cold War. And although the peasants of this world are certainly not going to usher in a reign of peace and justice, they could well become the agents of their own enslavement. Mao represents one of the most important trends in the developing lands, a totalitarian program of modernization.

There is, first of all, the reactionary potential of a Soviet-American alliance.

Toward the end of World War II Henry Stimson, a Republican member of Franklin Roosevelt's Cabinet, had an intriguing idea of a postwar settlement. Gar Alperovitz has summarized it in this way: 'The essence of Stimson's view was a conservative belief that the post-war power structure in Europe had to be acknowledged so that a *modus vivendi* could be established with Russia. Although he wished to preserve American economic interests in Eastern Europe, he took for granted Soviet special interests in the border countries just as he accepted American special interests in Latin America – the two areas were "our respective orbits." '

Secretary of War Stimson's perspective was not adopted; there was a Cold War instead. Yet it is important to remember that the Stimson approach was explored by another leading figure in those days: Joseph Stalin. 'The question of Poland,' the Russian dictator wrote to Harry Truman, 'has the same meaning for the Soviet Union as the question of Belgium and Greece for the security of Great Britain. . . . I do not know whether there has been established in Greece a truly representative government and whether the government in Belgium is truly democratic. The Soviet Union was not consulted when these governments were established there. The Soviet Union did not lay claim to interference in these affairs as it understands the whole importance of Belgium and Greece for the security of Great Britain.'

There was some ghoulish humor in this document. When Stalin acknowledged the legitimacy of the British – imperialist – claim to a sphere of interest in Greece, he was making a not so sly reference to an agreement he had made with Winston Churchill. The Briton and the Russian had coolly divided up all of Eastern Europe (the details are to be found in Churchill's memoirs of the war) and Greece was given to England. When there was a Communist-led insurrection in Greece, Stalin was as good as his word. He stood by while his comrades were put down in blood. He 'knew' very well what the character of the Greek government was and he had indeed been 'consulted.' He was simply advising Truman that he could be counted on to keep a bargain.

But Truman did not take up Stalin's proposal that the Communists and capitalists should recognize each other's spheres of exploitation. The idea, however, did not die out. It was, for example, the Presidential program of Henry A. Wallace in 1948. 'The real peace treaty we need now,' the former Vice President told a rally in 1946, 'is between the United States and Russia. On our part, we should recognize that we have no more business in the political affairs of Eastern Europe than Russia has in the political affairs of Latin America, Western Europe or the United States.'

In the 1950s and 1960s the atomic balance of terror imposed a *de facto* recognition of power realities somewhat along the lines that Stimson, Stalin and Wallace had proposed. In 1956 the American inability to intervene in Hungary constituted an admission of the fact that Communist power in Eastern Europe could not be rolled back. During the Cuban missile crisis of 1962 Khrushchev was forced to bow to the United States in the Caribbean. And no one in Europe any longer believed that they lived under the threat of Soviet invasion, a fact which was the basis of De Gaulle's attack on NATO.

In terms of world peace, this *détente* between the nuclear giants was most welcome. But it also gave potential substance to the Maoist vision of the imperialist 'cities of the world.' Now, as this entire analysis suggests, an America which is not inexorably fated to exploit the globe on its own is hardly driven to do so in concert with the Russians. Mao is onto a possibility, not a necessity. Yet it is particularly important that the democratic Left be aware of the element of reality at the center of the Chinese Communist's often fanciful thought. For, while the democratic Left has rightly understood that peace, in this nuclear age, is the precondition for all progress, it would be a serious mistake to think that peace is a sufficient condition for that progress. A *pax Sovietica-Americana* is to be preferred to a holocaust initiated by the two powers, of course, but it is not a genuine vision of justice in itself.

Therefore, the democratic Left must be concerned with the far side of disarmament. It cannot settle for a big-power deal in which Washington and Moscow refrain from destroying the world simply in order to exploit it. It must, as the next chapter should make clear in some detail, offer specific suggestions for remaking – or creating – that world. But if it should thus take Mao's half-truths seriously, it must also treat his illusions with great respect, for there is a very objective basis for their appeal to aspiring elites and despairing masses. I refer, above all, to the preposterous and powerful notion that the peasants of the Third World are going to build the socialism which the European workers failed to achieve.

For Mao, the contradiction between the rural areas of the world and its cities is the dynamic force in the history of this epoch. The Southern and poor powers are therefore seen as developing a common consciousness of their plight. At first, there will be wars of national liberation and defensive alliances (this is the 'democratic' stage of the process). But eventually the proletarian nations (which are really peasant) will be led to realize that nothing less than socialism will suffice. And, for the indefinite future at least, this drama is to be played out without the intervention of the Western working class, that old Marxian hero, which is said to have been integrated into imperialist society.

There are many reasons why this profoundly influential perspective is false. First, it is racist to assume that the Third World represents a unity, that all the non-whites, all the Southerners and all the poor are like one another. 'An African is no Tamil,' Stillman and Pfaff write, 'a Malay is not a Pathan.' More broadly, they continue, 'Asia is the domain of sophisticated and accomplished civilizations,' Africa has 'no culture comparable to Asia,' Latin America is an 'archaic Western society.' There are thus deep differences within the ex-colonies and sometimes they are even murderous, as the Chinese of Indonesia and the Indians of Africa have learned. Secondly, peasants may well be capable of greater political struggle than Marx imagined, but in the ultimate analysis they can only deliver power to the city dwellers who will rule over them. Scientific technology is urban, and one could almost define a modern nation by saying that it has succeeded in shifting masses from the fields to the factories and, eventually, to the computers.

But, most important of all, the determined collectivization of poverty can only produce poverty, not a society of justice and abundance. For all the righteousness of the anger of the poor of this world cannot will factories and a high level of mass education into existence. It was thus not for nothing that Marx insisted that the socialist future could be more liberating than the capitalist present only because it was to be built on the material accomplishments of that present.

Therefore, for all of its talk of 'freedom,' as soon as the Maoist ideology posits a revolution of impoverished peasants going it alone it must also opt for totalitarianism. If the new countries are to accumulate capital, or even keep pace with their expanding populations, and if there is absolutely no hope of genuine aid from the advanced lands, then a huge surplus must be extracted from the labor of the people. As Aneurin Bevan put it in regard to Western history, 'It is highly doubtful whether the achievements of the Industrial Revolution would have been permitted if the franchise had been universal.' Neither Western workers nor Third World peasants enjoy sacrificing present consumption to future investment while working harder than ever before. And the real meaning of the word 'socialism' in the Maoist vocabulary is a forced accumulation of capital more pitiless and systematic than that of Western capitalism.

This Maoist illusion has great appeal. It can inspire peasants who see no hope in a world order which condemns them to hunger and misery. It reaches out to African nationalists who came to power on the basis of classless, populist movement and who are therefore suspicious of democratic conflict which they associate with the ways of imperialism. It speaks to some Western intellectuals who discover in the ex-colonial peasant the miraculous resurrection of the God that failed, the capitalist worker (the unity of the Third World, Jean-Paul Sartre incants mystically, 'begins by the union, in each country, after independence or before, of the whole of the colonized people under the command of the peasant class').

And Maoism also has a message for aspiring elites. For the totalitarian industrialization is not carried out by an impersonal History but by men and women. In theory, the period of monolithic 'democracy' which accompanies this accumulation of capital is to be followed by an age of greater political freedom. In fact, as the history of Russia demonstrates, the elite that acts in the name of the nation develops common economic privileges and interests which eventually come into conflict with the needs of the great mass of people. After the first stage of totalitarianism there comes, with adjustments and thaws, the second stage of totalitarianism.

Thus, I would suggest that there is a strange dialectic of anti-democracy based on the *de facto* cooperation of

Western capitalists and Chinese Communists. By maintaining the international order of economic injustice, the West makes it materially impossible for the Third World to advance toward both modernity and freedom. And Maoism (and all the Maoist variants, for I take the theories of the Chinese Communist as symbolic of a political and intellectual trend which can be found throughout the Third World) is there to make a choice for totalitarian progress. The democratic Left commitment to helping in the creation of a new world aims at nothing less than utterly transcending the options which are now available – or at providing a new choice.

5

'The materialist doctrine that men are products of circumstances and upbringing, and that, therefore, changed men are products of other circumstances and changed upbringing, forgets that it is men that change circumstances and that the educator himself needs educating.' – Karl Marx, *Theses on Feuerbach*

America, the almost-imperialist, could act to change the imperialist order of things. This proves something, but not much.

American prosperity does not depend on the evil which this country does in the international economy. Or, put the other way around, this nation – and the West generally – could actually benefit by acting humanely in the world. But progress is certainly not inevitable and perhaps not even probable. For there are powerful institutions, like the world government of oil, which profit from the current injustices. There are vital myths, like those about a world market based on principles of 'reciprocity,' which must be given up. There is an imperialist, and often racist, Western psychology which has been some centuries in the making.

It is conceivable, then, that non-economic factors will keep America from doing anything decent for the world's poor. In his provocative, thoughtful article on 'Counter-revolutionary America' in *Commentary*, Robert Heilbroner argued that this was necessarily so. In Heilbroner's view, the 'social psychology' of the less developed countries is an even greater barrier to their modernization than their low levels of production. The ancient ways have to be rooted out, the social structure has to be overturned, and this requires 'some shock treatment like that of Communism.' 'Only a campaign of an intensity and singlemindedness that must approach the ludicrous and the unbearable offers the chance to ride roughshod over the resistance of the rich and the poor alike and to open the way for the forcible implantation of those modern attitudes and techniques without which there will be no escape from the misery of under-development.'

Heilbroner concedes, as noted earlier, that an American economy with $1.3 trillion in corporate assets could afford to lose the $16 billion of capital in Asia, Africa and Latin America without facing an internal crisis. But he doubts that the United States is politically able to tolerate the upheavals, the smashing of the old oligarchies, the violence, which is inherent in the development process. Therefore, he concludes, '. . . Communism, which may indeed represent a retrogressive movement in the West, where it should continue to be resisted with full energies, may nonetheless represent a progressive movement in the backward areas where its advent may be the only chance these areas have of escaping misery.'

There are two distinct parts of this thesis, one a description, the other a value judgment. The latter asserts that if a coercive, and even totalitarian, accumulation of capital is the only practical way out of the inevitably impoverished past into the possibly more just future, then one reluctantly endorses the 'progressiveness' of this tragic but unavoidable transition. There is, however, a perpetual danger that this attitude will lead to a surrender of morality in the name of the 'wave of the future.' Mussolini made the trains run on time, Hitler 'solved' the problem of unemployment, South Africa has the highest per-capita income for black men on the continent and Franco has recently presided over growth rates which would be the envy of many a Communist planner. Yet no one on the democratic Left would propose political support, no matter how critical, for these economically successful but fascist governments.

To generalize, the fact that a regime is economically progressive – i.e., it modernizes – does not give it any automatic claim to our approval. Karl Marx believed that the British Raj was performing a revolutionary function in India by smashing an old order so stagnant that it had no hope of change from within. At the same time, he denounced the military acts and the general policies of the British imperialists as crimes. For his morality, as Lesek Kolakowski has pointed out, was not determined by economics. He understood that the most important aspect of this process was human, the emergence of a new Indian consciousness that would rise up against the Empire. He therefore sided with the people and against the 'progressive' English and their unwitting revolution.

Even supposing, then, that Heilbroner's descriptive analysis is correct and there is no way for the developing nations to avoid the violence and agony of totalitarian modernization, that does not mean that democratic Leftists give their political support to the dictators who carry out the transformation. In Hungary before 1956, for instance, the real 'progressives' were the subversive students who came to form the Petoffi Circle and not the members of the Rakosi regime and the secret police even though the latter pushed economic development.

But, secondly, I think that Heilbroner's description is overly pessimistic. The gloomy pattern he outlines is a very real possibility, perhaps even a probability. But it is not fated, and by thinking that it is there is a danger of helping to fulfill a deplorable prophecy.

For one thing, it is not at all certain that America must

react with such hostility to the violence and turmoil of
the development process. Senator J. W. Fulbright is a
conservative in the old, humane and humanist sense of
the term. He believes that human nature will eventually
assert itself in the Communist world and produce a
Thermidor which will make the revolution more practical and realistic. He therefore favors a policy of watch-
ful waiting, and he is, of course, opposed to American
intervention into every upheaval. I disagree with Fulbright's analysis – particularly the discussions of human
nature and *Thermidor* – and tend to share many of his
conclusions. But the relevant fact here is that the Senator
from Arkansas has long recognized the reality Heilbroner describes and he has not recoiled from it in horror.

In *Old Myths and New Realities,* Fulbright wrote,
'. . . we must be under no illusions as to the extreme difficulty of uprooting long-established ruling oligarchies
without disruptions involving lesser or greater degrees of
violence. The historic odds are probably against the prospects of peaceful social revolution. . . .' The democratic
Left could be at least as candid as this conservative Senator – and it is not at all precluded that the American
people could come to accept these disturbing complexities
of international politics.

But even more basically, it is possible to temper with
the 'historic odds' which Fulbright (and Heilbroner) cite,
for they are, to a degree at least, man-made. For it is precisely the policy of the United States which sets in motion
a vicious circle. Because the world market transfers
wealth from the poor to the rich and foreign aid, far from
offsetting this tendency, exacerbates it, the developing
countries discover that they must accumulate capital
from their own, internal resources. And that means creating a coercive state, whether Communist or not, for
suppressing the opposition, not simply of the wealthy but
of the people who now must work harder, eat less and
give up the consolation of their ancient superstitions. The
attendant violence and impiety are viewed with alarm in

the United States and their existence becomes one more
reactionary argument for pursuing international policies
which will breed even more violence.

If, however, the direction of this spiral were reversed,
then the hopeful factors would reinforce one another.
For if some wealth were actually transferred from the rich
nations to the poor – and on this point details will be
forthcoming shortly – then at least some of the economic
compulsion toward coercion and violence would be removed. Consumption could, for instance, be gradually
increased without endangering the whole modernization
program. And the marvelous fact of ex-colonial people
rising out of their poverty should make it politically easier
in the United States to argue for redoubled efforts on
their behalf.

Heilbroner is a radical social critic with democratic
values, as are many who share his views: he sadly predicts the unfortunate relevance of totalitarian modernization in the Third World. There are others, on the
authoritarian Left, who enthusiastically hail the violent
accumulation of capital and super-exploitation of peasants as the flowering of the socialist hope. But perhaps
the strangest group arguing that communism may be
both inevitable and desirable in the ex-colonies is to be
found among American businessmen.

According to the July 8, 1967, *New Republic*, a news
letter privately circulated to Wall Street insiders speculated that it could well be to America's advantage if the
new nations would go Communist. If they then fail in
their modernization efforts, it is not America's fault; if
they succeed, they will then become soft, like the Soviets,
and the United States can then make profitable deals
with them (this is a variant of Fulbright's *Thermidor*
thesis). Now it is clear that there are enormous, and
crucial, differences which divide Heilbroner, the Left
authoritarians and the cynical businessmen from one another. But, keeping these distinctions carefully in mind,
we find there is one important thing they share in

common: a profound conservatism with regard to America's ability to intervene in the epochal event of the emergence of the Third World. I would argue, on the contrary, that it is at least possible that America might change itself and thereby the world and that, so long as that possibilty exists at all, the Left must struggle to make it real.

In summary, if America's imperialist heritage of economic interest, ideology and feelings of superiority were rooted in economic necessity, there would be no hope of overcoming it. Since it is not, there is some hope. But thus far in the postwar period, that is a most modest and theoretical consolation. Therefore the statistical possibilities for doing global good require radicalized politics if they are ever to be realized. An America which cannot even provide decent housing for its own 'well-off' poor is hardly going to lead in the bold measures that are needed to end the threat of starvation forever.

I have, in short, established only that we have the right to hope, not that we should begin to exult. And so the crucial issue becomes political, not economic, for trends do not create new societies even if they make them possible and 'it is men that change circumstances ... the educator himself needs educating.'

CHAPTER NINE
'THE FRONTIERS OF . . .
COMPASSION'

In undertaking to complete the creation of the world,
one must not expect too much.

It will take a radical new beginning to justify very
modest hopes. This cruel paradox, like practically everything else about the contemporary international disorder,
is a creation of man in history. The developing nations
were deprived of capital and skills, and both of these
deficiencies can be made up in part by capital and technical assistance from the advanced economies. But there
is also a heritage of backwardness which is not so easily
overcome. There are native oligarchies, tribalisms, anti-
modern cultures, and almost all of these reactionary
trends were vigorously encouraged by the West during
its imperial rule (the way in which Africa was Balkanized
to suit European needs is perhaps one of the most obvious
cases in point). And the optimistic sociology of Defense
Secretary McNamara in which stability increases along
with GNP is probably naïve. In reality, it is quite possible that an aspiring people engaged in transforming the
very conditions of their existence will be quicker to violence than a passive mass that is simply starving.

So, to paraphrase Keynes, a just world economy will
guarantee not civilization itself but the possibility of
civilization. And yet this problematic, unprecedented
course of action is the one, and only, chance the earth
has to close the gap between rich and poor.

First of all, there must be international economic planning which will allocate massive resources to the new

nations on the basis of their needs and capacities. To accomplish this, economic aid must obviously be freed from the priorities of generals, diplomats and corporation executives (or commissars). This clearly cannot be done so long as the appropriation of money is subject to the vagaries of annual political review in the donor countries. So the advanced powers must agree to some long-term mechanism of international taxation which will automatically provide the required sums. This would be, in short, a *contrat social* for the planet.

Senator J. William Fulbright put it this way in his *Arrogance of Power*: '. . . I suggest that we begin to replace bilateral foreign aid, which is analogous to private philanthropy, with an internationalized program based on the same principle of public responsibility which underlies progressive taxation and the social services we provide for our own people. I suggest that we extend the frontiers of our loyalty and compassion in order to transform our aid to the world's poorer nations from something resembling a private gratuity to a community responsibility.'

Secondly, the present 'laws' of the international economy must be repealed. Since these are the artificial creations of men, they can be turned upside down. Where the world market of the past century was brilliantly designed to transfer wealth from poor to rich, our ingenuity must now be devoted to building mechanisms with the exact opposite effect. This means, above all, understanding and applying Gunnar Myrdal's paradox: that only a double standard can ensure fairness. For it is now patently obvious that free and equal trade between unequal nations leads to systematic injustice. Therefore, in the name of equity and not of charity, there must be trade policies which discriminate in favor of the developing countries.

In addition to their economic effect, the trade and aid programs suggested here might constitute a substitute for the Cold War.

But here, once again, it is necessary to speak of possibilities rather than of utopias. For one thing, the Cold War has many causes, and the fate of the Third World is not even particularly pre-eminent among them. For another, even if the United States and Russia have discovered something of a common interest in not annihilating each other, they still represent different social systems with hostile ideas about how the globe should be organized. Moreover, the two countries could end their conflict with a gentleman's agreement between rich Northerners to keep the Southern part of the planet poor. And yet there is at least a hope of combining peace with a modicum of justice, and that is the aim of the proposals made here.

So two cheers, then, for the creation of a new world!

I

'There is no chance of agricultural development in the underdeveloped (and hence agricultural) country under systems of absentee landlordism where the workers or sharecroppers are confined by law and tradition to a minor share of a meager product. These feudal agricultural systems, moreover, extend their corrupting influence to government, to the provision of public or military sinecures to those who lack a claim on the land, and to the destruction of the moral fibre of the society itself. . . . The revolution that is required, we should remind ourselves, is less the Russian Revolution than the French Revolution.' – John Kenneth Galbraith, *Economic Development*

For some time the most thoughtful Americans have called for a democratic revolution in Asia, Africa and Latin America, both on grounds of justice and as an alternative to communism. And yet this familiar, excellent idea is more radical than its proponents realize. It requires, to use Galbraith's symbolic language, something much more profound than a 'French' revolution. In analyzing why this is so, I hope to develop a long-range perspective on the practical problems of creating a new world.

My point is not to argue for a 'Russian' revolution, an imitation of Lenin in 1917, much less of Stalin in the Thirties or of Mao in the Fifties or Sixties. It is precisely the material and spiritual agony of the totalitarian accumulation of capital initiated by the latter two leaders that must be made unnecessary. Nevertheless, a debate among the Russian socialist factions of over half a century ago has a peculiar relevance to the hopes and difficulties of the next decade. For between 1903 and 1917 the Russian revolutionaries quarreled over whether they should have a French or a Russian revolution.

In broad compass, the Mensheviks said that their country needed a 'French' revolution – i.e., the establishment of political, but not social, democracy within a capitalist economy. The Bolsheviks and Trotsky held that Russia was not condemned, or even permitted, to duplicate the evolution of the earlier Western capitalism. The Russian revolution, they said, would occur under unique conditions: within a backward, peasant and semi-feudal nation whose bourgeoisie was weak and in alliance with feudalism and whose working class was tiny but concentrated and radical. In such circumstances, they concluded, the capitalists would be incapable of leading a capitalist revolution and the escape from the feudal past would demand a leap into the socialist future.

There are many reasons why it would be preposterous to attempt to impose this reasoning on the Third World, among them the fact that the categories of Western Marxism were hardly designed to deal with tribes and castes. And yet the central point in this debate is quite apropos to the new nations. Lenin and Trotsky were right to understand that the capitalism which developed logically out of a given time and place – say, the French Revolution – could not be expected to reappear in utterly changed circumstances (they were, however, wrong in their expectation of imminent European upheaval, and their error prepared the way for Joseph Stalin). And this insight applies even more to ex-colonies, which are even more economically and socially distant from the late eighteenth- and early nineteenth-century West than the Russia of 1917.

What is involved here is not a scholarly wrangle over the past. The point is that to make a democratic revolution here and now, it is necessary to go well beyond the French model – e.g., to institute extensive economic planning; to ignore the allocation of resources which the market makes; etc. Now this clearly has anti-capitalist and socialist implications, but not in the ideologically neat way that Lenin and Trotsky imagined. For the times demand a new type of revolution which is neither French nor Russian. And this means that a central assumption of American policy from Harry Truman to the present – that a sophisticated and liberalized free enterprise could provide the economic basis for political democracy in the Third World – must be discarded.

Perhaps the best way to make all this theory and historical analogy concrete and accessible is to turn to an actual case in point: the Alliance for Progress. In 1966 Senator Robert F. Kennedy made a long, probing speech, 'The Alliance for Progress: Symbol and Substance.' It was an attempt to draw up a balance sheet on the experiment which his brother had initiated.

To begin with, Kennedy acknowledged that basic issues are at stake, for 'a revolution is coming – which will be peaceful if we are wise enough; successful if we are fortunate enough – but a revolution which is coming whether we will it or not.' This means that there must be a 'French' revolution: 'large-scale land redistribution necessarily implies major changes in the internal political balance of many Latin American countries – away from oligarchy and privilege, toward more popular government.' Thus, if literacy is broadened, so are the eligible electors in Brazil; if agricultural credit is made available to the masses, then the moneylenders are threatened; if higher education is democratized, then the upper-class monopoly of the universities will be broken. Yet modernization demands a more equitable sharing of wealth so as to create a large domestic market and massive investments in education and new industrial and economic infrastructures.

Now this is a call for wide-ranging change (even though, as will be seen, it falls short of what is needed). And Kennedy recognized that neither this dream nor the original ideals of the Alliance are anywhere near accomplishment. He noted that in the first period of the Alliance there has been no real increase in per-capita agricultural production; North American private capital has not participated in Latin American development as it was supposed to; and the economic aid of the United States Government was much too small and should be immediately doubled. In addition, Kennedy scored the reactionary effects of the oversubsidization of the Latin military and of the State Department practice of putting the interest of oil profits on a higher plane than those of a Peruvian domestic Peace Corps.

All of Kennedy's specific criticisms are sound enough, and so are his proposals to double economic aid and cut military subsidies. But on a conceptual level Kennedy retained Harry Truman's classic assumptions about Point Four: that the Government is to create a context in which American businessmen and ex-colonial entrepreneurs would cooperate, to the profit of all, in the work of modernization. As Kennedy stated the premise, 'private industry is the primary source of capital in all the underdeveloped regions; it is potentially the major source of development capital for Latin America. Secondly, private enterprise is also the principal repository of the technical and technological skills which Latin America needs.'

This is not true, and a failure to recognize the counterproductivity of private American (or advanced) capital in Latin America is the basic flaw in Kennedy's candid, sincerely motivated critique of the Alliance. For the market mechanism cannot be the mainspring of Latin American development in terms either of attracting foreign capital or of allocating domestic capital. There must be, in contradiction to 'French' revolutionary principles, conscious economic and social planning, not *private* enterprise. For the rationality of the profit motive directs the giant foreign corporations to distort the economic structure of the developing nation at best and to keep it eternally backward at worst.

To begin with, the basic infrastructural needs of the poor nations – roads, education, cheap mass housing, etc. – are simply not profitable investments. Indeed, no one is really interested in building decent homes for the poverty stricken *within* the United States, and smart money would shun such an undertaking overseas even more so. As T. C. Blair has written, '. . . the criterion of profitability when applied in Africa too often leads to high monetary receipts but low real social benefits. Investors channel money into profitable export produce and minerals and avoid investment in 'unprofitable' homebuilding, school construction and low-cost food protein production. Profitable external economies are created with a consequent stagnation of the domestic economy. Investment in the production of goods with a high utility for low-income African consumers continually lags behind other investment sectors.' This analysis fits Latin America perfectly.

In Venezuela, for instance, the urban population increased from 35 per cent of the total in 1936 to 63 percent in 1965, and the 1,632,000 citizens of present-day Caracas total more than all the people who lived in Venezuelan cities in 1941. This situation was precipitated by a foreign-sponsored boom in the oil industry, which, with the third largest output in the world, employs only 33,472 workers. Foreign capital utilized, of course, the most modern techniques precisely in order to maximize profit. This helped uproot the old traditions but it did not provide new employments, and so mass unemployment has been a chronic problem for the post-Jiménez and pro-Alliance governments.

But then it is not simply the foreign investor who thus distorts the backward economy. For the local oligarch follows the same rationale of profitability. As Thomas Balogh, cited earlier, points out, they often ship their capital to the wealthy countries and thus push up the interest rates at home. So if, as Senator Kennedy suggests, private industry is seen as the primary source of capital in all the underdeveloped regions, then both foreigners and natives with money will have a systematic tendency to invest in the wrong – i.e., highly profitable, distorting and not socially useful – enterprises. As Arthur Schlesinger, Jr, described the actual conduct of American businessmen in Latin America in the early Sixties, they pressured the Alliance 'to talk less about social reforms and more about private investment.' And, I would add, these men were quite right to regard social reform and private investment as often antithetical.

In a striking metaphor Celso Furtado summed up much of what is being said here: 'Big corporations with their advanced techniques and great concentrations of capital have the same effect in underdeveloped economies as those huge, exotic trees which drain up all the water and dry out the earth of an entire area. . . .' Therefore, Furtado concludes, '*in Latin America, development cannot be the simple result of forces acting within the market. Only a conscious, deliberate policy of the government can really lead to such development.* What we call the "Latin American revolution" is the growing consciousness of this problem and the effort, however, dispersed and discontinuous, to create political institutions capable of supervising the social changes which are essential if development is to be viable. Since the present ruling classes don't understand this problem and obstinately maintain the *status quo*, those in Latin America who fight effectively for development fill, whether they know it or not, a revolutionary role.' (Italics added.) In other words, even if there were a successful French revolution, even if the feudal relations and land patterns were broken, that would not be enough, for we are at the end of the twentieth century, not the eighteenth, and that makes all the difference in the world.

In its 1967 *Report*, the President's Council of Economic Advisers confirmed Furtado's analysis although, as can be imagined, they did not exactly linger over the point. After noting that, since 1963, the entire increase in American capital going to the developing countries has been mainly in the extractive industries, particularly oil, the Council commented that '... investment in technologically advanced, sometimes highly automated, extractive processes does not have the same stimulating effect on general economic activity as does investment in local manufacture.' But it is, of course, precisely this wrong kind of investment which excites private enterprise in the United States.

That is not to say that one is supposed to ignore the uncomfortable fact that the West is dominated by business, or even to argue that there is no role for private corporations in the work of development. But it does mean that free enterprise can participate in such a process only in a subordinate, and never in a primary, role. If, for instance, Eduardo Frei of Chile had followed the advice of the sophisticated executives of the Committee for Economic Development, he would never have 'Chileanized' part of the copper industry (a program designed to double output *and* to assure partial state ownership). In that case, one of the most hopeful governments on the continent would have lost much of its dynamic and popular support.

In short, the United States must abandon its ideological hostility to the public sector in the developing nations. In saying this I do not want to stand the free-enterprise myth on its head and argue that nationalization is some magic, painless way to modernization. There have been writers, such as the late Paul Baran, who essentially held such a view, but in the light of what has happened in countries like China and Cuba, it can no longer be seriously maintained. So there is no easy road out of underdevelopment, and one must talk pragmatically about some sort of international mixed economy. Yet there is a crucial point which can be rather simply put: the Third World cannot put its faith in Adam Smith or any of his heirs, for the market mechanism is a cause of, rather than a solution to, its poverty. Understanding this fact will require that the United States get over some of its favorite prejudices.

So the democratic revolution must build on economic and social foundations unknown, and even antithetical, to those of the great European capitalist transformations of the eighteenth and nineteenth centuries. And the generous vision of Robert Kennedy – and of American liberalism generally – must be amended so that it does not depend on private enterprise, either within the United States or inside of the emergent nations, as the prime mover in modernization.

But, once again, even while insisting on these far-ranging changes in American policy, the political limits of our intervention must be kept carefully in mind.

There is, as John F. Kennedy realized when he initiated the Alliance, structural resistance to positive change in the developing lands. The Latin American oligarchs are, of course, the most classic case in point. In its original, reformist version, the Alliance sought to meet this problem by making grants contingent on policy changes in the recipient nations, like creation of an equitable tax system. There was thus a hope in a revolution which would proceed from the top down. 'The leaders of Latin America,' President Kennedy said at Bogotá, 'the industrialists and the landowners, are, I am sure, also ready to admit past mistakes and accept new responsibilities.' In retrospect, this confidence was either naïve or ceremonial. The Latin American *status quo* is not even prepared to take a position of enlightened self-interest.

This intransigence means that, even as America provides massive assistance precisely in order to minimize the potential for bloody conflict within the Third World, there must be an expectation of turmoil and even violence. We might even find the United States sympathetic to armed revolutionists of the Left rather than, as so often in the past, to the military dictators of the Right. But it most emphatically does not follow that this country should adopt some democratic variant of the Maoist strategy and seek to foment wars of 'national liberation' all over the globe. The pretension to omnipotence which led to the tragic commitment in Vietnam is as dangerous in the service of a good policy as of a bad one. And that is why it is so important to specify exactly what is proposed in this activist notion of creating a new world – and what is not proposed.

Paradoxically, one of the most vigorous actions the United States could take in support of the democratic revolution simply involves ceasing to do the wrong thing. For during the postwar period America usually gave political, economic and military support to the confirmed opponents of social change. The list of recipients is dreary and familiar: Chiang, Rhee, Bao Dai, Diem, Ky, Franco, Batista, Jiménez, Trujillo and so on. And, as Theodore Draper has pointed out, the tragic conflicts of the Sixties which pitted the United States against popular upheavals – in Vietnam, Cuba and the Dominican Republic – were a consequence of previous American policy, such as the support of French imperialism and of Cuban and Dominican dictatorship. If it is sometimes difficult to locate the good guys of the Third World, it is easy enough to desist from a strategy of supporting the bad guys.

But it is not enough just to refrain from doing evil. For it is quite possible to establish political sympathy for revolutionary movements without sending agents to direct them. Even with all the failings of the *Alianza*, for instance, there is no question that in the period of its inception John F. Kennedy managed to identify his Administration's policy with the aspiration for change in Latin America. For that matter, Kennedy's speech in support of the Algerian right to independence was one of the few events of the Fifties which demonstrated that there were some Americans who were not bent on subordinating all democratic and anti-colonial principles to the political needs of the NATO alliance.

Indeed, the United States should follow the urging of the "Latin American revolution" is the growing con- (Frei, Lleras Restrepo of Colombia, Leoni of Venezuela) and restore the 'Betancourt doctrine' under which this nation refuses to recognize Rightist *coups d'état*. In this way, and through refusing to create and bankroll the armies of Latin America, America could make an enormous contribution to the cause of democratic revolution without pretending to be omnipotent.

And beyond these very crucial political and military acts, the very fact that the United States publicly commits itself to make a democratic revolution economically possible will be, in and of itself, an incitement to change. Over a century ago Marx realized that one of the factors which made the bourgeois revolution more dynamic than any previous upheaval was the great growth in the means of communication. But now this point is a thousand times more relevant, for all of the people of the world are being brought into listening distance of one another. The American word, if it is backed up with the kinds of deeds advocated here, could thus become a mighty force in its own right.

There is, however, a danger that America might adopt a policy of 'sentimental imperialism' (the phrase is Arthur Schlesinger, Jr's). Instead of assuming that our military technology allows us to intervene everywhere in the world, we would then act as if our social ingenuity and political institutions were universal models. There was more than a hint of this attitude when Lyndon Johnson proposed in 1966 to build a Great Society in Asia (since he had not yet built one in the United States, the announcement was, at a minimum, premature). Such a messianism would render the very best of programs ineffective.

So in keeping with the *sotto voce*, two-cheers mood of this chapter, let it be freely admitted that the concept of the democratic revolution relates only to the possibility of new possibilities. And that is more hope than one can find in the almost quarter of a century since World War II.

2

'The only force available for such counter-action [off-setting the inequities promoted by "free" exchange on the world market – M.H.] is some form of democracy applied between nations in a way analogous to that in which the democratic principle has been applied within [a few] nations.' – John Strachey, *The End of Empire*

Up until this point, the creation of a new world has been analyzed primarily in terms of what the United States could and should do. But perhaps the most positive and dramatic single action this nation could take would be to internationalize its economic aid. That would lay the basis for the global economic planning which alone can make the notion of 'democracy between nations' a meaningful reality. It is now necessary, as Senator Fulbright has said, to 'extend the frontiers of our loyalty and compassion.'

For, as all of the foregoing has shown, postwar aid, whether capitalist or Communist, has been inspired by almost every motive except one of orderly economic development for the earth's poor. In 1963, the OECD has reported, 84 percent of aid funds were bilateral – i.e., subject to military and political priorities. Thus it was that France used its disbursements to create a special, and advantageous, relationship with its ex-colonies, or that President Kennedy could say, 'Our assistance makes possible the stationing of 3.5 million Allied troops along the Communist frontier at one tenth the cost of maintaining a comparable number of American soldiers.' And even when the money was not so blatantly an instrument of the donor's foreign policy, it was regularly 'tied' to the needs of the advanced economy rather than those of the impoverished economy, and, more recently, the trend has been to loans rather than grants.

For historical reasons normally not of their own making, the impoverished nations are desperately short of human resources. Yet the political and military vagaries of postwar aid were so tricky that they would have taxed the abilities of the computerized planning process in a modern country, and did overwhelm the shaky planning institutions of the new countries. So it is obvious that funds must be allocated on some rational, predictable basis of need and capacity to use them. The United Nations has already begun the groundwork of developing econometric models of the world economy.* If the goal of closing the gap between the rich and the poor is taken seriously, this tentative undertaking must receive massive support and become the focus of a system of planned, internationalized aid.

To some it might seem grandiose and visionary to talk in this way of international economic planning. But, in point of fact, American private business is already engaged in precisely such an undertaking. Ford, General Motors and IBM favor 100 percent ownership of their overseas subsidiaries in order to plan their activities on a global scale from a single center. As Gilbert Clee and Wilbur Sachtjen put it in the *Harvard Business Review* in 1964, 'The really decisive point in the transition to world enterprise is top-management recognition that, to function effectively, the ultimate control of strategic

---

Studies in Long-Term Economic Projections for the World Economy (United Nations, 1964) is one example of the kind of work already in progress.

planning and policy decisions must shift from decentralized subsidiaries or division locations to corporate headquarters, where a worldwide perspective can be brought to bear on the interests of the total enterprise.'

The United Nations could be at least as imaginative in this regard as General Motors. It too should make global plans. There are, of course, different estimates of how much it would cost the advanced countries to make up the capital deficiencies of the developing lands.

In 1966 the Council of Economic Advisers optimistically figured that the new nations could use only $3 to $4 billion more than is now available. But there are much higher projections: Jan Tinbergen has set the needed funds at $7 billion, Michael Brower has argued that $12 billion in public grants are required, and the First Committee of the UN Trade and Development Conference predicted that the 'savings gap' would reach $20 billion in 1970.*

There is no point here in trying to settle on the correct estimate – a decision which, in any case, is beyond the competence of this writer. But two things are quite clear. First of all, however much these computations differ (because of different definitions *and* the fact that so little effort has been devoted to the task), economists consider that there is an objective basis of determining how much capital the developing world needs and how much it can absorb. If really massive intellectual and financial resources were invested in such an analysis, there is no reason why there cannot be rational planning and resource allocation on a global scale.

Secondly, even if the highest estimate is taken – the UN's $20 billion savings gap in 1970 – the amount of money at issue is well within the means of the advanced nations. By 1970 Europe, North America and Australia

---

*Goran Ohlin's study, *Foreign Aid Policies Reconsidered*, Chapter 4, summarizes much of the work that has already been done in computing the capital shortage of the poor nations (OECD, Paris, 1966).

will have a total GNP of over $1.5 trillion. A deficit of $20 billion would, in that year, be less than the 3 percent of American GNP which Harry Truman proposed to spend on the Marshall Plan and would approximately equal the extra appropriation which Lyndon B. Johnson asked for the Vietnam war in 1967. So one is talking about very large, but quite manageable, sums.

It makes, however, a great difference how this money would be raised. For one of the most important advantages of international economic planning is that it would make long-range policies possible. Capital in the developing lands should therefore no longer be at the mercy of the wild fluctuations of the world market in primary commodities or the political vicissitudes of the Cold War. It should be guaranteed over a considerable period of years to allow the local planners to make a much more efficient use of their resources. But then, of course, this massive, steady flow of funds could be assured only if foreign aid were put on some permanent basis within the advanced nations.

There have been proposals to commit all of the wealthy countries automatically to give 1 percent of their GNP for international economic development. This would be an enormous improvement over the trends of recent years when this ratio has been regularly declining in the United States (which possesses more than half of the total GNP of the rich, non-Communist part of the world). And it would yield almost three fourths of the $20 billion gap which the UN Conference predicted for 1970.

Yet there is a much better way of appropriating these funds: that of a progressive income tax. This notion has an obvious grounding in equity since the richer a nation (or an individual) the smaller the percentage of income that is devoted to necessities and the greater the ability to meet social obligations. Secondly, such an approach meets the problem of the gap between the rich and the poor head on by proposing (if quite modestly) some redistribution of income shares. But thirdly – and here Senator Fulbright has emphasized the crucial point – such a system would take foreign aid out of the realm of charity and philanthropy and make it a matter of right, like Social Security within the United States itself.

The details of such an international income-tax system need not concern us here. Experts, such as P. N. Rosenstein-Rodan, have already demonstrated that the details can be worked out if there is the political will (in Rosenstein-Rodan's computation, if all the non-Communist advanced nations with per-capita GNP of $600 or more were involved, the United States' share of the burden, on the basis of 1961 figures, would be 65 percent of the total).*

However, there is another problem in international economic planning that is anything but a technicality. It is essentially the same difficulty faced in the designing of the Alliance for Progress: What attitude would an international-aid agency take toward reactionary governments, toward Rightist or Communist dictatorships? Unless this question is answered, the whole enterprise could boomerang. For, as Victor Alba has pointed out, in the case of an agreement to regulate coffee prices, some of these reforms could subsidize local oligarchies, rotten power structures and economic backwardness. Therefore it is clear that some minimal conditions would have to be placed on the grants.

The UN cannot intervene into the political life of every developing country any more than the United States can (or, more precisely, it would be even more problematic for the UN to do so). Yet it can insist that there be regional planning in return for its aid; it can disallow dictatorial pyramid building and old-fashioned thievery; and it should even insist that nations, and regional groupings, show that there is a 'popular

* P.N. Rosenstein-Rodan, 'International Aid for Underdeveloped Countries,' in *The Strategy of World Order*, Richard A. Falk and Saul H. Mendlovitz, eds., Vol. IV, p. 517.

consumption criterion' (the phrase is Galbraith's) in their equations – i.e., that projects benefit the present, as well as the future, generation.

But, once again, it is much simpler to solve these thorny issues on paper than in practice, and there is no point in getting lost in rhetoric. Even under the very best system of international economic planning there will be waste, funds will be appropriated by the corrupt and the dictatorial, etc. It is not that such an approach will work perfectly but that, if one is serious about closing the gap between rich and poor nations, it seems that only something like this approach will work at all. Certainly the defenders of the conventional wisdom and the actual aid and trade policies of the postwar period have utterly failed in their professed goal of narrowing the chasm which divides the fat North from the hungry South.

It seems to me that the radical critic should sympathize with the usually ignorant, sometimes reactionary, popular irritation with foreign aid. The Marshall Plan was a success within its own terms for the most obvious of reasons: a free gift of many billions of dollars to an area rich in skill and work habits and only in need of money accomplished the reconstitution of capitalism in Europe. But then political leaders attempted to transfer the appeal of this achievement to their plans for a Third World which was, and is, in an entirely different situation than postwar Europe. The voters expected quick success and considerable gratitude. They received neither.

And although the Point Four verbiage persisted, the programs of the Fifties and Sixties were increasingly instruments of American military and corporate policy, not of genuine economic development. There are some right-wing critics of this process who are hostile to it for the worst of reasons: they want to turn their backs on the people of Asia, Africa and Latin America; they are sympathetic to the world *status quo* and to military rule. But there are others, a much more numerous group, who are simply bewildered by the seemingly endless, futile

appropriations in Washington. There is no use in pretending that these people can be easily convinced to support the regular allocation of even larger amounts of
money.

Yet this is the effort in political persuasion which must
be made. In the doing, it is necessary to explain that past
programs failed not because they were so exceedingly
generous and benevolent but because they were inadequate and manipulative. And in such a context international economic planning should not be proposed as a
utopia but rather as the only *practical* way to accomplish
ends which Americans have thought they have been supporting for more than two decades.

This new effort could be supplemented by changes in
trade policies which would not require such sweeping
innovations. They would represent a decision to reverse
the present reactionary priorities of the world market, to
create a mechanism which would automatically transfer
some of the profits of the international economy from the
rich to the poor. To accomplish this would mean that
the tariff policies of the advanced nations would have to
be radically changed. Yet there would be no need for
new institutions – all that has to be done is to turn the
old arrangement upside down.

These last reasons convince Gunnar Myrdal, one of
the most perceptive writers on the problem, that efforts
to restructure the world economy should concentrate on
trade, rather than aid, policies. The most persuasive
objection to this view is the paradox that Balogh raises:
that it is possible to change the inequities in trade and
thereby strengthen the position of those very oligarchs
and reactionaries who are a major block to economic
development. However, I think it is wrong to counter-
pose the two roads to reform. There must be international
economic planning if there is any hope of ameliorating
the travail and agony of the transition to modernity over
the long run; and there must be immediate and basic
changes in Western trade policies if the non-Communist,

advanced lands are not to be a rich man's club with windows looking out on a starving globe.

Basically what the developing nations need – and want, for they made these demands on GATT in the summer of 1966 – is a transition from tariffs which discriminate against them to those which discriminate for them (which is Myrdal's double-standard method of achieving justice). They asked the Kennedy Round negotiators to reduce the tariffs on their products in every case; to lower the rate on goods from the developing lands more than on those from the advanced economies; to make a maximum reduction of tariffs on tropical foods; and to compensate the developing countries for their loss of tariff preferences when these take place. They were turned down.

But the UN economists have come up with an even broader conception than the one embodied in these proposals. They have suggested that there be a development insurance fund based on the 'willingness of advanced countries to contribute on the understanding that their direct benefits will not equal their contributions.' Under this plan, all nations would pay into a central fund and each would then be compensated if it suffered a drop in its export proceeds. In a series of complicated calculations the UN Committee of Experts which outlined this system concluded that, had it been working between 1953 and 1959, the developing countries' claims would have ranged between $246 and $466 million a year (and the advanced countries would have received between $12 and $142 million a year). Such a program is clearly, even easily, within the bounds of the possible for the rich powers.

It might, however, be a little more difficult to persuade the well fed to stop making a profit from the hungry than to get them into an insurance scheme. As noted earlier, Nasser wanted the 1966 New Delhi summit meeting to advocate a freezing of the entire debt of the developing countries, but, for political reasons, neither Tito nor Mrs Gandhi could be persuaded to go along with his idea.

And yet it is abundantly clear that there is no possibility of justice so long as India must return about one quarter of the monies it receives in foreign aid just to service past debt. New Delhi is afraid to protest this outrage because it might then lose the three quarters of assistance which remains after the tribute is paid. Yet the advanced economies hardly need this offering from the impoverished. The debts of the developing countries to the governments of the West should be forgiven or else rescheduled in such a way as to make them effectively interest-free.

And indeed, it is high time that the big Western powers reverse the scandalous trend toward loans instead of aid which has been picking up strength throughout the Sixties. Goran Ohlin's report for the OECD (which is, after all, a most prestigious organization of the capitalist economies) put it this way: '*So far it is principally in the help of rich countries that grants have been given precedence.* Not only in war finance and lend-lease, but also more spectacularly in the Marshall Plan, recourse was had to grants in order to avoid the later complication of the transfer of repayments to a nation which was wrongly suspected of being internationally a creditor country. *For a similar wisdom to prevail in the field of finance, the readiness to shoulder a real burden must be considerably greater in the advanced countries than it is today.*' (Italics added.)*

Ohlin's last point really ties in all proposals about both aid and trade. For however it is done in a technical sense, the substance of every one of these ideas is the same: that the richest lands in history voluntarily surrender some of the advantages which *they* built into the very structure of the world economy and that money thus be transferred from rich to poor rather than, as now, the other way around. This does not mean that the wealthy nations are supposed to opt for poverty in order to fulfill a moral obligation to the less fortunate of the globe. It simply means that these affluent countries will enrich themselves

Foreign Aid Policies Reconsidered, OECD, Paris, 1966, p. 91.

at a somewhat slower rate and without pushing the majority of the world's population more deeply into misery.

This can be done. There are sober and intelligent proposals which have already demonstrated the possibility of creating a new world by changing the present injustices of aid and trade. So the crucial question is not technical but political.

3

'The developing countries are the unsung victims of the end of the cold war. America has become less anxious about Russia's highly inefficient penetration of the "third world." The rich countries of the West, zealously led by the Europeans, have settled back to quarreling among themselves rather than spending resources on the poor in what have come to seem the backstreets of power politics. The flow of funds to the poor, which doubled between 1956 and 1961, has since remained virtually unchanged. The tone of comment on the undeserving poor has become noticeably more acid. The impression that "aid" is a euphemism for throwing good money after bad has spread, especially in the American Congress where it matters most.' – The *Economist*, February 4, 1967.

The gloomy reality noted by the *Economist* could certainly be the model of the future. Here I propose to give two reasons – one economic, the other political – why this need not be.

First of all, it is in the long-range self-interest of the United States and the advanced countries generally to do justice. And this is true even on the melancholy but realistic assumption that private corporations and profit-seeking will be a major feature of the affluent economies over the next two decades or so.

There is an important historical point which Michael Barret Brown develops in his *After Imperialism*. Contrary to the 'classic' theses of Hobson and Lenin, the bulk of British overseas investment was not in the colonies but in the white dominions. For it was, in the long run, more profitable, more economically important, to participate in the creation of modern, capitalist societies like the United States, Canada and Australia than to exploit the cheap labor of Africa and Asia. So it was that, on the eve of World War I, 30 percent of British capital overseas was in the Dominions, 19 percent in the United States and only 10·5 percent in India and 2·5 percent in Africa.

The reason for this pattern was, as noted earlier, perceived by Marx at a very early point. A poor country could pay for only a relatively small amount of manufactured goods. Therefore a modern power, interested in trade rather than plunder, had to create a buying power in the world if it hoped to sell its exports. There was, then, a contradiction confronting the businessman on the international market (it had an analogue *within* each one of the capitalist powers; of that, more in a moment). As a producer, he might welcome the exploitable poverty of the backward areas, for it provided him with cheap raw materials; but as a seller he was faced with the problem that this very same poverty restricted the market for his goods. The British resolved the dilemma as outlined above. They invested massively in white Dominions where there were ties of language and culture as well as a relatively educated, modern labor force; and they speculated on the profitable misery of the non-whites, but less massively.

Now the British approach – and all the old, classic forms of imperialism, for that matter – is politically impossible. Yet the past does demonstrate a most important truth: that in the long run the appearance of affluence, or at least the end of poverty, on a world-wide scale would provide enormous opportunities for the industries of the advanced countries. An Africa which would need computers would be, among other things, a much more important market than an Africa fighting to overcome illiteracy and build the very rudiments of a sophisticated economy.

The corporate executive would be quite happy thus to be presented with a vast new market, but he is constitutionally incapable of supporting policies which would create it. He thinks, as George Ball put it in 1967 on behalf of Lehman Brothers (and in the spirit of his former associates at the State Department), that 'There are limits to what the public sector can do and then private capital has to step in.... The problem that the whole world faces is making the most efficient use of finite resources.' But, as the preceding analysis has made clear, this philosophy has led to modern and profitable enclaves in poor lands which distorted the balanced development of the economy and did not disturb the backwardness of the society but helped to institutionalize it. And what is proposed here is planned and essentially social investment (there is an international analogue to the domestic quarrel between the Smith-Keynesianism and social-Keynesianism). Private enterprise would benefit from the policies outlined here, but it cannot, and does not want to, initiate or control them.

There is, then, a sort of international Keynesian argument for the self-interest of America doing justice internationally. For, just as the vast increase in buying power, which was developed in the United States by the welfare state and the labor movement, laid the basis for an advance in the prosperity of the entire nation, so a decent life for the peoples of Asia, Africa and Latin America would be to the economic advantage of the entire world.

Secondly, now that the Cold War is, at last, coming to an end in Europe, it is possible for the first time to realize the values which most Americans thought they had been fighting for all along. To understand this point requires an analysis of the two anti-communisms.

There was at the very height of the struggle between the NATO West and the Warsaw Pact East a straightforward version of anti-communism. It was based on reac-

tionary politics and viewed the Soviets as only one manifestation of the godlessness and disorder of a world which
had taken leave of its fundamental values. From this
point of view, anti-communism was one, and only one,
way of defending a *status quo*. The alliances with Rightist dictators were, in this perspective, acts of virtue, not of
necessity. And lacking any sense of the economic, political
and social roots of both nationalism and communism, the
Rightist anti-Communists saw the enemy as a conspira-
tor, a subversive, an agent, who somehow drove otherwise contented workers and peasants to revolt.

The American symbol of this one-dimensional and
paranoid anti-communism was, of course, Senator Joseph
McCarthy. And it was no accident that McCarthy's hey-
day coincided with Stalin's last, and utterly demented,
years and with the Korean war. The American people
were bewildered and fearful in the presence of a megalo-
maniacal dictator and involved in a frustrating shooting
war only five years after World War II had ended in
Tokyo Bay. This was the political atmosphere in which
McCarthy rocketed to prominence.

But there was, and is, another form of anti-communism. It sought some alternative both to communism and
to the *status quo*, for it recognized the right, and necessity, of revolution but struggled that it might be democratic, not totalitarian. The views of Galbraith and
Robert Kennedy, discussed at length earlier, are obviously in this tradition. Indeed, this attitude regularly provided the official rhetoric for American involvement in
the Cold War itself. 'The seeds of totalitarian regimes,'
Harry Truman said in March 1947, 'are nurtured by
misery and want. They spread and grow in the evil soil
of poverty and strife. They reach their full growth when
the hope of a people for a better life ahead has died.'

The words were fine enough – but the President uttered
them in defense of the Truman Doctrine in Greece,
where the United States placed its enormous power at
the disposition of conservative forces fighting a popular

movement whose leadership had been won by the Communists. And this was typical of United States policy during the Cold War. There were many Americans who were committed to the fight against communism for excellent reasons of democratic principle and hatred of injustice. Yet, by far and large, the United States could not possibly fulfill the hopes of these decent people. For, as this entire analysis has attempted to make clear, the essential conservatism of the American economy in an artificially unjust world subverted most of the nation's progressive political aspirations. At the same time that we preached 'freedom' to the Third World we were busy eroding the material basis of the very possibility of freedom.

In practical terms, as long as America's economic and social policies frustrated its political visions, the country regularly turned to the authoritarian Right even as it talked in the words of the democratic Left. Thus the militarization of American foreign policy and its association with so many dictators and anti-democrats is not the result of a particular malevolence of this or that politician but is related to massive structural trends both within the United States and in its dealings with the world.

But now it is possible to demilitarize our thinking and to redeem our own pledges. For a massive commitment to international development does not provide simply an economic substitute for the arms economy. It is also an emotional and political substitute for the reactionary passions of Rightist anti-communism; it is the one way peacefully to implement the decent values which motivated the anti-communism of the democratic Left. However, it must be most emphatically said, this proposal is not primarily 'anti.' It cannot be, for a new world will hardly be constructed out of hostility. One wants to save the workers and peasants of the Third World from the horrors of totalitarian capital accumulation, to be sure, and, in a social and economic sense, that is an anti-

Communist program. But in an enterprise that requires such ranging construction the stress must be positive, and the challenge is, in Fulbright's moving phrase, 'to extend the frontiers of our loyalty and compassion.'

The world market, like the domestic American economy, has been carefully structured to benefit the rich and harm the poor unless there is conscious political intervention to overcome the heritage and mechanism of injustice. This fact has subverted America when it honestly sought to be generous in its foreign-aid programs, and when an exception to the rule has been made it has been accomplished in the name of military priorities and a reactionary anti-communism. Yet, as Chapter 8 showed, this trend describes an instinctive, but not an inevitable, direction for American policy. There could be structural reform on a global scale.

The United States and the Soviet Union, having brought mankind to the brink of a nuclear holocaust, could simply walk away from the Cold War, retreat into their separate self-interests and respect each other's injustices. Or the United States could take the lead in a gigantic international effort for the reconstruction of the world. There are economic arguments for such a course, and they should be stated. But ultimately if this is to be done it will happen because the deep-running force of American idealism bursts the channels in which the generals and executives have confined it and takes its own direction. That is the politics of hope.

CHAPTER TEN

FOR A FIRST PARTY

America needs a majority party of the democratic Left.

This is not a proposal for a tightly disciplined party on the old European model (I see no reason to add to the amusement of the political scientists who have been setting up, and shredding, that straw man for a generation). It is simply a recognition of the fact that, to solve problems which the Government passively records, there must be radical departures and a political movement capable of initiating them. The real ideologues in this period are those utopian pragmatists who believe that the society can bumble its way through a revolution. They are fanatics of moderation.

The experts will not save us. A corporate end-of-ideologist like Max Ways thinks that there are no longer passionate issues which are settled by 'taking from group A to give to group B,' but only neutral problems which the private sector will now contract to solve. In the next breath he cites the Appalachia policy as a shining example of the new day. That program is based, of course, on highway building, which is supposed to generate wealth the region's businessmen will let trickle down to the poor people whom they have been fighting for years. More broadly, all the evidence in this book demonstrates that, in the absence of organized popular counter-pressure, public moneys are spent according to the priorities – and interests – of the powerful. So there must be a dynamic political movement if only to force the welfare state to promote the general welfare.

Unfortunately, the mere existence of a desperate need for change does not guarantee that it will take place. There may even be a dark truth concealed in the idylls of the utopian pragmatists. For they do not simply assert that the avoidance of principle is the beginning of civic wisdom. They also hold that this attitude is deeply rooted in American history and reality. The nation, they say, is so heterogenous that it must operate by deals between a myriad of factions and is therefore incapable of programmatic politics. If this is indeed the case – and it might be – then American history is tragic, for it does not permit the people to make the sweeping innovations upon which the survival – which is to say the deepening – of democracy depends.

I do not accept this pluralist fatalism. There is a certain unconsciousness of class in this country, there are Madisonian institutions rigged against the majority, the land is incredibly vast and varied – and yet there is also an objective basis in American life for the creation of a party of the democratic Left. One aspect of this realistic hope is admittedly old-fashioned: the material self-interest of working people, Negroes and the poor can be satisfied only through united political action. Another is unprecedented: a new social stratum is being formed by modern technology which could well have a non-material interest in basic change. These are possibilities, not inevitabilities, since the groups which should coalesce into a new political movement also have a great potential for fratricide.

But still there is a hope. America desperately needs a majority party of the democratic Left – and if there is a political will to form it, there is a way.

I

I am not here advocating a third party. I propose a first party which will be the instrument of a new political majority in the United States. There are two reasons for stressing this point. One has to do with some radicals of the 1960s, the other with some conservatives of the 1780s.

During the Fifties, American radicalism was all but destroyed. The Cold War made any form of social criticism suspect as an act of subversion, and McCarthyism made most people fearful of joining any organization of the Left, even of the anti-Communist Left. Then, toward the end of the decade, there was a modest revival of radical sentiment among the college youth. It first focused on ethical issues, such as abolishing the House Un-American Activities Committee or fighting capital punishment. In 1960 the civil-rights sit-ins triggered a wave of campus activism which all but liquidated the vestiges of McCarthyism and gave a profound social dimension to the student concern.

By the summer of 1963 the courage of black Americans had shamed a vast coalition into existence. In August of that year more than a quarter of a million blacks and whites marched in Washington, and for a breathless moment it seemed that unbridled conscience might triumph over the outrage of racism. In the beginning of 1964 the declaration of the War on Poverty made the young even more conscious of the economic and social foundations of racism and injustice. Thousands of students went to Mississippi or into the Northern slums. With the Johnson victory and a clear liberal majority in the House for the first time since 1938, it even seemed that the campaign promises would be redeemed.

By 1967 most of the bright hopes which these events inspired were in shambles. The ghettos erupted in violence and the militant Negroes turned their backs on integration. The idealistic young whites decided that America was the most hypocritical nation in history and that liberals with whom they had only recently marched were the arch-liars. Some were so disillusioned that they opted out of the society altogether as hippies. It was in these disenchanting circumstances that two small but significant groups – Black Power advocates and the white youth of the New Left – proposed minority strategies for the conquest of political power.

For the Negroes, the basic fact was that no white could be trusted. Therefore, black men had to change the society on their own. This was to be accomplished by creating so much disorder, using whatever means were necessary, that the whites would be forced to make reparations for the historic injustice of racism. The Negroes, they held, were a colonial people, their proper movement was one of national liberation, and they would have to adapt the guerrilla tactics of China and Cuba to an urban context. At times this logic drove straight through to an apocalyptic vision in which the black militants would help to bring the country down and a triumphant Third World of the non-whites would then build a decent society out of the ruins.

The radical white youth had a different, but similar, perspective. All of the agencies of social change from the previous generation, they said, had been corrupted by affluence and co-opted by the Establishment. The function of the 'corporate liberals' is not that of securing reform but of providing just enough ameliorations to keep radical discontent ineffective. Therefore, they concluded, a new movement would have to be built around those who had not been tainted by prosperity or power: the poor, the Negroes, the alienated, the rebellious young, the hippies and the outcasts generally.

In essence, then, the New Leftists and the black militants were, for quite different reasons, proposing that a minority make a revolution. Bizarre as it may seem for people to urge such a perspective in the name of either democracy or equality, it is important to understand the genuine desperation which motivated them.

The civil-rights movement in the Fifties and the first half of the Sixties was struggling against a sectional prejudice of American society. But, as I noted in Chapter 3, at the precise moment when the Jim Crow statutes were defeated, Negroes confronted the much more subtle and vicious injustice of the new racism with its concealed economic and social mechanisms. Now the central issues touched on some of the most basic premises of the *status quo*. For it would take massive, planned public investments, and not just a spirit of brotherhood, to provide jobs, housing and education for the black poor. In short, the years of marching, of non-violent sacrifice and of soaring hopes had not changed the essentially degraded place to which the black man was assigned in the society. It was small wonder that disillusionment set in.

Even more important as a cause of demoralization was the tragic war in Vietnam. When Lyndon Baines Johnson declared his 'unconditional' war on poverty in 1964, the sums he proposed were, in accord with the Federal liturgy of the 1960s, utterly inadequate to deal with the problems he defined. But at least there was Presidential recognition of a national scandal, and one was allowed to hope that the skirmish he ordered would turn into a battle. But with the sharp escalation of the American involvement in Southeast Asia in 1965, money, political energy and Federal talent were mobilized to destroy the Viet Cong rather than the slums. In economic terms, the country was rich enough to fight a domestic and an international war at the same time; in political and psychological terms, it was not.

In short, the Government had raised up the hopes of the Negroes, the poor and their middle-class sympathizers and then dashed them down. The militant blacks and the radical young concluded that the entire society was therefore dishonest and that they would have nothing to do with the traditional reform movement. Having thus cut themselves off from the majority of the people, they had forfeited the possibility of a democratic perspective even though some of them – the young radicals – spoke in the name of ultra-democracy. It is necessary to sympathize with the emotions at work in all of this and impossible to approve of the logic which they inspired. The objections to a theory of radical, minority change are both practical and moral.

Black America shares traits with the Third World countries in the days of white rule – there is one crucial difference. In the colonies, the nationalist movement embraced, or represented the aspirations of, 80 or 90 percent of the people. Their struggle against white imperialism had a mass base and a democratic legitimacy. In the United States, Negroes are a minority of between 12 and 15 percent (as noted earlier, the Federal statisticians are not quite sure of the actual figure). This means, first of all, that they cannot possibly win on their own and, secondly, that even if they did prevail, they could only establish a minority dictatorship or else sell racial 'protection' to the society. In LeRoi Jones's play *The Slave*, there is an unhappy prophecy that armed Negro revolt will only substitute black tyranny for white. Jones may well no longer be sad about the prospect, but his fantasy contains a hard truth.

But even if one adopts the integrated perspective of the young radicals and seeks to unite both black and white left-outs, the fundamental problem remains. The poor constitute, at the highest estimate, somewhere between 20 and 25 percent of the people, and that figure includes the majority of Negroes. There is no census of the alienated, but even if they could be recruited to activism, they hardly represent another quarter or third of the population. Moreover, poverty demoralizes people at least as much as it incites them to rebell. That is why there is a lower level of political participation in the other America than anywhere else in the country. But in the New Left vision, a minority of participatory democrats are supposed to govern the corrupt majority of the nation.

And it is important to have a proper respect for that white power structure which the Negro militants excoriate. It will savagely repress violence if it becomes convinced that such a tactic is necessary, and it cannot be dislodged non-violently except by a politically organized majority. The Third World is hardly a unified phenomenon and, as Chapters 7, 8 and 9 make plain, both the fat capitalists and Communists are successfully substituting economics for gunboats to maintain the dependent status of the disadvantaged nations. The masses of Asia, Africa and Latin America will thus not be able to save the people of America from themselves, and indeed the democratic Left must do much more for them than they can possibly do for it.

Thus, on grounds of both practicality and democratic principle, nothing less than a new political majority will be able to make the sweeping changes which America needs. But – and I turn now from the radicals of the 1960s to the conservatives of the 1780s – the mere fact that 51 percent – or even 60 or 65 percent – of the people are actively in favor of a policy does not mean that it will be turned into law.

Out of an exaggerated fear of majority rule, the Madisonians built checks and balances into the Federal system which favor determined minorities. In modern times, this fact has been exploited by a secret party, the Dixiecrat-Republican coalition, which does not hold conventions, adopt programs or normally run Presidential candidates but which does rule the Congress of the United States. In 1964, when Barry Goldwater brought the coalition out of the Congressional corridors and let the people vote for and against it, his audacious strategy elected so many liberals that it moved the entire nation to the Left. How can the partisans of social change do for themselves what Goldwater did for them in 1964?

In the myths of utopian pragmatism, it is un-American to seek a party opposition, of Left and Right (in present American terms, of liberalism and conservatism). But the 'deadlock of democracy' which existed for the generation prior to Goldwater's campaign defeated every major social innovation proposed between 1938 and 1964 even though the polls and the 1964 election showed that the majority of the American people were in favor of them.

And in the legislative year which followed Goldwater's temporary realignment of the party system, there was more change than in the previous quarter of a century. It was a measure of how far behind the nation had fallen that even this burst of Federal creativity was far from adequate.

This is why there must not be just a new majority but a new party as well. For the old party system is based on some of the most conservative aspects of American life: the one-party South; the Congressional seniority system which gives the long-lived and safe-seated Dixiecrats a disproportionate influence; and, until quite recently, the anti-democratic power of rural minorities in state legislatures. So the democratic Left must propose both a program and a party realignment, for the first cannot be passed into law without the second.

It is certainly no easy matter to realign the politics of the nation. But it is not impossible. After all, such sea changes have occurred before. To take two of the most recent examples, there was an 'upthrust of a potent new force in American' life at the turn of the century, as James MacGregor Burns describes it. The 'new middle class' of professionals, salaried people and small-business men took their place on the political stage and helped make America a Republican country. In the Thirties the industrial workers and the Negroes were indispensable elements in forging a 'natural' majority for the Democrats.

But the Rooseveltian alliance of labor, big-city immigrant machines, Dixiecrats, Negroes and liberals was so contradictory that, by 1944, Roosevelt himself was thinking of joining with Wendell Willkie, to build a new, realigned party. Both Roosevelt and Willkie died before anything could be done, and the Dixiecrat-Republican coalition proceeded to dominate Congress for a generation. Now, however, there are new possibilities. There are hopeful openings in the bread-and-butter wing of the social-change movement: among trade-unionists, Negroes and the poor. And it is possible that conscience is acquiring an economic and social, and therefore political, weight in the society that it never had before.

In advocating that the new majority which might be built out of a coalition of these forces seek a new party, the important thing is to allow the public a choice of liberal and conservative alternatives. The names by which the options are called are not crucial. Indeed, currently the drive toward realignment is expressing itself mainly within the Democratic Party, where its Left and Right wings have been engaged in a bitter struggle for some time. And it is therefore quite possible that a new party will bear an old label: the Democratic Party.

Finally, a word about the conservatives is in order. The Republicans will not, in all probability, repeat the Goldwater adventure in the near future. But then the democratic Left can hardly content itself with waiting around until some reactionary ideologue once again proposes a choice rather than an echo. In any case, a 1964 type of realignment which is inspired by the unsophisticated Right drives the sophisticated Right into an alliance with the Center and the Left. The voter was asked during the Goldwater campaign whether he approved of what had been done in the Thirties rather than what he wanted in the Sixties and Seventies. So Walter Reuther and Henry Ford could agree on not going back to the days of Hoover, but their profound differences over the present and future were obscured in the process.

A good deal of the problem derives from the paradoxical history of the New Deal, when the wealthy blindly fought the savior of capitalism as a traitor to his class. However, now that the businessmen have become Keynesians of a sort, a minimal political rationality is possible. If the nation ever gets around to facing its crises, then the realistic conservatives would be corporate New Dealers committed to managing the economy by tax cuts and more private consumption and to contracting the solution of social ills to the private sector. The leaders of such an intelligent defense of the *status quo* would properly be men like Rockefeller and John Lindsay rather than Barry Goldwater. And the democratic Left would move beyond the New Deal with a program of planned social investments.

In short, it is no longer a political issue in the United States as to whether the state should intervene into the economy. The question is how it should do so. The conservatives propose a reactionary Keynesianism which shores up, rather than disturbs, existing power relations; the Negroes, trade-unionists and liberals seek to make Federal action an instrument of positive social goals to benefit the poor more than the rich. This very real counterposition already exists, and it provides a starting point for a party realignment.

Many editorialists and professors say that the picturesque American people are constitutionally incapable of tolerating such choices between moderately principled parties with serious programs. But there are important forces moving in this direction, among them an incipient new trade-unionism and perhaps an unprecedented social class.

2

The American labor movement, one has been repeatedly told in recent years, is either dead or dying. In fact, it may well be stirring to new life.

The main reason for all the funeral orations over the unions is the changing character of the American work force. In the Fifties white-collar occupations became more numerous than blue, the class sources of labor strength diminished and the proportion of organized workers in the country declined. Even among liberals with historic ties to the AFL-CIO, the trend has been taken as proof that the unionists no longer have a dynamic role in the society. In his *American Capitalism*, John Kenneth Galbraith saw the labor movement as a

major source of 'countervailing power' which challenged
the corporations. A little more than a decade later in his
New Industrial State, Galbraith dismissed the unions as
relatively uncreative agents of industrial rationality
which exact a certain price for making the work situation
more disciplined and stable.

Galbraith mistook a possibility for a fate. The unions
have indeed organized a decreasing percentage of the
labor force. Yet, in terms of numbers, they are, and will
remain, the largest institution in the country committed
to domestic social reform. Secondly, and much more
positively, the Seventies could see a vast growth in collective bargaining among groups which previously have resisted unionization. The very same technology which
reduces the proportion of factory workers in the bastions
of labor strength also industrializes the professionals and
opens up new sectors of union recruitment. It is important to see both these tendencies in greater detail.

To begin with, the reports of the disappearance of the
American working class are quite exaggerated. In 1965
there were over nine million skilled workers and foremen
and over thirteen million operatives. In 1975, according
the Department of Labor projections, the skilled will
number eleven and a half million, the semi-skilled fifteen
million. There is, in short, a continuing mass base for
classic unionism in America. Even if labor does not score
a breakthrough in new areas of organization, it will still
represent the largest organized body of Americans committed to economic reform.

Moreover, the factory has not become a pleasant place.
There were radical commentators in the Sixties who
noted that some workers had achieved middle-class income levels, homes in the suburbs, and the like. They
concluded that these people are no longer workers – and
forget that the assembly line is a miserable, alienating
place to work and generates a consciousness quite distinct
from the gripes of the office employee. This fact was an
element in a cruel joke which American conservatives

played on themselves when they helped write the Landrum-Griffin Act. They believed their own fantasies in which class-struggle leaders were inciting contented workers to strike and so wrote some protections into the law for rank-and-file dissidence. The result was a whole series of disputes in which the union membership rejected their leaders' proposals and insisted on more militant action. It would be an unpardonable irony if the Left also believed the fairy tales about happiness in the plants.

But the new departures for the labor movement are hardly dependent on the simple persistence of the old grievances. That, to be sure, gives the unions a bedrock of institutional stability. What is, however, even more significant is the stirrings of a laborite consciousness in utterly new areas of the society. Among those who have moved toward collective bargaining (though not necessarily toward affiliation with the AFL-CIO) are priests, graduate students, blind employees in 'sheltered' workshops, athletes, nurses, doctors, airline stewardesses, social workers, welfare clients, slum tenants, neighborhood communities and nuns. The American Federation of Teachers is, of course, the most dramatic case in point. It has not only signed up well over a hundred thousand teachers in the labor movement but has effectively forced the rival National Education Association to act like a union.

As far back as 1960 Jack Barbash identified an underlying cause of these trends toward collective bargaining (they were much less pronounced then than now). 'The largest factor working in favor of unionization,' he wrote, 'is what might be called the socialization of the work situation. The individualistic bent which constituted the hard core of the professional's values is having to give way to the realities of industrial discipline. The realities are first the technological requirement of concentration of numbers of workers in one place. . . . The second reality stems from the first – that where you have large numbers of persons concentrated at one worksite, you need to develop rules, regulations, measurements, standardizations, evaluations, procedures.'

These new conditions create the basis for a middle-class insurgency on the job (and on the campus). They also could promote an unexpected consequence of white-collar unionism: the organization of the working poor.

The poor are dispersed in jobs which are difficult to organize because of scattered, small units, seasonal employment, etc., and where the potential membership is so impoverished that it cannot even finance a basic union structure at the outset. Where these workers have succeeded in creating their own organizations – in the hospitals of New York and the fields of California, for instance – they have done so by being a labor-oriented civil-rights movement and not just a union. The people belonged to minority groups (Negroes, Puerto Ricans, Mexican Americans) and, as such, they were able to appeal to a broad segment of the community, to the rest of labor, the churches, the middle-class liberals, the idealistic young and so on.

So far the college-educated unionists have demonstrated a particular sensitivity to the plight of the working poor. Some of them, such as the teachers and welfare workers, are in daily contact with the other America and have made the quality of public services a contract issue along with questions of wages and working conditions. Others have participated in that resurgence of conscience which the civil-rights movement evoked among the students, the religious and the liberals. Thus it is quite possible that, as the proportion of organized professionals grows, middle-class militancy will speed the unionization of the working poor.

So perhaps there will be a new labor movement. As it stands today, the AFL-CIO is committed to social investments and even formally advocates democratic planning. If labor were to grow by recruiting more professionals and working poor people, its economic program would probably become even more innovative. At that point, the revivified unions could have a deep community of interest with the poor generally and with Negroes, since the work of destroying the ghettos and building a decent America would provide full employment for a generation at least.

The old-fashioned economic drives and reawakened conscience of the middle class might converge. The reinvigorated labor movement which could result would be a crucial element of a new political majority in America.

3

The perspective I have just described might be a road map to a fool's paradise. In order to guard against this possibility, it is important to understand how very real it is.

The labor movement could refuse to grow. Instead, it could build strong, parochial unions composed of workers in the most advanced industries, a labor aristocracy for the age of automation. Since this sector of the economy is characterized by enormous productivity increases, these unions would be able to better the living standards of their members even if life in the slums were becoming worse. They would, in such an event, find it necessary to defend these comfortable jobs against the handful of black and white poor who would emerge from the inferior ghetto schools with enough education to qualify for them. And such an evil could be perpetrated in a fairly routine and bureaucratic way.

In politics, the worst racist tendencies in the working class would come into their own. Since the unions would be going it alone, there would be no economic rationale for subordinating backlash emotions in the interests of defeating an anti-laborite like Goldwater, as happened in 1964. Negroes would be seen not as allies but as enemies seeking to take away the white man's job or devalue working-class neighborhoods by integrating them. The historic split between the black and the white workers which reactionaries did so much to promote in the past would once again be a national fact of life.

The Negroes would thus be driven to confirm some of the worst of the white workers' fears. Since the old, liberal-labor-Negro coalition would have fallen apart, there would not even be significant ameliorations of life in the ghetto. So Negroes would desperately demand hiring practices which would substitute white unemployment for black; and they would seek to break out of the ghetto by a violent struggle for a larger share of the inadequate stock of working-class and lower-middle-class housing. Within the Negro community itself, the first reaction would be an angry mood of black power. But even if Negroes succeeded in controlling their own neighborhoods, they would capture black poverty, not white affluence. (This is why Barry Goldwater and William F. Buckley, Jr, have been sympathetic to the Black Power slogan.) In reality, however, the collapse of domestic liberalism would not make radicals out of the ghetto dwellers. In the long run, defeat would lead to despair.*

Meanwhile, the white poor would once more become invisible. In the Sixties, attention was focused on their plight largely because of the Negro civil-rights movement. But none of the various ethnic solidarities among the white poor – Puerto Rican, Appalachian, Mexican American and others – generated the force of black race consciousness. And without the labor support or middle-class sympathy inspired by the civil-rights movement the white poor would be unable to transform their own misery.

The professionals and the liberals would become more and more horrified by the jungle world at the bottom of the society, which would imbue them with fear rather than compassion. The teachers and social workers would

---

*I documented the interrelationships between economic progress and militancy in 'The Economics of Protest' in *Employment, Race and Poverty*, Arthur Ross and Herbert Hill, editors (Harcourt Brace & World, 1967).

effectively organize against their students and welfare clients and, more broadly, the impulse toward collective bargaining among college graduates would result in craft organizations of the upper class, on the model of the AMA. Campus idealism would survive these rude shocks for a while, since it is based on philosophic values more than on self-interest. But youth cannot build a private world in the midst of public disaster for too long. Eventually, as in the McCarthy period, the students would succumb.

As a result of such events, the American crisis would become literally intolerable. There would be incredible problems of urban life, race and automation but no progressive political force capable of resolving them. In the circumstances, violence would be used to suppress the justified rage at the bottom of the society, and fear and cynicism would permeate every level of national life. The moment would be counter-revolutionary, a sort of American analogue to the German breakdown of 1932 and 1933.

I have written this scenario as a social horror story, and it is unlikely that it will come true in this extreme form. Yet every tendency which is here magnified somewhat out of proportion already exists. What direction they will take depends on which basic strategy the people adopt.

The key to the dark vision is this: that trade-unionists, Negroes and the poor will struggle against one another for scarce resources, such as housing, jobs and adequate education. Their strife will make even traditional, liberal reform impossible, a fact which will guarantee that there will be even less to go around and therefore more reason to fight. The poor, both black and white, will suffer most egregiously, but the organized workers and middle class will have to become paranoid in order to hold onto their possessions. The social fabric of the nation will, of course, be torn to shreds.

But this catastrophe need not happen, for there can be

an alternate strategy of the democratic Left. If, instead, these groups united to produce an abundance they would reduce, and even eliminate, their own antagonisms. An oversupply of good housing would do more to end segregation than all the ordinances, executive orders and sermons put together. A decision thus to create enough housing for all would generate the jobs which would employ every worker now in the construction industry, require the hiring of newcomers, both black and white, and even permit technological change and reduced costs. Such a policy would meet the needs of both Negroes and the building-trades unions. It could unite groups which have so often been hostile to one another.

In other words, a rational analysis of the material self-interest of organized labor (including its new middle-class adherents), Negroes and the poor indicates that they should cooperate in a gigantic effort to remake America. But powerful irrational forces, race hatred pre-eminent among them, could drive the same groups toward an internecine struggle for scarce goods in which each of them will lose. History has not, and will not, decide which of these tendencies will prevail. Men will.

4

It may be that the emergence of collective-bargaining impulses among professionals is something more than a new attitude within a traditional social class. Perhaps it is one portent of the appearance of a social class which has never existed before and which will play a significant role in the formation of a new majority of the democratic Left.

In 1951 C. Wright Mills wrote of the 'new middle classes': 'They are a chorus, too afraid to grumble, too hysterical in their applause. They are rearguarders. In the shorter run, they will follow the panicky ways of prestige; in the longer run, they will follow the ways of power, for, in the end, prestige is determined by power.

In the meantime, on the political market-place of American society, the new middle classes are up for sale. . . .'

In *Power in America: the Politics of the New Class*, published in 1967, David Bazelon asserted: 'So the great new mass of more or less educated people, primary beneficiaries of the postwar "income revolution," devoted worshippers of children and automobile culture, has become the decisive swing group to mediate and perhaps finally to resolve the classic American conflict of the city-dweller and the small-town agrarian, the immigrant and the WASP, and at last to dispel the effects of agrarian ideology.'

If one assumes that Mills's new middle classes and Bazelon's suburbanites describe the same social groupings, their theories are on a collision course. But perhaps the most important thing about Bazelon's thesis, and whatever reality lies behind it, is that he is not talking about Mills's white-collar world at all. He claims that the American economy is creating nothing less than a new class which could either make a technocracy or else ally itself with the poor in a movement for democratic reform.

But then it is not just Bazelon who suspects that a new class may be in the offing. Fragments of this thesis appear all over the political spectrum. There are New Leftists who argue that well-paid engineers and technicians constitute a new working class since they, like the factory hand, have no control over their job (Mills took up that idea, too, but the data have changed so rapidly that his critique of it cannot be compared to this new statement of it). In *Fortune*, Max Ways uses some of the same trends in describing the conservative revolution which idealistic, hardheaded businessmen will make. For Daniel Bell, the 'new men' of the post-industrial society are not engineers or businessmen but scientists and researchers.

Here are just a few of the Government statistics which provide the basis for all these theories. In 1947 there were about 3,800,000 'professional, technical and kindred workers,' and they made up 6·6 percent of the work force. There were 5,800,000 managers, 10 percent of the total, and 7,200,000 clerical employees accounted for 12·4 percent of the labor force. The 3,300,000 sales people were 5·9 percent of the employed. By 1965 the professionals had more than doubled their numbers to nine million and were 12·3 percent of the jobholders. Managers had increased their proportion by a fraction, from 10 percent to 10·2 percent, sales personnel had gone from only 5·9 percent to 6.5 per cent and the clerical workers had reached 15·5 percent.

It was obvious enough that an historic turning point occurred when the blue-collar workers became a minority of the labor force. But what was not so obvious was that as the gross proportions changed, so did the meanings of the categories and particularly that of the white collar. For Mills in 1951 the most important groupings within the class were schoolteachers, office and sales people. By 1967 office and sales were much less important; education was, along with health care, the fastest growing department of the economy, and scientists and technicians were making the most rapid occupational advances. And all the data point to an intensification of these trends. In the next decade, as the Department of Labor predicts it, professional and technical jobs will grow faster than any other, and their increase will be concentrated in education, space, urban problems and medical services. The traditional office worker will not be in demand, but the computer specialists will be.

It is much too early to say that these figures prove the appearance of a new class if one is speaking high sociologese. But with the caveat that dry statistics are being flavored with a bit of metaphor and drama, the phrase is useful. There is a large, growing group of educated people and they do not belong to either the old, or the new, middle class. Some of them have been created by the evolution of the corporation, others are more a consequence of the spread of higher education. If the speculations about them are true, then contemporary technology is giving rise to politically and socially unprecedented types of human beings.

The conditions of corporate life are a main element in many of these theories. As Bazelon sees it, the new class skills are essentially social, for they are based on a 'great number of people who mostly organize, and administer and criticize and comment on the activities of others.' Galbraith makes a similar definition of the members of the corporation 'technostructure,' and Bell pictures his 'new men' in like fashion. All of these analysts point out that such an experience predisposes people toward planning. They are therefore seen as potential recruits for movements of social change.

It was one of Karl Marx's very few brilliant American disciples who first anticipated this point, but in a negative way. Writing in 1905 and 1906, Louis Boudin described a new middle class which was not so much professional as corporate. The control of big business, he said, was not in the hands of the managerial employees. Since they were not owners, they were not truly bourgeois – they lacked the love of economic independence and enterprise. Their position depended on income, not property, and any one of them was 'ready at any moment to change this windy existence for a governmental job, service of a corporation, or any other occupation, provided his income will not be diminished, or even if it is diminished to a certain extent, provided that it is assured to him for any length of time.'

And then, in an extraordinary intuition of the point Bazelon, Galbraith, Bell and the others were to make more than half a century later, Boudin went on to talk of how this new middle class was attracted to planning. Even though it presided over borrowed power, he said, it was still beset by insecurities of both income and status. So 'it feels the need of a stronger hand than that of the individual in arranging the field of battle for the struggle for existence. If such a makeshift may be dignified into an ideology, its ideology is State Socialism.' The present-day theorists of the new class are more optimistic than Boudin (and they do not have the luxury of expecting a proletarian revolution to solve all problems as he did). But all of them recognize a profound ambiguity in this emerging social formation. Its corporate-induced prejudices in favor of planning could be put in the service of the workers, the poor, the Negroes. Or they could serve a kid-gloved authoritarianism.

In Bazelon's version of the ominous alternative, the new class would 'proceed woodenly to administer everybody and everything. The latter choice would indicate that the Soviets do in fact, unmistakably and unalterably, proffer the image of the future technological world order.' Plannified capitalism would then come to resemble liberalized totalitarianism. This is the possibility which the young radicals of the Sixties excoriated as 'corporate liberalism.' And there are indeed strong economic tendencies in the direction of equating corporate and national purposes, as Chapter 5 detailed. The question at this point is whether or not they can be resisted through political action. And a good part of the answer depends on whether the new class will be the ally or the manipulator of the older classes struggling for a decent life.

First of all, insofar as the new class acts *through* the corporation, it will tend to be technocratic and hostile to democratic change. As I documented in Chapter 4, the mature, sophisticated, neo-Keynesian corporation will, when acting on its own and in the absence of a dynamic popular movement, serve its own narrow, and often antisocial, interests. Textron, to cite that case again, devotes much brilliance to speculating on a Federal agricultural policy which has worsened the life of the ghetto. A broiler chicken has, in that company's view, something in common with a rocket engine: it is a source of publicly subsidized profit. For that matter, the not-for-profit corporation, such as the New York Port Authority, is often infected with the pervasive egotism of the business world and makes public service a means of empire building.

When Daniel Bell asserts that in the post-industrial society 'production and business decisions will be subordinated to, or derive from, other forces in the society' (that is to say, the 'new men'), the ambiguity of his two verbs masks the possibility of alternate social orders. It is almost mathematically certain that basic choices in the future will 'derive from' scientists, technicians and professionals in the sense that they will draw up the blueprints. But it is not at all clear that these decisions will be 'subordinated to' them, that the new class is the bearer of new values and not just of new techniques.

So the American corporation gives rise to a stratum of people who believe in long-range planning, economic rationality and the like. But as long as they express these attitudes through the corporation, they will act bureaucratically and use sophisticated means to keep the black and white poor in their proper place. Therefore, it seems to me that the new class is not a subversive and conspiratorial underground inside the corporate structure. Its positive political potential can only be realized outside of and indeed in counterposition to, the corporation. And there is, I believe, reason to hope that these professionals and technicians will indeed bite the hand that feeds them.

For the new class is not simply corporate, and, in fact, only a minority of the group is to be found in this sector. And even more important, it is educated and in such a way as to transform the political meaning of education.

Up until this generation, college training was reserved for a tiny elite and a relatively small middle class. For this reason it was not until the Johnson landslide of 1964 that a majority of college graduates got around to the mildly liberal step of voting Democratic. Now, however, the class content of a degree is being changed. Almost half of the potential age group is enrolling in institutions of higher education. In 1965 the median educational level of the professional and technical workers was 16·3 years – i.e. it extended into graduate school. And this figure is obviously going to rise in a society which now calculates that a worker must have fourteen years of schooling to succeed in the labor market.

In part, these trends reflect some of the worst aspects of American life. There is the competitive, dog-eat-dog scramble for the good schools from the nursery to the graduate degree which was analyzed in Chapter 6. Middle-class parents understand that academic achievement is a guarantee of future income within both public and private bureaucracies, and they drive their children with this thought in mind. So if the value system which has motivated the current passion for education determines the content of that education, then the new class will use all of its learning to maintain its special privileges.

But a school is a dangerous place, for it exposes people to ideas. Indeed, the best students at the best universities have been the ones who went to Mississippi or marched against the war in Vietnam, and for some of their mothers and fathers this must have been, to put it mildly, an unintended consequence of the struggle for Harvard or Berkeley. In the spring of 1967 *Newsweek* reported that in the previous year the Peace Corps had recruited most of the top 2·5 percent of graduating seniors, that their 1967 target was 3.5 percent and, for 1968, 4 percent. This is why General Electric's personnel ads on television stress public service and social good and make a venerable price-fixing corporation sound like a scientific Community Chest.

Increasing education, all the data indicates, means greater political involvement. Bazelon is right, I think, to consider the various reform movements from New York to California as political expressions of the new class. And study after study documents a correlation between high educational attainment and libertarian views on civil liberties, capital punishment, open occupancy –

and the war in Vietnam. The suburbs, James MacGregor Burns has written, may well be 'more responsible to bold leaders who stress issues of the mind and heart, and not just of the stomach.'

Moreover, the growth of unionism among the professionals is also probably another aspect of the emergence of the new class. And so is the insistence of the collegiate activists that they have a role in determining curriculum, university policy and the conditions of their academic existence in general. In each case a new, conscious community is acting to change traditional relations of power.

But perhaps the most unexpected new-class insurgency has taken place within the Catholic Church. For years secular liberals had wrongly seen Catholicism as a political monolith, ignoring the liberal trends represented by such magazines as *Commonweal* and *Cross Currents*, passing over the massive working-class Catholic component in the New Deal coalition. But when the papacy of John XXIII finally did bring the internal struggles into the open, even the most partisan advocates of the Catholic Left were amazed at the creative vitality that had been pent up for so many years. It would be a mistake to interpret this development as simply a reflection of the changing class structure of Catholicism, yet there is no doubt that education, emigration from the ethnic ghettos and contact with the larger society played an extremely important role in the event. And these are precisely some of the most important forces at work among the new class.

But the burst of religious conscience has not, of course, been confined to Catholicism. In the late 1950s the Negro upsurge challenged the conscience of all the religious hierarchies, Catholic, Protestant and Jewish, and an ecumenical political unity unquestionably was a major factor in the passage of the civil-rights acts of 1964 and 1965. And even though the religious activists, like everyone else, have been affected by the recent swing to the Right, there is no question that they provide an enormous source for ideas and for recruitment to the democratic Left.

From Marx to Mills, the Left has regarded the middle class as a stratum of hypocritical, vacillating rearguarders. There was often sound reason for this contempt. But now it is possible that a new class is coming into being. It is not the old middle class of small-property owners and entrepreneurs, nor the new middle class of managers. It is composed of scientists, technicians, teachers and professionals in the public sector of the society. By education and work experience it is predisposed toward planning. It could be an ally of the poor and the organized workers – or their sophisticated enemy. In other words, an unprecedented social and political variable seems to be taking shape in America.

There have always been both conscience and cotton wings in American politics, and even upper-class reformers, like the Abolitionists. It is now possible – not assured, but possible – that the economy is creating a social structure which vastly enlarges the conscience constituency. If this is indeed the case, it is one of the most optimistic facts the democratic Left can find.

5

So the daily concerns of working people and the poor must merge with the values of the college-educated and religiously inspired in a new majority party.

There are many ways in which this is an undramatic, and even tedious, strategy. It would be much more emotionally satisfying if there were some majoritarian proletariat with internal cohesion and solidarity seeking to find its own mighty voice. There isn't. So one is forced to the politics of coalition not because it is an ideal instrument to make sweeping changes but because it is the only way available to American society for the foreseeable future. Given this perspective, there is no point in papering over the difficulties in the proposal. For, as in any coalition, there will be tensions and even open conflicts among its various constituent elements.

Non-economic issues will be a particular source of internal antagonism on the democratic Left. When it comes to civil liberties, aesthetics, capital punishment and the like, profound differences divide the poor and the workers from the middle-class liberals and radicals. In general, the more educated a group, the greater is its sensitivity to 'ethical' questions in politics. People whose work and/or neighborhood are rough do not, for instance, instinctively defend the speaking rights of a hated opponent. There are powerful impulses toward solidarity and brotherhood among people who have been denied a decent education, but they do not ordinarily extend to strangers and certainly not to enemies. It was one of the great triumphs of the Negro religious spirit in the civil-rights movement that, for a while, it inspired masses to non-violent struggle and an exception to this rule.

But even more important, in terms of the strategy of the democratic Left, there are potential conflicts in the area of foreign policy. On disarmament, as on civil liberties, almost all of the polls describe a decline in positive sentiment as one descends the educational scale. For this reason, a mass party of the democratic Left cannot be initially organized in response to international issues where there is a maximum potential for discord among its various constituencies. It will develop first out of domestic stirrings and crises. This emphatically does not mean that the peace activists should become quiescent and cite sociology as an excuse for doing nothing. It is just that they should not expect that a new party will accept their views at the outset.

But there is hope in the long run. If a movement arises which challenges corporate power within the United States, its members could come to question the myths of free enterprise on a global scale. The civil-rights movement is again a hopeful precursor. Negroes in the ghettos of the Sixties were much more concerned about the issue of war and peace than the white poor. One reason was, of course, that the solidarity of color extended to the Third World. But another was the fact that, in creating their own movement in this country, they became much more sensitive to struggles going on in distant places. If the empire of oil can be defeated at home in the Seventies, the new majority may well understand that it is necessary to defeat it abroad as well.

In the fall of 1967 this possibility became actual in the San Francisco elections. Some peace activists had placed a purist resolution on Vietnam on the ballot. By demanding that the voters choose between an either-or of immediate withdrawal or Lyndon Johnson's policy, they forced many opponents of the Vietnam tragedy, even including some pacifists, into attitudes of opposition, boycott or qualified support. But even though a marvelous opportunity to repudiate Washington's policy was thus lost, the response of the poor people in areas where community organization had taken place was most instructive. For contrary to sociological expectation, it was these neighborhoods and not those of the middle class which returned the highest percentages against the war. For the people in them had understood the relationship between the retreat from social goals and the escalation of the killing in Southeast Asia. If there were a vital movement of the democratic Left on the national level which was first rallied into existence by domestic concerns, it might well make the same kind of connections between the injustices structured into the American system at home and those which we export abroad.

These possibilities clearly concern over-all strategy and not the problems of immediate action. There is a certain necessary vagueness since it is impossible to second-guess the next twenty years. Yet there are some specifics that can be outlined.

At the present writing, the main arena in which the struggle for a new majority party is taking place is the Democratic Party. It claims the allegiance of the overwhelming bulk of the organized reform forces, largely because it was the instrumentality of the last two effective majorities in American history, the Rooseveltian coalition of 1932–1938 and the Johnson consensus of 1964–1965. It is also the supreme national example of an unprincipled, and now impossible, compromise. In the Congress of 1967 and 1968, the leading foes of the social programs of the Democratic President were the Southern Democratic committee chairmen. And so long as a liberal victory on the Presidential line thus strengthens Congressional reaction, there is not the least possibility of confronting the issues analyzed in this book.

At this time, then, the best strategy for the democratic Left is to seek to win the Democratic Party in such a way as to exclude its Right wing permanently. Whether this situation will persist into the future is, it must be emphasized, a tactical, not a moral, question. It is an unhappy, but compelling, fact of American life that membership in a political party does not constitute a commitment either to its program or leadership, and it is precisely the aim of the democratic Left to overturn this tradition. However, this unfortunate reality cannot be transformed by pretending that it does not exist. Therefore, as long as major party politics, with all their lack of principle, offer the best point of departure for basic change, that is where one must work.

So the democratic Left does not work in the Democratic Party in order to maintain that institution but to transform it. The lack of political principle which it finds there is most certainly an indictment of the American party system generally *and* a dynamic contradiction which can be used to challenge that system. There is obvious danger when those committed to a new morality thus maneuver on the basis of the old hypocrisies. Yet, as the New Politics Conference in Chicago in the summer of 1967 so cruelly demonstrated, a relatively small coalition of enthusiasts, black-power militants, idealists and Communist machine politicians cannot create a nation-wide movement by fiat. More poignantly, the ethical anarchism of the hippies in recent years often led them to underestimate how hostile to love the society can be, and the result in some cases was drug addiction or even death.

It would be neater, and more ethically appealing, if American politics allowed the Left to make a total break with the past and start a party of its own. And indeed such a strategy might be required. But if it is, the moment will be signaled by the actual disaffection of great masses of people from the Democratic Party. Such a vast shift in political habits cannot be sermonized into existence, a point which middle-class activists with their philosophic loyalties and motives do not always understand. Before raising the banner of a new party, in short, there must be some reasonable expectation that significant forces will join it. That could happen in the next twenty years; it is not presently imminent; and the dispute over whether it is indeed approaching will turn upon fact and not morality.

It sounds radical to take an intransigent position. It is radical to go among the people as they actually are and work with them to create a new majority party. For apocalypses are easy to proclaim but the structural reform of the most powerful nation in history is much more difficult and not so dramatic.

But there will almost certainly be disputes within the democratic Left on these tactical questions. The various social groupings involved have different attitudes and passions and, moreover, there are often grounds for honest difference in the complexities of the moment. Yet, however vigorous the internal debates of the democratic Left may be, the various partisans must remember that their unity is the only eventual hope.

As the 1968 elections approached, many of the potential partisans of the democratic Left had almost totally lost sight of this point. The trade-unionists, with some exceptions, viewed President Johnson as a man of domestic social accomplishment and certainly the best realistic candidate from the wage workers' point of view. There were some in the labor leadership who were ideological hawks, but most supported the Administration in Vietnam because they approved of what it was doing in the United States. On the other hand, the overwhelming majority of the middle-class liberals, reformers, religious activists and college students were passionately opposed to Mr Johnson because of his policies in Southeast Asia. As a result, the advocates of social change often fought more bitterly among themselves than with their enemies on the Right.

There is no easy resolution to this split. It will almost certainly last as long as the tragic military intervention in Vietnam and while it persists America will continue to retreat from its most fundamental commitments both at home and abroad. And yet both sides in this fratricidal dispute must be reminded over and over of the electoral mathematics of the United States. The middle class, even with its qualitatively new dimensions, is not a majority; neither is the labor movement; and black America is 12 or 13 percent of the nation. To obtain the massive popular support required for radical transformations in the very structures of American life requires that these movements once again come together in a coalition. And in debating the profound tactical differences which in the late Sixties exist, no one can ever forget that this eventual unity is the only possible road to democratic change.

Yet the coming coalition, this chapter should have made plain, cannot be patterned on the old, New Deal model. The Left must go beyond Franklin Roosevelt in political strategy as well as in social and economic program. The Dixiecrats must be excluded, the progressive Southerners included; the Negroes are going to organize and speak for themselves and not be voted by white politicians; the middle class (or perhaps new class) elements will have a much greater weight than in the Rooseveltian coalition, for they are much more important now; and there is realistic hope for the renewal of labor's domestic social idealism. And even though practically every one of these groups is quarreling with every other as the Sixties come to an end, they will either come together or else America has no hope.

But with all these problems it is realistic to work toward a majority party of the democratic Left. The country is not fated, as so many academics claim, to a mindless politics which never poses basic issues. The majority is not so corrupt, as some black militants and young radicals argue, that nothing can be done save to shake the pillars and bring the roof down on the whole decadent scene. For there is even a possibility within American society of actually building a political movement equal to the monumental tasks we have so casually defined for ourselves.

There can be a first party.

CHAPTER ELEVEN

EPILOGUE: TOWARD A DEMOCRATIC LEFT

Pragmatically, America must have a new vision.

The international aims of the United States are largely subverted by its own policies. Foreign aid and trade accentuate that gap between the rich and poor nations which the Secretary of Defense fears as a source of global instability and war. By thus making a democratic revolution economically impossible in the Third World, this country acts as a recruiting sergeant for totalitarian modernizers even while it is the ally of the world's counter-revolutionaries.

The domestic crises which now threaten to rend the very fabric of the society are usually financed with public funds. A welfare state which has generally followed corporate priorities in the name of the common good has furthered urban decay, intensified poverty and racism and left the middle class frightened and bewildered. While all this was being done there was talk of a Great Society.

So common sense has become radical. To make modest progress posssible in the ex-colonies, the creation of the world must be finished in a different way than it was begun; to achieve reforms which will deal with the immediate problems of American society requires first steps toward a new civilization. But then a new civilization is coming in any case. The only real issue is whether we want to decide what it will be like.

These pragmatic arguments for the visionary are typically, and in many ways unfortunately, American. As I noted earlier, this country is embarrassed by its own generosity and demands that the good be disguised as the profitable, which is why Harry Truman gave his Leninist rationale for foreign aid. Moreover, in recent years the collapse of so many faiths prompted scholars to proclaim the end of ideology, and businessmen used the thesis as a further excuse for privatizing the public sector. So from both the professorial and corporate point of view, programs derived from a systematic analysis of society are suspect. Finally, the contrast between the soaring phrases and mundane practices of the Johnson Administration has made many people wary of any large idea.

In anticipation of these various skepticisms, the argument of this book in no way rests on philosophic premises about the nature of man. Instead, every accusation made against Washington has been confirmed by Washington. The case for radical innovation in the United States today is, in short, available to the public at the Government Printing Office.

The democratic Left should thus use all of these Government-certified catastrophes to show why a certain humanization of the life of man has become a practical necessity. It should be willing to cajole, and even frighten, the society into minimal decency, and the Federal card file of social tragedies can be a valuable tool of the visionary's trade. But as a movement with the conviction that there is more to people than greed and fear, the Left must also speak in the name of the historic idealism of the United States.

I

For America, even this actual America without a democratic Left, is also the most radical country in the world.

As the Sixties come to an end, this seems a preposterous statement. This country appears to have degenerated into a war of each against all, of black against white, lower class against lowest class, suburbanites against

metropolis, and the whole relatively fat, smug, complacent nation against the millions of Asia, Africa and Latin
America. There are violence and racism everywhere, and
perhaps never before has there been less of a mood of
social solidarity.

And yet these reactionary hatreds are vicious expressions of that very impulse which, in other circumstances,
makes America so radical. There have never been fixed
hierarchies in this country, and a man therefore had to
assert his worth and establish his identity for himself.
When there was hope, people joined together for militant
action which proclaimed their dignity. This was the way
of the original revolutionists, of the Abolitionists, the
Populists, the trade-unionists, the civil-rights activists and
all the others who constitute the living tradition of the
American Left. But when fear predominates, as today,
this very same independence of spirit drives a man to
defend his own equality by attacking his neighbor's.
American fraternity and fratricide both derive from the
national conviction that a man must stand up on his own
two feet.

So it was that workers poured into the unions authori-
ized by the National Recovery Act in 1933 – and poured
right out of them. It was a time of layoffs, and once the
new unionists saw that the law did not really protect
them from management retaliation, it was every man for
himself. But in 1935 and after there were hirings rather
than firings and a national sense that something could
be done. There was renewed hope, and the very same
workers moved with courage and audacity and permanently altered the social relationships of the society.

In some ways it is precisely this fierce knowledge of the
individual's own value that has kept the American labor
movement from class consciousness on a European model.
The worker on the automobile assembly line has always
known that Henry Ford is more privileged than he is and
not because of any personal accomplishment. Yet he has
also felt that he is just as good as Henry Ford. It was this

pride, rather than passivity, that kept him from adopting a philosophy based on the inherent differences between classes. And the left-wing character of the American social experience has been one of the greatest obstacles to the emergence of a consciously left-wing political movement.

I say this sociologically but I have also seen it with my own eyes. The American worker, even when he waits on table or holds open a door, is not servile; he does not carry himself like an inferior. That openness, frankness and democratic manner which Tocqueville described in the last century persists to this very day. They have been a source of rudeness, contemptuous ignorance, anti-intellectualism, violence – and a creative self-confidence among great masses of people. It was in this latter spirit that the CIO was organized and the black freedom movement marched.

So the American character is complex and dialectical, and it would be a mistake to generalize from only the present demoralization. Moreover, it is the larger social context that determines which aspect of the national personality will come to the fore. A brief sketch of some recent history should make this point clearer.

Somewhere in the 1950s – the Montgomery bus boycott of 1955 is probably the best date – the United States began to recover from McCarthyism. In the 1958 elections there was a liberal sweep, and the 1960 sit-ins helped create a dynamic movement in the South. With John F. Kennedy's victory there was a new sense of optimism even though the Dixiecrat-Republican coalition thwarted most progressive legislation. Kennedy's death hallowed many of his proposals, and the first, neo-New Dealish days of the Johnson Administration saw more Congressional action than at any time in a generation.

Throughout this period the ugly American emotions were still very much alive, yet the country was too hopeful for them to dominate. In the vocabulary of the 1964 elections, 'front-lash' solidarity prevailed over 'back-lash' prejudice. But in 1965 the war in Vietnam took over American politics, and by 1966 Lyndon Johnson had run out of the New Deal, Fair Deal and New Frontier. The reactionaries seized on both these opportunities, and the mood of the nation was transformed. There then appeared what Bayard Rustin has called the 'politics of fear and frustration.' As the possibilities for significant change declined, Negroes, whose hopes had been raised on high, desperately and unsuccessfully demanded their just due. This frightened whites, who became more repressive, and new gains were thereby made even more difficult and the Negroes even more frustrated. By the summer of 1967 each side was arming.

There is one consolation in this sorry narrative. Today pessimism reinforces pessimism, but tomorrow, were the nation to move but one inch toward the democratic Left, hope would corroborate hope, and the best in the American character would once again be liberated. Something like that happened during the tragically brief Presidency of John Kennedy. The 1960 margin of victory was barely perceptible, yet it tipped an historic balance. The country somehow did understand that it was necessary to get moving again. And even after the defeats and retreats of the recent years, that popular idealism which Kennedy touched is still among us. When the moment comes, it could take the nation beyond the New Deal.

So the democratic Left does not simply deduce the practical necessity of change from the official figures. It also has, in Silone's phrase, a sense of the seed beneath the snow, of the radicalism of the American experience.

2

Being economical is a luxury America and the world can no longer afford.

Keynes, as brilliant an economist as he was, looked forward to the relative obsolescence of his own discipline. He believed that 'the day is not far off when the Economic

Problem will take the back seat where it belongs, and that the arena of the heart and head will be occupied, or reoccupied, by our real problems – the problems of life and human relations, of creation and behaviour and religion.' But what Keynes did not realize was that, within a generation, America would have no alternative but to take advantage of these utopian opportunities. The old traditions – the calculus of loss and gain, the cult of efficiency, the assumption that the most profitable use of a resource is the best use – are not only unnecessary. They are profoundly anti-social as well.

According to these economic criteria, it is utterly rational for the world market to redistribute wealth from the poor to the rich and for aid and trade policies to facilitate this abomination. In the global system of injustice created by the nineteenth-century West, it is logical that the Third World perform the most brutal tasks for the least possible remuneration. It also follows quite rigorously that the most costly items in this whole process are not even entered in the ledger: violence, instability and the constant threat of World War III.

Within the United States, whatever the social industrialists may think, justice is not a sound business investment. The poor *are* a bad financial risk and so are the Negroes, central cities, beauty, civility, clean air and all the rest. The new society – that second America which the Government tells us must be built within little more than three decades – cannot be designed according to the commercial priorities which brought the first America to crisis.

So there must be many more planned, social investments, both nationally and internationally.

The scandalous and dangerous gap between the rich and poor nations can be closed only if the advanced economies contract, on a regular and progressive basis, to supply billions of dollars for world economic planning and to restructure the world market in favor of the developing lands. And here at home the physical and spiritual torment of the other America and the fear and discontent of the well-off require democratic investments and imagination.

There are, however, powerful institutional forces in the United States that do not want such changes. The men who articulate them are doubtless sincere and honest and even genuinely moved by starving Asians or rat-bitten children in a Northern ghetto. It is not that they are personally evil but that they are the agents of the old, and disastrous, economics. To them oil profits are more important than the domestic Peace Corps of Peru; a good price for fertilizer takes precedence over food shipments to India; and a real-estate windfall weighs more in the balance than the fate of black America.

There is no consensus possible with such men as long as they hold to their institutional values. The Left must therefore attack their power democratically and non-violently and thereby widen the areas in which people organizing themselves politically are stronger than money. For when a free society avoids conflict, that is not an act of civic prudence but a surrender to the manipulative elites which work behind the façade of unanimity.

All this, one will be told, is un-American. For a long time all kinds of people – from the conscious friends of injustice defending their privileges to the sincere academics – have said that the Left is either a foreign conspiracy or a mawkish daydream or perhaps both. Sometimes they were aided in their work by Leftists who allowed their libertarian ideals to be identified with totalitarian movements. But now the old caricatures of the Left are even more unreal than ever before.

For America has indicted America. We have meticulously documented the fact that by acting in the old ways we shall increasingly betray our ideals. To redeem our own promises to ourselves, Americans must move toward the democratic Left.

THE ROAD TO 1972

When four years of Republican rule end in January 1973, the United States of America is likely to be even more torn by internal crisis than it was in the last shambling days of Lyndon Johnson's Administration.

I write this prediction less than two months before the scheduled inauguration of Richard Nixon and in the waning days of a year which has been disastrous for prophets. In the winter of 1968 the Viet Cong Tet offensive subverted the credibility of both the American military and Lyndon Johnson himself, and helped Eugene McCarthy to confound all the soothsayers in the New Hampshire primary. In the spring, Martin Luther King, Jr. was shot down while fighting for the rights of sanitation men in Memphis and Robert F. Kennedy was assassinated as he campaigned for the Presidency in California.

In the summer, the Democrats and the Republicans measured up to times of tumult and tragedy by nominating two representatives of the old politics and by early fall it seemed certain that a non-campaign was going to elect Richard Nixon by a resigned, unhappy acclamation. Hubert Humphrey, it seemed, might even come in third behind the most powerful Rightist (and even semifascistic) leader in recent American history, George C. Wallace. But at the last moment all the polls had to be revised, Humphrey nearly won the popular vote, and there were several hours in which it appeared that a Constitutional crisis was in the offing.

Under such circumstances, the emergence of a frightened and bewildered political agnosticism would be completely understandable. Yet if men are to control events rather than be subject to them – and that is a major goal of the democratic Left – it is necessary to try to discern the underlying trends which are at work in these various surprises and shocks. To get some insight into this process does not, as will be seen, guarantee that political victory can be calculated and planned. But it is the precondition of even beginning to put our destiny under our control. Thus this Afterword is neither star-gazing nor an exercise in academic futurism, but an attempt to help the Left better transform the immediate future by better understanding the immediate past.

What is needed is a new majority political coalition of the democratic Left capable of winning the Presidency in 1972. But before turning to the tactics of such an effort, let me suggest in broadest outline what I take to be the probabilities and tendencies of change as America enters the seventies under Republican rule.

When this Administration completes its term, the United States is likely to have more social problems than now, more racism, more urban deterioration. In saying this, I do not picture Richard Nixon as some kind of a Rightist demon but as a moderate conservative in a time when basic problems cannot be solved without radical departures. And I make the optimistic assumption that the horrible war in Vietnam will be over and that a chastened America will not rush to make another such tragic commitment. So, I project that crying domestic needs will be unsatisfied even though the conflict in South East Asia, which destroyed Lyndon Johnson's Great Society at home, is decisively ended.

For even with the billions which will be freed for construction when the carnage stops in Vietnam, there is no sign that the Republican Administration and the conservative Congress will do anything but commit the worst mistakes of their Democratic predecessors. Indeed, in the campaign of 1968, Richard Nixon formally promised the American people that he would step up the expenditure of Federal funds for the creation, and socialization, of public crises while cutting back on the token programs which sometimes even helped a bit. At a time when there is so much official evidence of the utter inability of Adam Smith's invisible hand to solve systematic, ingeniously devised problems of man's conscious making, there is this resolute call to further privatize a Government which has already done so much for corporations at the expense of citizens.

If these projections are at all accurate, they make diametrically opposed political developments quite possible. On the one hand, there could be a bitter struggle between the have-nots and the have-littles, the whites and the blacks, the organized and the unorganized, the poor and the ex-poor, for scarce jobs, housing and education (this is the bleak variant discussed in Chapter Ten). That would make it totally impossible to build a progressive majority in America, and it would feed the emotions which made George Wallace the most successful Rightist demagogue in modern American electoral history. Or, if there were an emergent movement of the democratic Left, these very same conditions could radicalize millions of Americans and persuade them to follow a new leadership calling for political realignment and innovation.

The trends will not decide which of these tendencies, the ugly or the hopeful, will prevail. Men will. Within this context, let me attempt to map out a democratic Left road to 1972.*

---

* For the historical record, one uncertainty which existed when this book was completed in the fall of 1967 has been most happily removed. The 'next generation', to whom it is dedicated in part, was born on 23 March 1968, and is named Alexander Gervis Harrington.

I

One of the many myths propagated by Republicans in the political battles of 1968, and credited by far too many liberals, was the notion that our crises had intensified because Washington, with pretenses to omnipotence, had 'done too much'. Some of the most pertinent contrary facts were documented in Chapter Six but since this delusion has been announced as a leading idea of the Republican Presidency, it is well worth taking up some of the recent data. For in housing, transportation, agriculture, job generation and welfare, 1968 corroborated one of the central themes of this book: that Washington, while talking massive programs, has acted timidly and, worst of all, that there has been a real tendency for these inadequate programs to exacerbate, rather than alleviate, the miseries and inequities of the society. It is because the Republican Party has a principled position in favor of such counter-productive policies that I feel the outlook for the early seventies is gloomy.

In February of 1968, Mr Johnson put the seal of Presidential approval on the crisis figures about housing need and said that the country had to construct 26 million units in ten years, 6 million of them governmentally subsidized and low-cost. He thus increased the target of the White House Conference in 1966 by 20 per cent but then the Administration and Congress had ignored that more modest proposal anyway. Ironically, the architect of the Great Society announced at the same time that he was determined to fulfil Robert Taft's 1949 low-cost housing goals but did not mention that the nation had dropped fifteen years behind that conservative Republican's expectations. The *New York Times* rightly noted that the Johnson message was 'essentially conservative'. When the Housing Act was passed, many editorialists were pleased with this or that item in it but almost all agreed that it was most unlikely that these new ideas would really be funded.

So it was that, in November 1968, the cover of the trade journal *American Builder*, asked 'Who Really Gives a Damn About Housing?' and answered, 'Not the cities; they're headed for a decade of failure. Not the Suburbs; they couldn't care less. Not the rural areas; everyone's leaving them. Not the power structure. All they do is talk, talk, talk.' In its proposals for positive action, the *American Builder* had advocated reforms like a national land policy and land bank, an end to un-planned and socially catastrophic highway construction, taking zoning power away from suburbs (it is primarily used to keep out the poor and the black), Congressional appropriations for programs it passes on principle, and so on.

But perhaps the most daring, radical idea was put forth by Dwight Eisenhower. Addressing himself to the issue of slums and ghettoes, he wrote, 'We shall never solve these problems simply by tearing out vast areas of sub-standard dwellings and stacking people vertically in new high-rise apartment complexes.' Instead, he went on, 'The first essential of any realistic housing plan is to reduce the density of population by encouraging large numbers of people to relocate in new, more wholesome communities. These new towns would have their own schools, shops, clinics and hospitals, their own light indus-try and recreational facilities. For those who do not find employment locally, swift mass transportation should be created to take them to jobs in the cities. Needless to say, these new areas must not be just added enclaves of segre-gation. They must be open and made inviting to decent people of all races.'

It is not exactly clear why the former Republic Presi-dent thus adopts a solution which might have been borrowed from the European socialists. However in de-fense of Mr Eisenhower's conservative credentials, he goes on to suggest that his scheme will be carried out by private enterprise. That, as the analysis of the Social–Industrial Complex showed (and there will be more recent evidence in a moment) is simply not going to happen. But it is still significant that Eisenhower has some perception of the radical changes which present conditions demand. The National Commission for a National Land Policy has advocated the construction of twenty-five new cities which would, in forty to sixty years, reach populations of 1 million each. At the University of Minnesota, researchers have been designing a new city which could be built on open land, a hundred miles from any other urban area, and housing 250,000 people at a cost of $4 billion. In one version of the scheme, there would be no vehicles on the surface level and all deliveries would be made underground.

So the practicality of radically solving the urban crisis is not only obvious to intellectuals and planners but to a former Republican President as well. But a Johnson Administration, which was somewhat more sympathetic to such an approach than the Republicans are likely to be, could only legislate pathetic tokenism in this area. And to get an idea of how dramatic the break with the past must be, consider the shocking figures of the National Commission on Civil Disorder's 1968 Report: that in thirty-one years, the United States Government subsidized 650,000 units of low-cost housing, while in roughly the same period (thirty-four years) it provided invisible supports, like cheap credit and handsome tax deductions, for the construction of more than 10 million units of middle and upper class housing. If the nation were to honor the President's 1968 goal of housing for the poor, it would have to build ten times more units for the poor in ten years than it has built in the previous thirty-one. If the target of the Riot Commission is taken, then that rate must be doubled.

It does not take a seer to suggest that the Republican Administration of the late sixties and early seventies will not undertake such a sweeping re-ordering of social priorities. It will, Richard Nixon promised in the 1968 campaign, give subsidies to private business instead. This book has already set out a critique of this proposal, but some 1968 data is so vivid that it should be noted. In April 1968, David Boldt wrote an article for the *Wall Street Journal*: 'Industry in the Slums? It's not that Easy'. He told how the Watts Community Redevelopment Agency had come up with a plan for a thirty-five-acre industrial park. The Watts Citizens Committee, led by Ted Watkins, an Autoworkers Union activist, turned the scheme down. Watkins said, 'And what we don't need is a bunch of low pay sweatshops that don't give a man enough incentive to get off of welfare.'

Even more pertinently, the people of Watts were suspicious of a Southern Pacific Rail Road Plan which would have cut a five block swath through the center of the community. They did not find this an efficacious way of saving their neighborhood, particularly if it was going to be financed with the help of 'anti-poverty' funds.

Another revealing report appeared in the Journal in October. Albert R. Hunt described the – much-touted, government-supported, panacea-to-end-panaceas – efforts to use the Federal carrot to persuade the private sector to create jobs. It was discovered, Hunt said, that ghetto costs were several times that in prime labor areas and taxes were high. When a company goes in to such a rotting neighborhood the plants are small and the products simple (they are a cut above the sweatshops Watkins feared, but only a cut). Four big companies had indeed gone into the slums: Westinghouse, AVCO, IBM and Control Data. Their investment had yielded a total of 870 jobs. Westinghouse, to take a striking example, held a big press conference to publicize its Pittsburgh plant in a poor area which would put seventy-five people to work. At the same time, and without a lot of publicity, it was building a $65 million facility in the outskirts of Charlotte which will employ more than 1000 workers and make turbines for atomic electric utility plants. The employees there, one might guess, will not be poverty stricken.

Therefore during the year when Mr Nixon was making
the private sector panacea for the solution of social problems a centerpiece of his campaign, that very private
sector, as viewed in the business press, was indicating that
it was not very interested beyond a token gesture here or
there ('fire insurance' in the ghetto, some cynics called
these installations). Or else, like the corporate interests
who wanted to cut Watts to pieces, free enterprise was
too interested in the worst possible way.

One other case should also be noted. In Detroit, the
Federal Government has successfully urged the auto industry, and Henry Ford in particular, to hire 'unemploy-
ables' from the ghetto. In this way some 5000 jobs have
been created at Ford with much celebration. Yet an
analysis by Robert C. Albrook in the August, 1968, issue
of *Fortune* put this happy development in a somber perspective: 'With unemployment rates of below 4 percent
recently, job creation on a big scale may have been
rational and profitable for a big company. But if the rate
moved back up toward 5 percent, hiring the hard-core
unemployed might mean turning away experienced
workers.'

This prediction takes on an almost sinister cast when
one considers that the Business Council – that group
whose ubiquitous, semi-official power is attested by Gar-
diner Ackley – at its October 1968 meeting, proposed to
combat inflation by raising unemployment to 5.5 percent
or 6 percent. Of the 100 corporate chieftains who met at
Hot Springs, Virginia, to propose that the poor thus
suffer to save the prosperity of the affluent, 80 percent
were estimated to be supporters of Richard Nixon. They
were also prominent advocates of the capitalist conscience who had not bothered to consider that their defla-
tion nostrum would almost certainly wipe out all the
labor market gains of the war on poverty – and more.
Henry Ford's recruits would be back on the streets, only
more bitter.

In other words, massive job generation to do away

with the Depression-like underemployment of the impoverished, and particularly the blacks among them, is simply not going to take place in the private sector even with Federal subsidies. There are, of course, the millions of public service, non-profit occupations identified by the Automation Commission and re-emphasized by the Riot Commission. Congress could begin to fund them any time it wants to, but there is little likelihood that the humane bills of Congressman James O'Hara and former Senator Joseph Clark will be acted upon by a Republican Administration and conservative Congress.

There are other determinants of our public woes which will, at best, stay as bad as they are under Nixon. After hundreds of official speeches about the need for an integrated transportation policy, Congress in 1968 passed a law which enshrined the highways-over-all approach, mandated the Los Angelization of Washington, D.C. (some people there had asserted their rights as against freeways and had to be put down by a Federal law), made the beautification program even more of a joke than it had been, and struck a blow against wildlife. And in November 1968, the road-building industry was fighting furiously against new Federal rules which would allow a modicum of public participation before decisions are made on highway design. At the end of September, thirty Republican Congressmen changed their vote in order to help the Nixon campaign and thus defeated a $20,000 ceiling on agricultural subsidies. In 1967, some 9,952 farmers had received 408 million dollars – James O. Eastland, the impartial plantation owner on the Senate Agricultural Committee, took in $211,364 that year – and this had helped, of course, to displace even more undereducated rural poor people who would soon be showing up on city relief rolls.

But then welfare was in its usually impossible state. The Riot Commission discovered that in 1967 in Newark, Detroit and New Haven (three important centers of riot), the medium percentage of ghetto inhabitants covered by

Federal programs in manpower, education, housing, community action and relief was one-third (similarly, the Council of Economic Advisors estimated a year or two earlier that two-thirds of those officially classified as poor get no public assistance). The Commission also noted that welfare provides an average of one half of what people desperately need throughout the nation and in some places gets down to 25 percent of need.

So the 1968 statistics bear out the patterns described in this book. Washington admits that there must be a most dramatic break with the lethargic, low-cost housing programs of the past, affirms that there must be socially conscious transportation and agricultural policy, and publishes detailed figures on the minimum requirements of human decency. It then proposes a pittance for housing, reaffirms catastrophic transportation and farm programs, and lets welfare rot. Since Richard Nixon seems likely to follow the very worst of these trends, and to try to make the private sector ethical when it either doesn't want to or will act only when it can use public monies to institutionalize the old injustices, the probabilities are that the United States will be in worse condition on 20 January 1973 than on 20 January 1968.

It is this domestic reality which, short of another Vietnam or worse, will create the background of American politics in the coming period. Foreign policy, as I noted earlier in the book, does not generally determine who wins or loses elections unless, as in the case of Vietnam, it upsets the internal equilibrium (there is, as we have seen, a much larger 'conscience constituency' reacting to such issues but it is far from decisive). So I will only remark here that 1968 brought a further retreat in foreign aid and that the Republicans have promised to rely more on trade, which is rigged to the advantage of rich countries and therefore a root cause of backwardness in the Third World, than upon aid.

In other words, it is almost certain now that the 'Development Decade' of the United Nations will end as a complete failure, and even with the prospect of increasing famine. At the same time, the celebrants of American corporate virtue have recently been lavishly praising one of the causes of this tragedy: the multi-national corporation. As I wrote in Chapter Nine, the big companies have for some time been working out schemes of international economic planning for private profit which have the profound, and incidental, effect of perpetuating the miseries of the ex-colonies. After all, General Motors has the eighteenth largest GNP on the globe (at $20.2 billion in 1967 it ranked ahead of Argentina, Belgium, Switzerland and Czechoslovakia, among others), Ford is the twenty-third richest industrial power, Standard Oil of New Jersey the twenty-fourth, and General Electric, at the thirty-fourth, has more of an output than Greece.

As Sanford Rose described these world businesses in *Fortune*, 'Carrying multi-nationalism to the logical extreme, a corporation will concentrate its production in the area where costs are lowest, and build up its sales where the market is most lucrative.' Should a developing country with foreign exchange difficulties object to such a calculus – which, as the argument of this book shows, intensifies all the injustices of the international division of labor – then a multi-national corporation could veto the decision of such a supposedly sovereign power. It could, Rose says, 'simply "take out" its dividends by raising prices on intracorporate sales proportionately', and thus nullify the local Government's refusal to repatriate profits.

It is, once again, clear that if General Motors is able to engage in international economic planning for its private purposes, the United Nations should be able to do so for public and social ends. And it is just as clear that a Republican America will not support such a minimal step toward global decency but, with its links and commitments to the private sector, will accentuate the worst trends abroad as well as at home. This will mean a prolongation of the agony of the majority of the people of

the world, a condition which might lead to another
Vietnam.

2

So the economic and social perspective for the early
seventies is not exactly cheering. But it would be a serious
mistake to think, as some on the American Left have
argued, that a radical failure to respond to the needs of
the poor, the blacks and the social sector generally will
necessarily give rise to a progressive movement seeking
radical solutions. As Chapter Ten showed, the exact
opposite reaction is possible and, with the frightening impact of George Wallace in 1968, that ugly alternative is
already a part of reality.

Trotsky said of the German communists before the
rise of Hitler that they infuriated all classes and won
none. There is something analogous to that insight (and
much, of course, that is not) in the way that Lyndon
Johnson provoked such widespread hostility only four
years after his landslide election. He made extravagant
promises to the poor, and particularly the blacks, which
raised militancy and hope and, when he accomplished so
little, incited anger. Meanwhile, many white workers and
members of the lower middle class did not realize that
the bold programs were more rhetoric than substance.
They thought that they were being discriminated against
and the consequent backlash sentiment gave Wallace
shocking support in the industrial North early in the campaign. And the best children of the affluent were horrified
by the war and disillusioned by all the broken social promises which it occasioned, and their anger helped create
an opposition which held a third of the seats at the Democratic Convention.

There were some Leftists who mistakenly then concluded that a Nixon victory would make it easier to win
the Democratic Party in 1972 than Humphrey's election.
They were wrong, perhaps tragically so. For if the Nixon

record is only as bad as Eisenhower's in the fifties – unemployment chronic in order to get price stability, growth at a snail's pace in the name of fiscal responsibility, and so on – then the economic omens could be conducive to a George Wallace. For under such conditions, there could be even greater incentives to fratricide at the bottom of the society since there could be militant movements disputing scarce goods.

One reason this point is not so widely understood comes, paradoxically, from the heightened consciousness of poverty. For once the economic underworld was rediscovered, there were those who pictured the society as divided between the poor and the affluent. Yet, as I pointed out in Chapter Three, there is a huge 'at risk' population hovering just above the poverty line. And, even more pertinently, two-thirds of the families in America have less than the $9,191 a year required to maintain a 'moderate standard of living' as computed by the Department of Labor (it used 1966 figures and, given inflation, the actual income would have to be higher today). That means that the have-nots and the have-littles, the impoverished and the struggling, comprise the overwhelming majority of the population. If, as is certainly possible, the economic policies of the Republican Administration drive this vast mass to a civil war against each other, rather than to a confrontation with the real power in the land, Rightist demagogery could have a field day.

But this Rightist trend need not prevail; there is a road to 1972 for the democratic Left. And, though I was as surprised as the next man by the incredible, unpredictable events of 1968, I would argue that they corroborate the strategy for building a majority party with a radical program described in Chapter Ten.

To begin with, there has clearly been a vast expansion of the political power and influence of the college-educated, a phenomenon so striking that it might indeed herald the appearance of the 'new class' discussed in

Chapter Ten. To some the appeal of Eugene McCarthy and the late Robert Kennedy in 1968 seemed to be a fad among the 'kids' and not much else. Yet by the fall of 1968 almost every practical pol in America, including many hacks, was proclaiming his loyalty to the 'new politics'. This was a professional recognition of the importance of this new constituency. But these young people were not up for grabs. They were activist and concerned with issues and, through the reform movement they helped bring to the Democratic Convention, they won historical changes in the party structure – ending the unit rule, changing the mode of election of delegates, and so on – even though they lost the Presidential nomination and the Vietnam debate. And though the vote on the latter issue went against them, they could properly claim credit for having been a factor in changing their country's foreign policy.

But if 1968 dramatically revealed the mass potential of this new conscience constituency, it also defined its limitations. The McCarthy campaign never really reached out to the poor, the blacks or the white workers. Robert Kennedy did (which is why I supported him, joining the McCarthy campaign after his death), but the assassin struck him down before he had the chance to prove his case and candidacy. So, as it turned out, the opposition at the Chicago convention was much too exclusively college-educated and not at all representative of the other groups in America which need social change. As one who worked in that movement, I feel that its greatest danger is a tendency toward self-righteousness and elitism, a lack of sympathy for those who view politics as a bread-and-butter necessity rather than as an idealistic avocation.

This was also true of the ultra-Left and anti-political confrontationists in 1968. That Mayor Daley denied them the effective right to assemble, and encouraged the police to assault them – and even bystanders – in a sickening, fascistic show of force was, of course, an outrage. But at the same time, one must be critical of those who, sometimes in the name of radicalism, adopted modes of political language and shock tactics which were guaranteed to provoke the vast majority of Americans to anger and to the Right. The Hippie philosophy of 'doing one's thing' is appropriate to a drop-out and may even have an integrity of its own; but it is a disastrous precept for those who want to change society by winning a popular majority to end the misery of the slums and ghettoes.

Yet the main impact of the conscience constituency in 1968 was positive. Therefore it is all the more clear then, in assembling a new majority for 1972, that 'kids' have to be treated as an adult political force which, for reasons of demography and economics, is likely to have an even greater impact on society as time goes on. If there is a certain disillusionment among this stratum as a result of the outcome of 1968, it is a major task of the democratic Left to win them back to political activism.

Secondly, as I remarked in Chapter Ten, the news of the disappearance of the American working class is premature.

I disagree with the political stance of most of the AFL-CIO unions in 1968 prior to the elections: support for the horrible war in Vietnam and for Lyndon Johnson, and then an alliance with the big city machines and the Southern establishment to obtain the nomination for Hubert Humphrey. Yet the fact remains that in the campaign labor provided the best organized, most cohesive mass base for Humphrey, liberal congressmen and progressive social programs. For when the moment of truth came, the Northern white workers, including many who were deeply prejudiced, voted their economic self-interest rather than their race hatreds. So it is crucial to understand the persistence of 'old' (that is, one generation old) political motives in the midst of furious change. A factory is still a deeply alienating place and even though wages are up – but not as much as profits in the sixties – the typical worker has a tough time with debts, taxes and the cost of living. There is therefore a consciousness of the need for social change which arises out of the very conditions of working-class life. And it was this factor which dominated the politics of the industrial North-east in Mr Humphrey's surprising bid for power in 1968.

Therefore the 1968 campaign makes a central point of Chapter Ten even more compelling: the organized workers must play a major role in the creation of a new majority. And, as was pointed out earlier, the best point of contact between the middle-class conscience constituency and the politics of practical working-class necessity is on domestic social and economic issues. Therefore when the war in Vietnam ends, the effecting of such a unity with a labor movement will be a basic task for the democratic Left. Above all, college graduate activists must neither act, nor think, contemptuously toward those who, through no fault of their own, were denied a higher education.

The poor, and particularly the black poor, were in motion in 1968, but there were some ambiguities. In the South, black voting strength increased tremendously and one result was that the Democratic Convention was forced to give more recognition to Negroes than ever before in history. During the California primary, Mexican-Americans, led by Cesar Chavez of the farm workers, succeeded in turning out massive majorities for Robert Kennedy in their areas. So it is plain that the poor can become a force in their own right. That, however, does not mean that such a development is easy or inevitable. Earlier in the book I remarked on the many factors which keep the other Americans from developing a class consciousness and organization. For instance, even though the most articulate and visible spokesmen of the black ghetto in 1968 were militants who scorned and detested the Administration, Hubert Humphrey received the overwhelming bulk of the Negro votes. In much the same way as Northern white workers refused the Wallace adventure on their Right out of a deep sense of the need to defend their economic and social position, so Negroes rejected the ultra-militant appeals on their Left.

However, it must be candidly recognized that the Northern ghettoes are, to considerable measure, still unorganized. This is probably one of the reasons why some of the most energetic, youthful blacks are insisting upon community action at the grass roots. If this positive aspect of the black power ideology unites more and more Negroes in on-going organizations, that will be a major contribution to all of American life. But there is a danger that such activists will be taken in by 'black capitalist' panaceas such as Mr Nixon proposed. Big business refuses to go into the slums, or does so on a token basis, on sound 'economic' grounds (if one understands that 'economics' within America and the world are historically designed to favor the rich against the poor rather than being a natural law). The rents are high, the public services run down, the labor force has been systematically under-educated through no fault of its own, and so forth. If Negroes try to create their own entrepreneurial enclaves they will run into the same bitter, racist facts of economic life.

To be sure, there should be government support to black business, but that should not give rise to the illusion that the number of Negro companies which can succeed on the poverty market of the ghetto are going to pull up well over twenty million Americans by their bootstraps. What the Negroes must do is to change the definitions of economics, i.e. through massive, planned social investments see to it that no American, black or white, lives in a deteriorating backwater which is only attractive to cockroach capitalism and exorbitant gougers. And to do that, as I argued throughout this book, requires that a black-led mass movement join in a democratic Left new majority.

And 1968, even with its terrible disappointments, does

show that such a majority coalition is possible – and the only way to get progressive social change in America. Hubert Humphrey won the Democratic nomination on the basis of the classic Rooseveltian united front: labor, the South, the big city machines. But that united front is no longer really able to deliver, for Wallace took the deep South, Nixon the border states, and Daley could not even deliver Illinois to his candidate. Indeed, one of the reasons that Humphrey did so much better than expected – aside from his own dogged determination and courage to persevere – was that he veered in the direction of a new coalition once he began to run. He was almost immediately deserted or snubbed by his Southern allies, and his association with the Chicago machine was clearly costing him dearly. So he concentrated on a bread-and-butter appeal to workers and poor people, an anti-Wallace emphasis which strengthened his hold on the black vote, and an attempt to win back the McCarthy–Kennedy forces. His belated new politics almost carried the day.

In short, it would take a foolish practical politician to try to resurrect the New Deal strategy. And a majority coalition of the democratic Left has become, not simply desirable, but the only way to move the nation in a progressive direction. The Dixiecrats increasingly refuse to maintain their alliance with the liberals except when Congressional seniority is involved. They should be given their walking papers and the 'loyalist' forces of the Chicago Convention, both black and white, should be recognized as the new South. The machines are coming to an end in any case. And the labor movement, the conscience constituency, the blacks and other poor groups, and the new South are, in any case, an incipient, dynamic majority – if they can unite. Building that unity is the central task of the democratic Left on the road to 1972.

Finally, 1968 gave the answer to those who urged the Left to break, for once and for all, with the corruptions of the Democratic Party and to plant its own independent banner as a rallying point for the masses. As I said in Chapter Ten, I wish that politics could be so logical and straightforward; but they are not. And in 1968, the people gave such a massive demonstration of their political identification with the liberal wing of the Democrats that, despite a disastrous Convention and a badly split party, Hubert Humphrey very nearly won a three-man race. And until there is decisive evidence of a new trend, the Left must be where people are actually struggling to resolve the problems of their daily lives. That means that the road to 1972 moves through the winning of the Democratic Presidential nomination to a victory for the new majority in November of that year.

At some McCarthy rallies in the summer of 1968, I spoke of the extreme contrasts of the year – a vast outpouring of youthful sentiment in the mainstream and against the war; the deaths of Martin Luther King and Robert Kennedy; and so on – and I quoted the famous opening passage of *A Tale of Two Cities*. Dickens wrote in a conservative mood, yet his words define what confronts the democratic Left as the Sixties end: 'It was the best of times, it was the worst of times . . .' It is the worst of times because we have lost brave leaders and the nation has moved to the Right; it is the best of times, if we have the audacity to hope and act, because it is possible to assemble a new majority, because there is a road to 1972 which runs toward the democratic Left.

INDEX

*Some other books published by Penguins and
Pelicans are described on the following pages*

THE ACCIDENTAL CENTURY
Michael Harrington

Michael Harrington, whose *The Other America*
stirred the nation to action against poverty,
turns, in his new book, to the cultural and
intellectual crisis confronting the United
States and the rest of the Western world in
the 20th century. The crisis has been brought
about by the "accidental revolution," in which
an unplanned social and creative technology has
haphazardly reshaped our lives and put in doubt
all our ideologies and beliefs. The resulting
decadence threatens to destroy Western civilization and with it the Western concept of man.
The technological and social revolution of the
20th century will continue; but, says Mr.
Harrington, it must cease to be accidental. It
must become conscious, planned, and democratic
through the political intervention of man. An
exciting and provocative book by one of the
most brilliant social critics of our time.

THE OTHER AMERICA
Poverty in the United States
Michael Harrington

The book credited with sparking the government's
War on Poverty. Michael Harrington gives a
vivid description of America's poor—the unskilled
workers, the aged, the minorities, and the other
rejects of the affluent society. He analyzes the
nature and causes of the Other America and
warns that in the U.S. today poverty is becoming
a self-perpetuating culture, a way of life. He
calls for an integrated and comprehensive
program to conquer it. The government has
responded with the War on Poverty.

"It impressed Jack Kennedy . . . it is clear that
(this) book contributed to Johnson's new
drive."

—Time

"*The Other America* has been credited with
helping to open the Administration drive on
poverty . . ."

—The New York Times

"It is an excellent book—and a most important
one."

—The New Yorker

URBAN CHOICES:
the city and its critics
Roger Starr

Urban Choices deals with the ultimate questions
of city life in the United States; it attempts
to establish a set of values by which the decisions
of urban governments can be judged.

Roger Starr insists that social values must be
related to the ways in which urban residents
actually behave. He is impatient with oversimplified or Utopian solutions to city problems
and contends that even the best-intentioned, most
sensitive of the cities' critics—critics as diverse
and distinguished as Lewis Mumford, Jane
Jacobs, Herbert Gans, Victor Gruen, Marya
Mannes and Peter Blake—are severely limited
in their approach to the predicament of
America's urban centers in this time of
unprecedented social and economic change.
Mr. Starr strips away the folklore that has
obscured the real issues. Drawing on his
experience as Executive Director of New York's
Citizens' Housing and Planning Council, he sets
forth his views in several major areas which
require immediate, difficult, perhaps unpopular
choices. Among the problems he deals with are
housing, unemployment, racial tensions, poverty,
transportation, architectural planning, air and
water pollution, and urban politics.

Trenchant, relentless, asking the hard questions
and demanding the hard decisions, *Urban
Choices* presents a clear assessment of the nation's
urban ills and makes specific and sound
suggestions for their cure.

WHY THE DRAFT?
The Case for a Volunteer Army
edited by James C. Miller III

The Vietnam War has made the draft one of the most controversial issues in American politics and therefore difficult to consider objectively. In WHY THE DRAFT? *The Case for a Volunteer Army,* however, seven young political economists have succeeded in taking a critical but objective look at the draft in all its aspects and at the alternatives to it. After carefully summarizing the cases for and against Selective Service, National Service, the Lottery, and the Volunteer Army, they weigh these alternatives on the basis of equity, feasibility, national tradition, and social balance and democratic ideals. Their conclusion is that conscription in any form is inequitable, for it places a special 'tax-in-kind' on those forced into service, and while each of the alternatives is feasible, the volunteer army has the lowest real cost. They then examine the whole question of a volunteer army in detail, relating it to the national tradition, considering the cases of Britain and Canada which already have volunteer armies, and answering the critics of 'an army of mercenaries'. They end by calling for an immediate raise in military pay with improved living conditions, in order for us to return to what they see as our heritage of a volunteer army.

THE MOST PROBABLE WORLD
Stuart Chase

One of America's foremost social critics and economists charts the great trends and forces of our time to draw a realistic profile of the world we are shaping for the twenty-first century. Stuart Chase examines the achievements and hazards created by science and technology and sets forth the social, political, and scientific problems which we must solve if the most probable world is to be peaceful and secure.

Overpopulation, pollution, and new weapons could make a wilderness of the world. Yet the same imagination and skill of which these evils are by-products could free man from drudgery, sickness, famine, and armed conflict. Today the dangers and the potentialities are dovetailing with unprecedented speed.

Using the most up-to-date information, Mr. Chase discusses the arms race, environmental pollution, urban problems, human psychology, the uses of atomic power, the UN, automation, East-West economic differences, the influence of the automobile, and a promising new program of education which can prepare the leaders of future generations for coping with the complexities of a dynamically changing society.

This arresting study is not science fiction but an expert's hard look at the world of the future— a world near enough to be a challenge for our time.